JURISPRUDENCE AND STATECRAFT

The Wisconsin Development Authority

and Its Implications

THE WISCONSIN DEVELOPMENT

Jurisprudence and Statecraft

AUTHORITY AND ITS IMPLICATIONS

Samuel Mermin

1963

THE UNIVERSITY OF WISCONSIN PRESS | MADISON

Published by
The University of Wisconsin Press
430 Sterling Court, Madison 6, Wisconsin

Copyright © 1963 by the
Regents of the University of Wisconsin

Printed in the United States of America by
George Banta Company, Inc., Menasha, Wisconsin

Library of Congress Catalog Card Number 63-15054

To Lora, Pete, Dan, and Kathy

PREFACE

This study centers around a project launched by the Governor Philip La Follette administration in 1937 for the public financing of a private corporation's promotion of public power and rural electric cooperatives. Terminated in 1939 by a decision of the Wisconsin Supreme Court, the project attracted much attention as an important element in the political-economic life of its time.

Its significance outruns, however, the contemporary setting. There are broad implications for constitutional theory and public policy bearing on efforts at state promotion of enterprise; there are lessons for the historian concerning the role of law; and there are jurisprudential lessons for those interested in learning how our American system of judicial precedent operates. The present volume explores all these facets of the problem, after analyzing the background, nature, and legal-economic history of the Wisconsin Development Authority project.

I am greatly indebted to the Rockefeller Foundation and to the Research Committee, Graduate School, University of Wisconsin for financial assistance, and to my colleague Willard Hurst who first suggested the research and has helpfully criticized the manuscript. I am grateful also to my former student, Donald Heaney, for helping to insure substantive and formal accuracy in the interpretation and citation of reference material.

S.M.

Madison, Wisconsin
December 15, 1962

CONTENTS

JURISPRUDENCE AND STATECRAFT

The Wisconsin Development Authority

and Its Implications

INTRODUCTION

The story of the WDA is a neglected story. It offers much of interest to the student of political-economic history, and of constitutional and juristic theory. It affords an instructive example of the interplay of the many factors that go into the making of social reform and into the solution of resulting "legal" issues. The story has color: it involves, for instance, one of the most spectacular floor fights in modern Wisconsin legislative history. It includes also an elaborately argued, much-discussed "great case" in Wisconsin's Supreme Court, which offers much of interest for juristic theory on the legal process, and is vital to the consideration of one of Wisconsin's permanent constitutional problems, viz., the scope of certain constitutional limitations (prohibitions as to "private purpose," "local purpose," "internal improvements") on the use of state resources for promotional purposes.

Organized in 1937, the Wisconsin Development Authority was a private, non-profit corporation. Its purposes were to promote the operation of electrical and other utilities by non-profit co-operatives and by governmental units, including municipalities and municipal power districts; to construct, acquire, and operate utility facilities; and to engage in research and informational activities with respect to the efficient utilization of the state's utility resources.

As corporate purposes go, these were uncommon purposes. But not so noteworthy as to make the newspaper headlines. What did make the WDA a regular subject of news stories and public debate was the fact that *public* funds were appropriated to this *private* corporation to further its promotional and educational purposes. This hybrid political technique for achieving legislative objectives was born of a desire to avoid constitutional difficulties —though it died as the victim of another and unforeseen constitutional difficulty.

CHAPTER I

THE BILL AND

ITS BACKGROUND

Forerunners and Origins

The stress on public power and on cooperatives, in the functions of the WDA, had its roots in prior events. While cooperatives as such had not begun to emerge as an important factor in the utility problem until a year or so before the WDA (with the birth of a federal rural electrification program), the public power issue was one of long standing.

PUBLIC POWER

Since the first explicit legislative authorization for municipal operation of certain utilities, in 1895, the law of Wisconsin has steadily reflected the importance of the public power issue. Governor Davidson's 1907 message to the legislature acknowledged that there was "a growing sentiment in favor of municipal ownership, and encouragement should be extended in this direction, especially with respect to water works and gas and lighting plants . . . ." The public utility law passed at that 1907 session, which has been characterized by Clemens as "the first modern statute providing for the regulation of public utilities," involved the principle of granting a monopoly to the utility company, but subject to certain limitations. Thus, the company was subject to regulation by the Railroad Commission, which might, among other things, allow a municipality to compete with the company if the commission found such competition justified by public convenience and necessity, or the municipality might undertake proceedings to acquire the existing utility. "It apparently was the intent of the framers of the law," says Crow, that regulated monopoly should be the rule, with municipal ownership an easy method in case regulated monopoly was not workable or failed to give consistent satisfaction . . . ."[1]

Again, in 1915 when a water power law repeated the 1911 provision for the Railroad Commission's permit control over private companies' development of water power facilities, it included a "recapture" provision. Under this, states and municipalities could for compensation acquire the water power site and property thirty years after granting of the private permit.[2]

In 1927, reflecting its increased interest in the potentialities of public power, the legislature passed Assemblyman Alvin Reis's [R., Madison] resolution for appointment of an Interim Committee to investigate the power problem. In its report to the 1929 legislature, the committee took cognizance of several contentions: that savings would result from allowing municipal competition with the utilities in exploiting the state's water powers, from allowing cities to join together in power districts, and from permitting the state itself to operate power projects; that the existing rate schedules of the utilities varied widely throughout the state; and that the constitutional limit on municipal indebtedness in article IX, section 3 (5 per cent of the municipality's taxable property) presented a practical barrier to municipal acquisitions of utilities. The recommendations joined in by all five members of the committee failed to meet most of these contentions. But the Majority Report called unequivocally for a joint resolution looking towards a constitutional amendment authorizing the state itself to engage in power operations, and for legislation "authorizing municipalities and intervening rural areas to form electric light and power districts."[3]

The latter recommendation was explained in terms of greater economic efficiency and also in terms of meeting the debt-limitation problem faced by the municipalities. From the report's statement of the proposals made by the Wisconsin League of Municipalities, it is evident that the committee majority was largely recommending the League's proposals. The report stated, however, that the recommendations were intended not to give public ownership any advantage, but to endorse the principle of "the original public utility law that the people of any community should be enabled to decide for themselves whether they desire public or private ownership."[4]

In the 1929 legislature, these recommendations for authorization of state operation of utilities passed the Assembly, but were defeated in the Senate; and the same was true of the recommendations as to power districts. It was also true of a measure embodying the public-ownership advocates' proposal that municipalities should have the *right* to compete with utilities rather than be compelled to meet the heavy burden of convincing the Railroad Commission that convenience and necessity required the public competition. The only measure of substantial benefit to the cause of public power in the 1929 legislature was a joint resolution to amend the constitutional limitation on municipal indebtedness so as to allow municipalities to finance public utilities by mortgaging the utility or its income, instead of incurring a general indebtedness to be paid from taxes.[5]

However, almost complete success came with the 1931 legislature. While the 1930 election, like that of 1928, was a victory for the Republicans, this time the Progressive wing of the Republican party was in the saddle, led by Philip La Follette. He was elected governor on a platform which attacked the "Power Monopoly," called for "extension of public ownership and operation of utility plants" and blamed the 1929 legislative defeats on "reactionary members of the state senate." In fact, Governor La Follette's message to the legislature in January 1931 was largely devoted to the power issue. He extolled the virtues of public power and the need to bring electricity to the farm in order to lift the rural standard of living, to halt the flow of population from country to city, and to open up a new market for businessmen. He declared that "the experience of other communities demonstrates the wisdom of two forms of public competition: direct municipal ownership of smaller units, and publicly owned corporations capable of supplying wider market areas, and of integrating the local and district public systems with the private utilities." But at present "by a combination of constitutional and statutory prohibitions, both of these projects are effectively shackled. Under existing law, we are practically limited to private ownership of power production and distribution. This has hitherto meant high prices to the consumer with high profits to financial manipulators."[6] His program included not only an overhauling of the Railroad Commission's controls over such matters as rates and holding companies, but also several public-power recommendations.

First, he recommended that this legislature pass the same resolution passed in 1929 on mortgage financing of municipal utilities, so as to put the constitutional change to popular referendum in 1932. This recommendation was followed and the change was approved at the 1932 referendum.[7]

Second, he asked for legislation which he said was "prepared and ready for your consideration," designed "to give municipally owned plants larger opportunities for economic development through the organization of power districts." This, too, was followed.[8]

Third, he asked for "a constitutional amendment authorizing the State of Wisconsin to provide, if it so desires, a state-wide publicly owned power system." This was acquiesced in by passage of a joint resolution (which, however, did not eventuate in a constitutional amendment because the analogous resolution of the succeeding legislature had somewhat different provisions and was not followed by any successful similar resolution in the 1935 legislature) and supplemented by a statute creating the State Utilities Corporation of Wisconsin.[9]

The latter body, which exemplified Governor La Follette's above-quoted reference to the use of public corporations, was intended to function as an advisory group until the constitutional amendment was passed, whereupon it would become the active agency for operating state-owned power plants. Since there was no constitutional amendment, the corporation never undertook the ambitious program outlined for it, and its statutory authorization was repealed in 1939.[10] As for bills to make municipal competition easier, these, as in the case of the 1929 bill, were successful only in the Assembly (and this was true of succeeding legislatures as well).[11]

Thus, the 1931 provisions for power districts and for easier financing of municipal utilities were the only successful aspects of the La Follette legislative program for public power up to the time the Governor pressed for the Wisconsin Development Authority bill in 1937. In the intervening election campaigns, too, his program had stressed public power.[12] But as we have noted, the legislature had not followed through on the resolutions for constitutional amendment with respect to power operations by the state or by a state corporation. According to the governor's counsel, Gordon Sinykin, it was *primarily to deal with this constitutional obstacle* that the WDA bill was drafted. At hearings on the bill, he pointed out that the State Utilities Corporation, created in 1931, was prevented (by the constitutional prohibition against a state contracting debts for, or being a party to, internal improvements) from performing practically all functions provided for in the WDA bill; that the attempt to get a constitutional amendment had failed in the legislature and another attempt would take too long; and that "for that reason we worked out a plan whereby the state could go ahead with the kind of a program embodied in the State Utilities Corporation Act without the necessity of waiting for a constitutional amendment to be adopted, and for that purpose we have employed the device of the private corporation."[13]

There were additional motivations for the WDA bill. Its authorized promotion of power districts would vitalize the power-district law—which was being little used, probably for want of an active agency to implement it,[14] as well as invigorate the still sluggish municipal ownership movement.[15] The other major reason behind the WDA lay in the desire to have the Authority coordinate state activities in the promotion of rural electric cooperatives and utilize federal funds therefor—a motivation which is discussed in the section below.

COOPERATIVES

Bringing electricity to the farm had long been an American dream. In the slow process of realizing the dream, the major push came when an item for "rural electrification" was included among the hundreds of millions of dollars appropriated for relief by the Roosevelt Administration in 1935. In May of the same year, by executive order, President Roosevelt created an agency known as the Rural Electrification Administration to use the funds in question; in August of 1935, the President made this a loan agency; and in 1936 Congress established it as a long-term loan agency, authorized to make self-liquidating loans, for up to twenty-five years, with preference given to governmental units, peoples' utility districts, and "cooperative, non-profit or limited-dividend associations."[16]

To make efficient use of these federal funds in Wisconsin, some state machinery for guiding and coordinating farmer applications seemed necessary. But the Progressive efforts in this direction were beaten by a Republican-Democratic coalition in the 1935 legislature, which also buried numerous work-relief projects, including a La Follette rural electrification program. Governor La Follette did, however, obtain an emergency federal grant for setting up state coordinating machinery, which was called the *Rural Electrification Coordination,* or REC.[17]

Under its first director, Orland S. Loomis, a Progressive Senator (31st District) with strong public power views, REC carried on a vigorous campaign. The field staff went out before farm groups to spread the word on organization of REA projects and filing of loan applications. They had the help of a 1935 survey by the Wisconsin Emergency Relief Association which had mapped the potentialities of rural electrification within the state. Encouragement in the promotional effort came from local bankers and merchants, who were likely to benefit financially from a new REA project, whereas a contrary pressure came from private utilities, whose representatives at project organization meetings would raise troubling questions in some farmers' minds, questions, for example, about the scope of personal liabilities entailed by co-op membership. Another source of opposition was the advertising campaign during 1935–37 by manufacturers of rival methods of electrical generation, home generating plants, wind chargers, and storage batteries. Opponents could also point to financial difficulties experienced by some Wisconsin electric co-ops in the early twenties.[18]

But the inadequacy of REC's narrow coordinating and promotional functions was soon apparent. REC was in no position to offer technical engineering or legal service, or to supervise construction, or to negotiate contracts for wholesale electric service. So in April 1936, at the urging of REC itself, representatives of the sixteen Wisconsin REA projects formed a central agency to discharge these additional functions—called the *Wisconsin Rural Electric Cooperative Association,* though usually referred to as "Statewide." The organization, for its fee of 3 per cent (later raised to 4 per cent) of the total cost as defined by the REA loan contract, introduced many cost-reducing methods in the first several months of operation. Thereafter, however, it suffered several losses; REA rejected REC's and Governor La Follette's requests to permit raising the fee to 6 per cent; and REA Administrator Carmody in 1938 made clear to Wisconsin REA project directors his hostility to Statewide's manager, J. Morgan Wilson, and to its engineering "monopoly." The result was Statewide's reorganization into the *Wisconsin Electric Cooperative* which in 1940 began merchandising electric appliances, line materials, office equipment, etc. Its engineering staff was largely taken over in 1938 by WDA, which had begun functioning after protracted litigation starting in 1937. Statewide was not to render engineering services successfully again until after it in turn took over engineering functions from WDA in 1944; after some initial reverses it participated actively in the post-war expansion of electric co-ops.[19]

A 1938 REC report on its activities indicates that while Wisconsin did not receive its first federal REA funds until May 1936, by the beginning of 1938 almost $6,000,000 had been received, of which about $5,000,000 had been allocated for constructing 5,595 miles of electric lines to serve about 17,000 rural families— the remainder being granted for wiring and plumbing loans and construction of a cooperatively owned generating plant. With the single exception of a $60,000 loan to the village of Bangor's municipal plant, all REA loans had been to *cooperatives.*[20]

Evolution of the cooperative idea in electricity had not been a steady, early rooted growth. Nationally, "small electric mutuals had arisen in a number of rural areas shortly after the first World War, although by 1934 only 45 of them survived; most of the others had been absorbed by private companies. Some had been quite successful. The idea was picked up by the TVA, which had sponsored and was supplying a number of cooperatives. It became part of the REA program through people directly acquainted with the original undertakings (of whom [Nebraska's] Senator [George] Norris was one), through TVA, and especially through organized farm cooperative groups, some of which saw the possibilities at once and began to set up electric cooperatives. The TVA-sponsored cooperatives seem to have provided the early general form (in respect to by-laws, etc.), with modifications made necessary by the limitations of the Executive Order establishing REA and, later, of the Rural Electrification Act."[21]

In Wisconsin the cooperative idea itself was, by this time, far from novel. The state had long made special provision for the incorporation of cooperatives of various kinds, for promotion of agricultural cooperatives, and even for the required teaching of the essentials of cooperative marketing and consumers' cooperation in school curricula.[22] But *electric* cooperatives were fairly new and they had to fight their way.

The bitterest opposition in this fight came from the private utilities. They solicited the same customers sought by the co-op, and used various weapons, including rate-slashing, disparagement of the co-op, and "spite line" extensions into proposed co-op territory. The latter device picked off the cream of the potential customers—the remaining customers being rejected as unprofitable business, and being at the same time insufficient for a practicable co-op project by themselves. The utilities were also able to take over a number of co-ops, often as a result of the protracted delay and uncertainty incident to negotiation of the wholesale rates they were to charge the co-op.[23]

In the continuing struggle between utility and co-op, the Public Service Commission played an important role. After pointing out that "under existing statutes and court decisions" (1) utilities could not be granted exclusive franchises or permits, hence "rural territory is an open field as far as franchise rights are concerned," and (2) co-ops serving only members were not public utilities subject to commission regulation, the commission in 1936 declared, "In this situation common sense dictates that some rules be established whereby this competition in rural areas may take place on a fair plane of equality.... We hold no brief for or against any agency in this competitive struggle. Our primary concern is in seeing that the maximum number of farmers get service at the lowest cost consistent with the requirements for adequate and continuous service. We feel that the agency which should serve, assuming minimum requirements of service standards, financial responsibility, etc. are met, is largely a matter of choice with the farmers themselves, as long as wasteful competition or duplication of facilities will not result."[24] The commission encouraged negotiation between utilities and co-ops in territorial disputes, and established various rules of the game. In 1936, for instance, it required that under certain conditions utilities had to obtain commission permission before making a line extension more than a mile long; and it put limits on utility invasion of territory in which the co-op proposed to serve a majority of prospective customers and for which project the co-op had received a loan contract.[25]

Other controversies included those over the issue of whether utilities were required to serve the cooperatives at all, and, if so, at what wholesale rates. The commission in 1936 rejected the utility's argument in the *Madison Gas & Electric* case, that it was not compelled to render service to a cooperative whose service area lay outside of the utility's service area, and the argument in the *Wisconsin Public Service Corporation* case that the utility could not be required to serve a cooperative whose service was competitive with its own. The latter case also rejected the argument that variations among co-ops precluded the filing of a rate schedule for all co-ops on an "open order" basis; and in turn denied the co-ops' contention that rates must not exceed 1.5 cents per kilowatt hour if loans from the REA were to be forthcoming. The commission said that under Wisconsin law, "major consideration must be given to the cost of furnishing such service and the relation of such a rate to the rates available to other classes of customers"; that serious discrimination may result from rates to co-ops lower than those to a municipal wholesale customer.[26]

Not only from the commission did the co-ops attempt to win safeguards for their expansion. The previously mentioned 1938 REC report was able proudly to cite a substantial list of 1937 legislative enactments for which the co-ops had fought—principally the Rush Act. This prohibited utilities from beginning constructions, extensions, and the like, in an area of a proposed electric co-op until six months after the co-op had filed with the commission a territory map and statement showing that a majority of the prospective customers were included in the project; and this six-month period was to be extended for another year when the cooperative entered into a federal loan contract. It has been argued that the Rush Act as well as commission policies concerning utility extensions retarded rural electrification in Wisconsin because electrification by utilities would have been more rapid then by the co-ops; but there is evidence, on the other hand, that utilities were primarily interested in developing the more profitable areas, and that on these they already had enough of a foothold to prevent much adverse impact from the Rush Act and commission policies.[27]

As we have noted, the co-ops were receiving organizational guidance as well as representation before the commission, from the state executive agency, REC. At the time of the hearings on the WDA bill in April 1937 it was pointed out that REC funds were expiring, and hence it was "necessary to pass this [WDA] bill so that we can continue taking part in the Federal Rural Electrification program."[28] The Wisconsin program, at this time, was still in swaddling clothes. Though many projects were underway, the first Wisconsin co-op had not yet begun to service customers. Not until June 1937 did this event occur. It was in 1938 that the co-ops began to out-distance the utilities in increase of rural customers.[29]

In a perspective look at the WDA bill, its role becomes clear as a continuation of (1) an indigenous movement for governmental utility operation, and (2) a newly stirring movement primarily of federal origin, for rural electrification through cooperatives. In the bill's particular technical *form*, it mirrored the effect of a rigid constitutional barrier coupled with the fact of insufficient political power to demolish the barrier by the normal amendment process. In its motivations, the bill reflected the political-economic values of "liberalism" represented in the federal New Deal program and the Progressive program of Governor La Follette.

Indeed, the role of state executive initiative is particularly prominent. In relation to two of the later sections of this essay (treating the respective roles of legislature and court), this section could almost be titled in terms of the executive's role, for a recent study has shown that La Follette played an unusually dynamic role in the initiation of proposals for legislative action (as well as in driving them through the legislature).[30]

Nature of the Bill and the Corporation

The WDA bill did not set up the Wisconsin Development Authority, It provided state funds for the Authority, which was a previously formed private company, organized by twelve Wisconsin residents on March 30, 1937, as a non-stock, non-profit corporation, under chapter 180 of the Statutes.[31]

The lengthy articles of incorporation revealed that the corporate purposes were (1) to *promote or encourage* the organization of municipal power districts, the organization of cooperative and non-profit production or distribution of utility services (the Articles refer to the furnishing of "light, heat, water or power, the transmission of telephone messages, or the rendering of street or interurban railway or bus services"), and the construction, acquisition, or operation of facilities for such production or distribution by cooperatives, non-profit corporations, municipal power districts, or other governmental units; (2) to *make studies* of the state's utility resources, studies looking to a cheap and abundant supply of utility services, and studies for the coordination of water power and fuel power development with the regulation of rivers for water supply, flood control, and other uses; (3) to *collect* and *disseminate information,* and to *engage in research,* planning, and educational activities pertinent to its corporate purposes; (4) to *construct, acquire, improve,* and *operate* plants and facilities for production and distribution of utility services, and in connection therewith to condemn real and personal property; (5) to *enter into contracts* and to *furnish technical services,* including engineering, accounting, management services, and other services useful for carrying out the corporate purposes; (6) to *recieve, spend, and account for expenditure of, funds* given it by the federal or state government or other source—such government funds to be spent only pursuant to such terms as the grants might set; (7) to exercise *miscellaneous* powers, such as the power to borrow money, acquire and dispose of securities, sell or otherwise dispose of property, and to cooperate with governmental and non-governmental persons or groups. The designation of purposes and powers was stated to be not exclusive; and it was declared "that this corporation shall have and exercise all powers conferred upon it by law." However the charter forbade the corporation to engage in the business of banking, or of an investment association under chapter 216 of the Statutes, or of a building and loan association under chapter 215.[32]

The WDA bill itself was introduced on March 31, 1937, a day after the incorporation of the Authority (by Senator Roland E. Kannenberg [P., 25th District] as 266S and by Assemblyman Andrew J. Biemiller [P., Milwaukee, 2nd] as 608A). The bill appropriated to "the Wisconsin Development Authority, a Wisconsin corporation, on the effective date of this section, $10,000, and annually thereafter beginning July 1, 1937, $60,000, for the execution of its duties and functions under Sec. 199.03." WDA was designated as a state "instrumentality," whose authority to discharge the designated functions was to terminate if its non-profit character were to be changed by amendment of the articles. The duties and functions designated were, word for word, the promotional, research, and informational functions listed in the corporate articles (summarized in the preceding paragraph, in parenthetical clauses (1)–(3)),[33] and the function of cooperating with the federal government and its agencies in the execution of the foregoing functions.[34] In addition, the bill gave WDA the right of access to existing "collected" information from state officials and agencies, together with authority to request advice and assistance from them, and the right to seek from the public service commission information not yet collected.

Thus the legislation did not subsidize all of the corporate functions: no state funds were provided to finance any construction, acquisition, or operation of utilities by WDA, or any furnishing of engineering or other services (other than educational) to other groups. Section 199.02 of the bill made this clearer by providing that the WDA "shall not use or expend any of the funds appropriated to it by the state for any activities or functions which would be repugnant to the constitution of the state if carried on by the state" (the state was and is prohibited by article VIII, section 10 of the constitution from being a party to carrying on "internal improvements"). On the other hand, Section 199.02 further declared that "nothing in this chapter shall be construed to prevent said corporation from using or expending funds which it may derive from other sources than the state to works of internal improvement or such other lawful purposes as it may deem proper." All WDA activities carried on with state funds were to be reported to the governor in annual reports by WDA, and the Authority was to keep its accounts and records "so as to distinguish clearly between the uses made of funds appropriated by the state and the uses made of funds derived from other sources, and all disbursements of funds appropriated by the state shall be audited by the Secretary of State in the manner provided by law."

Not all of WDA's powers were intended to be immediately exercised. As a contemporary newspaper commented on the impending introduction of the bill: "The important power to acquire and construct utility property, according to administration spokesmen, will not be employed for some time. For the present, it was explained, the principal functions of the development authority would be to promote municipal and cooperative ownership of utilities and to supervise and advise municipalities in the power business or preparing to enter such business ... apparently with eventual state operation of power facilities as the objective."[35]

CHAPTER II

THE BATTLE

IN THE LEGISLATURE

Hearings on the Bill

On April 8, 1937, one week after the bill's introduction the Assembly Committee on State Affairs and the Senate Committee on Corporations and Taxation jointly held a three-hour public hearing on the bill. With opponents complaining of rush tactics that, according to press reports, were causing the bill "to be more talked about than anything else before the legislature," the Senate committee immediately reported out the bill with recommendation that it be sent to the Joint Finance Committee for a thorough hearing; and the Assembly (after an unsuccessful attempt by its committee to refer it to the Joint Finance Committee), referred it again to the State Affairs Committee for another hearing in two weeks. Both houses approved a resolution for printing and distributing five thousand copies of the bill and of the WDA articles.[1]

THE FIRST HEARING

According to press accounts of this unrecorded initial hearing of April 8, Attorney General Loomis (who had been REC's first director) referred to WDA as an instrumentality for receipt of federal funds for certain power projects being considered by Congress in the St. Croix River Valley, the Wisconsin River Valley, and the Kickapoo River Valley. Loomis argued that "Wisconsin needs such projects if its industry is to compete with other states.

He explained that one of the purposes of WDA is to promote such projects." And, "reciting failures to amend the Constitution to permit state utility ownership [he] said the new authority is 'the way out. Under this bill we won't have to wait.'" Together with Thomas Duncan, the governor's secretary, Loomis also stressed WDA's importance for continuance of the rural electrification program. John Becker (REC's second director) emphasized the importance of developing power districts through WDA; Professor Beuscher of the University of Wisconsin Law School compared WDA to a "little TVA," which could establish rates to serve as a yardstick, forcing private rates down; Assemblyman Biemiller said the bill meant cheap rates for the masses, and that utility officials received too much money; Mayor Hoan of Milwaukee declared that "with all the nationwide propaganda against municipal ownership financed by the power trust, the small municipalities need some help so that the true facts can be brought to the public"; and studies by the Public Service Commission were presented to show that rates of municipal electric utilities were lower than private utilities' rates.[2]

These and other reported proponents[3] met with opposition. Kenneth White, of River Falls, expressed the fear that under its articles, WDA would be able to sponsor a huge public works program of the kind which had been defeated in the 1935 legislature. And a number of utility and industrial and retail business representatives expressed, principally, a concern that WDA would have authority to compete with all other kinds of business.[4]

THE SECOND HEARING

On April 22, 1937, the Assembly Committee on State Affairs and the Joint Committee on Finance afforded the bill a more extensive hearing, of which a transcript is available. Senator Kannenberg, sponsor of the Senate bill, emphasized that lower rates from public power would help industry and keep Wisconsin a great industrial state. Assemblyman Biemiller, sponsor of the companion bill, declared that the bill brought "to a focal point, the fight that has been going on for many years in this state between the people on one hand and the power trusts on the other," and that it would allow the "people of Wisconsin to develop their own resources and . . . use them for their own benefit" rather than allow holding companies to continue to "milk the people of . . . Wisconsin and take huge sums from this state and carry them to Wall Street."[5]

Legal motivations and implications of the bill were discussed by Gordon Sinykin, executive counsel to the governor, and John Ernest Roe, Madison attorney—who were described at the hearing as the two attorneys having most to do with the drafting of the bill. We have previously noted in Chapter I Sinykin's explanation at the hearing of the use of a private corporate instrumentality as a means of avoiding the constitutional restriction on state participation in internal improvements, and thus saving the time that would be involved in a second attempt at constitutional amendment. He further declared that there was nothing new in using a private corporation as an instrumentality of government, citing such federal corporations as Reconstruction Finance Corporation, Home Owners' Loan Corporation, Electric Home and Farm Authority, and Federal Deposit Insurance Corporation.[6] He put particular stress upon "the TVA which seeks to do for the Tennessee Valley on a far greater scale what we are seeking to do by this program for Wisconsin. Some of these corporations are organized as stock corporations; others of these federal corporations are organized just as the WDA has been organized, namely, as a non-stock, non-profit corporation." Moreover, he said that Wisconsin in the past had practiced "calling on private corporations or private agencies to carry on various functions of the state government and [appropriating] money to such agencies and corporations for various functions and purposes," including the State Historical Society and various agricultural societies. "Some of these societies carry on these functions together with some other functions, and some of them perform only the functions provided by the appropriations made to them by the state. Most of these societies receive appropriations from the state to carry on various types of promotional work in agriculture."[7]

Sinykin referred to misunderstandings which had developed over WDA's powers and duties. The clause in WDA's articles which stated that the enumeration of its powers was not exclusive, and that the corporation might exercise all powers conferred upon it by law, would not authorize WDA to engage in any kind of business; WDA was confined to the *utility* field. The clause was intended, he said, to avoid a narrow construction of the powers granted within the utility field. He described it as a provision common in corporate articles, particularly in articles drawn by the Attorney General of the United States for federal government corporations. Might WDA *amend* its articles in order to go into other business? Sinykin replied that under Section 180.07 of the Wisconsin Statutes, no non-stock corporation might substantially change the original purposes of its incorporation.

He then considered the charge that WDA's duty of making an annual report to the governor would be insufficient, since it would cover only activities financed by state funds. Sinykin's reply was that the Authority's other activities would be separately covered, since, like any other corporation, WDA would have to make reports to the secretary of state and to such other agencies concerned with its activities as the Public Service Commission and Tax Commission; moreover, chapter 182 of the Statutes reserved to the legislature and the attorney general large investigatory powers over corporations. He concluded by pointing to the accomplishments of TVA and predicting that WDA "will serve to do the same sort of thing for Wisconsin and make Wisconsin the first state in the union to embark upon a comprehensive public ownership program on a state-wide basis."[8]

Supporting Sinykin was the statement of Attorney Roe. He too attacked the assertion that WDA could go into any business it pleased and then considered the objection that the only businesses specifically excluded by WDA's articles were banking, investment, and building and loan associations. These had been expressly designated, he said, because statutes covering those businesses made certain requirements as to stock, and it was deemed important to insure the non-stock, non-profit character of WDA by this "specific prohibition as to these types of business requiring a specific capital structure, particularly in view of the fact that the WDA is authorized to finance its activities."[9]

In further support of the bill was the statement of John Becker, one of WDA's incorporators and REC's director. He stressed the importance of a central guiding agency such as WDA by contrasting the lack of advance under the municipal power district law of 1931 (the State Utilities Corporation being inactive) and the progress of rural electrification under the active guidance of REC.

He felt the WDA could not only carry on the program for rural electrification but would also "do for the farmers of Wisconsin who are in smaller groups and for the municipalities, exactly what the Coordination Office has done for the farmer in the rural areas that were able to organize cooperatives."[10]

Other supporting witnesses were mayors of municipalities interested in municipal ownership and farm representatives interested in rural electrification. Mayor S. W. Slagg, of Edgerton, detailed the delays in the still-pending proceedings following Edgerton's vote in 1933 to acquire the private utility operating there. He thought WDA could help cities both in acquiring plants and after acquisition, though he acknowledged that delays occasioned by utilities' going to court would not be obviated. Mayor F. L. Brewer, of Richland Center, said that his city had a successful municipal power plant for thirty years and had arranged to supply an REA cooperative with electricity. He thought there would be no further municipal ownership in Wisconsin for ten years if the bill were not passed, since a coordinated state program was required. Stockholders in private utilities would not suffer, either directly or from taxes consequent upon municipal ownership; not taxes but the "water" in utility stock after municipal plants were bought up for more than their worth would hurt the stockholders. Kenneth Hones, President of the Farmers' Union, Wisconsin, and one of the WDA's incorporators, said that "without the assistance of a bill of this nature, it is going to be impossible for us to carry on and carry out the rural electrification program in this state." The whole state, he said, would benefit, since with lower rates more industry would be attracted into Wisconsin and farmers would buy more electric appliances. That electric cooperatives are basically American was emphasized by Thomas Stodola of the Cooperative League of Wisconsin; moreover, they had brought down utility rates. Likewise, Otto Woerth, representing about nine hundred farmers in Langlade County organized in a cooperative plant, declared that utility rates came down when the REA project began to be talked about.[11]

Opposition to the bill came from some large utilities, the Wisconsin Manufacturers' Association, some taxpayers, and miscellaneous retailers. Most of the retailer group based their opposition on the fear that WDA would go into the coal or oil business, in spite of the prior attempt which Sinykin and Roe had made to allay such fears. A few of the retailers stated a general opposition to government in business.[12] The latter attitude was also presented by certain Racine taxpayers, through Dr. R. J. Miller, and by United Taxpayers, Milwaukee, through Richard Lehmann, who warned, "If you want to . . . bankrupt every poor farmer and home owner with some millions of dollars more of experiments, go ahead, but get ready for the storm which is coming." For the Wisconsin Manufacturers' Association, R. O. Wipperman argued that the bill would narrow the tax base, since private utilities paid substantial taxes (almost $7,000,000 in 1933), and helped keep things going in the Depression; that the bill would violate the "pledge" in the 1907 indeterminate permit law, that utilities might operate indefinitely as long as they rendered ample service at reasonable cost; that it was undesirable to encourage the buying and operation of plants by local bodies when the ability of these local bodies to do so was unknown; that if the Public Service Commission were regulating public utilities inadequately, the remedy was to make the regulation adequate rather than enact this bill; that if the bill's proponents were sincere in saying that it did not go beyond the utility field, they should be willing to amend it specifically to make that clear.[13]

Opposition by utility companies was presented first by C. E. Kohlhepp, of the Wisconsin Public Service Corporation. He asserted that private utilities were doing a good enough job of rural electrification, and that an electric cooperative could get federal funds without any state agency. If the purpose were to continue the work of the Rural Electrification Coordination, then "why don't you bring in a bill to appropriate the funds necessary to keep it going—why hook it on to this propagandized frankenstein?" And why so much fuss about the cost of electricity, when this cost represented only about 2 per cent of the average home budget? As for the alleged high cost of electricity to industry, he asserted that no industry had ever left the state because of too high power costs. The latter issue provided the main theme of L. F. Sibold, of the Milwaukee Electric Railway and Light Company. He offered charts based on Federal Power Commission data, to show that Wisconsin ranked well up among the states offering low power rates. The factors keeping industry out of Wisconsin, he said, were not power costs, which were a small part of a manufacturer's total costs, but Wisconsin's state income tax and the fact that taxes paid by utilities, in terms of percentage of gross revenue, were higher in Wisconsin than in most states. The allegedly lower rates of municipally owned utilities were illusory; if their hidden advantages through subsidies and tax advantages were enjoyed by private utilities, then (even though the latter must build long lines to reach farms far apart, as compared with the closely contiguous customers of municipal utilities) the private rates would be lower than municipal rates. He ended by warning that there was no economic Santa Claus; the taxpayer would have to pay for losses suffered by WDA.

For a group of locally owned telephone companies, J. H. Sanderson, of Portage, reiterated some ideas already expressed: if utility performance was inadequate, the Public Service Commission had ample regulatory authority to deal with the situation; WDA's powers were broad enough to let it enter any business; it was an entering wedge for socialism; there would be a loss in tax revenues from private utilities. He expressed one additional thought, which is interesting for its relation to the crucial questions in subsequent litigation: "Why," he asked, "should $60,000 be spent annually in propaganda for public ownership only; why not educate the public on both sides of the issue?"[14]

Considerable newspaper space was given to summarizing the testimony. And more than one paper made the point that "a surprising feature of the hearing was the fact that the greatest opposition came not from the private utilities, but from independent oil dealers and coal operators who saw in the bill a menace to private ownership."[15] Whether this was a matter of private utility strategy did not appear.

The Bill on the Floor

As could be expected, the bill stimulated considerable lobbying by the utilities—enough to require a direction to the Assembly sergeant-at-arms to "clear the assembly parlor and corridors of all lobbyists." But on April 29, a week after the second hearing, both committees recommended passage. Five days later, by Resolution 49A, introduced by Assemblyman Palmer Daugs [D., Ft. Atkinson], the Assembly sought Attorney General Loomis' opinion on WDA's powers under the bill.[16]

Two days thereafter, the attorney general replied in the following manner to the specific questions asked in the resolution: (1) The exact scope of the constitutional restriction against the state's contracting debts for, or being a party to, internal improvements was not settled, though a review of prior judicial constructions was deemed helpful; (2) under WDA's articles it might engage in works of internal improvement within the public utility field only; (3) under the bill, WDA might not use state funds for such operations, though state funds might be used for educational or promotional activities in relation to such internal improvements in the utility field; (4) funds other than state funds might be used by WDA to engage in works of internal improvement as well as for its other corporate functions.[17]

Next came a batch of proposed amendments. In the Assembly, between May 4 and May 13, the opposition proposed seven amendments, all of which were rejected; the Progressives proposed three amendments, all of which were adopted. The first rejected amendment would have subjected WDA property to the general property tax (an apparently unnecessary provision in view of the absence of any exemption for this private corporation's property). Another, which received almost no support, would have required that, in order to qualify for state funds, WDA must drop all functions other than those mentioned in the bill as state-financed functions (that is, WDA would be limited to research, educational, and promotional activities), and that its annual report to the governor must cover all its activities, rather than only those financed by state funds. An amendment described as "taking the steam out of" the administration's argument that rural electrification would be jeopardized by failure to pass the bill, would have created a state agency, the Wisconsin Rural Electrification Authority, which would limit itself to rural electrification activities, that is, would help cooperatives and non-profit corporations qualify for federal REA loans and furnish engineering and accounting services to them. This amendment, however, was held "not germane."[18]

Rejected also was an amendment which would have expanded beyond the state-fund restriction the restraint on WDA activity in internal improvements, and would have restricted its permissible promotional functions to rural electrification. The Assembly further rejected a less restrictive amendment, intended to confine to the utility field the internal improvements which WDA might engage in with non-state funds. A request for delay to permit wider official distribution of the transcript of the second hearing was defeated after Assemblyman Biemiller objected that all members were fully informed as to the bill's contents.[19]

The three amendments *adopted* to the Assembly bill (1) made clear that the state was never to be liable or responsible for any debt or obligation of WDA; (2) struck the "transmission of telephone messages" from the listed fields of WDA's activity (apparently because of the feeling that the telephone business was largely interstate); and (3) declared that the powers given by the bill would terminate if the corporate articles at any time authorized WDA to engage in activities, and WDA then actually engaged in activities, specified neither in the bill nor in the existing articles. The last amendment, said Assemblyman Biemiller, clearly confined WDA to the utility field, and would compel the private utilities to stop fighting the battle against WDA behind the representatives of small non-utility business. To the latter charge of duplicity, Assemblyman Vernon W. Thomson [R., Richland] replied that the bill's sponsors were enlisting the friends of REA to fight their battle; and he also deplored the amount of "propaganda" coming out of the office of the governor's secretary, T. M. Duncan.[20]

About a week after these rejections and adoptions, the Assembly on May 20 passed its bill, 55 to 36. But in the Senate, 608A did not get beyond the Joint Committee on Finance. The Senate chose to press its own 266S, which was to pass the Senate June 16 and the Assembly on June 25. The same three amendments which had been successful in the Assembly were successful in the Senate as amendments of 266S.[21]

Of several amendments rejected in the Senate, two were rather similar to two rejected in the Assembly: one would have confined WDA's activities to promotion of rural electrification; another would have limited WDA to assisting in construction, purchase, or operation of cooperative, non-profit and municipal enterprises in the light, heat, and power field only, as well as terminating its powers under the bill, if (as the existing articles would have permitted) its activities went beyond these service functions. A requirement that these services should be rendered only on request of the municipality, cooperative or non-profit corporation was also defeated. The remaining rejected amendments were of a different sort. One would have killed the bill by striking out the enacting clause. Another would have prohibited WDA's use of state funds for election or referendum purposes. And one, which would have included "ownership and operation of radio stations" in WDA's functions (of research in, and promoting operations by, cooperatives, non-profit corporations and governmental units) was apparently not offered seriously; a newspaper comment was that "its author humorously remark[ed] that this seemed to be the only line of activity which had been missed."[22]

In an uproarious session on June 16, the details of which are given below, the Senate passed the bill and it went to the Assembly, where six amendments were offered and rejected. These included the counterpart of the radio station amendment rejected in the Senate; another attempt by Assemblyman James T. Cavanaugh [D., Langlade] to get enacted his rejected amendments which would have confined WDA to activities constitutionally open to the state itself; the counterpart of Senator Edward J. Roethe's [R., 16th District] rejected effort to restrict WDA to rural electrification; an attempt to condition the bill's effectiveness upon its approval at the polls in April 1938; and efforts to control WDA's membership and indebtedness and to confine its use of non-state funds to internal improvements. On June 25, the Assembly concurred in the Senate bill 56 to 21; and then by 51 to 30, it refused to reconsider the vote.[23] The governor approved the measure on July 1, 1937.

But the happenings in the Senate on June 16 are worthy of some further note. A contemporary journalist told this story of the day's events:

Final passage by a vote of 17 to 15 came at 4:37 p.m. . . . It came almost as an anti-climax to an incredibly disordered five-hour fight in which nearly a dozen opposition senators risked arrest in a mad scramble to block passage.

Furious because they had been tricked into a trap by a resourceful if shifty minority, progressives obtained the signatures of 17 of their number to a petition in the form of a resolution which assailed democrats and republicans as a bunch of "cattle" ordered about by the "power trust".

The five-hour Senate performance which would have needed no brightening or imagination for Gilbert and Sullivan to have translated it into an operetta, was the most spectacular ever conducted in the past two decades or more, veteran senators and legislative employees declared.

Three times the bill reached a final vote. Twice, by prepared plan, most of the opposition Senators raced out of the Chamber, leaving progressives in complete control of the vote, but constitutionally unable to pass the bill, since the constitution requires a quorum of 20 members for vote on an appropriation bill.[24]

The first walk-out occurred just before the first attempted passage of the bill, which was by vote of 15 to 2.[25] Senator Kannenberg, apparently aware of the quorum difficulty, moved successfully for reconsideration of the order messaging the bill to the Assembly, and then moved to expunge from the record all proceedings on final passage. During discussion of whether the latter motion involved a suspension of the rules, requiring a two-thirds vote, Senator Nelson rose to a point of order. Less than the constitutional quorum (three-fifths) for appropriation bills had been present at the vote, he said, so that the passage and the messaging to the Assembly was void, and the bill therefore remained in the condition just previous to the void passage—engrossed but not yet passed. The chair's ruling that this point was well taken was, upon appeal by Senator Coakley, sustained, 16 to 13.[26] The "walk-out" senators participated in this vote. According to a press comment, they had, "tipped off by their sentries, [come] pouring back to the chamber. The sergeant-at-arms' staff had been unable to locate them anywhere until that time." But when a new vote on passage was about to be taken,

Senator Maurice Coakley (Rep., Beloit) quarterback for the opposition team, led his teammates dashing wildly through the chamber again. Spectators gasped. Could this be the Wisconsin Senate?

Fighting mad by this time at the fact that a minority could forever block the majority, progressives ordered the arrest of the senators who had taken a second "run-out powder." Lieutenant-Governor Henry A. Gunderson and Chief Clerk Lawrence Larsen signed 10 subpoenas ordering the arrest and immediate return of the absent senators.

Sergeant's assistants and police swarmed through favorite haunts in search of the missing Senators.[27]

Though roads leading out of Madison were scoured, the senators were all the time two blocks from the Capitol in an East Main Street tavern-restaurant. One story has it that they sauntered leisurely back to the Capitol after dining and conducting a council of war; another, that they rushed back because of a telephone message that Progressives were preparing to pass a bill forbidding discharge of teachers for political or economic opinions.[28]

When the Republicans and Democrats did come back, Progressives refused to be caught asleep at the switch again. They slapped on a call of the Senate, which requires locking the doors of the chamber, so that no Senator can leave.

But before he let the bill come to a final vote once more, Senator Coakley rose to pronounce the curse of unconstitutionality. The Senate was not about to pass the bill, he insisted, because the bill had legally been killed when the Senate unconstitutionally voted to pass it, 15 to 2, earlier in the day [so that the only appropriate motion now was for reconsideration of the vote by which passage had been refused].

Lieutenant-Governor Gunderson banged him out of order. Progressives did not bother to reply. The roll was called. The bill passed, 17 to 15, with one Senator E. Merwyn Rowlands (P.) Cambria, not voting because he was absent.[29]

The margin of victory in the Assembly had been greater than in the Senate, though the Progressive membership had a greater handicap to overcome in the Assembly.[30] Though there was but a slim margin in the Senate, afforded by the support of Senator Nelson [R., Maple] and Senator Zimny [D., Milwaukee], the margin had never been seriously in doubt. Apparent disaffections in Progressive ranks had resulted at most in delays rather than withdrawal of support.

Early in the fight, it was said that "if Progressives can get the votes of Senators Arthur L. Zimny (Dem., Milw.) and Philip Nelson (Rep., Maple), the bill is as good as passed in the Senate. Zimny and Nelson went along with the Progressives on the labor relations bill and the budget, and it is understood they will join the administration on the WDA bill." But it was "no secret to the Governor's office that certain Progressives would duck a roll call on public ownership if they could. A few have voted for amendments on municipal competition bills knowing that the amendments emasculated the bill." The same newspaper reported later that in retaliation to one of its stories ("that legislators were reluctant to vote upon the Senate 'TVA' bill because it was sponsored by Kannenberg and would prefer to act upon the assembly measure") Senator Kannenberg was seeking to withdraw his bill and had pointed to "a determined effort on the part of a certain group to promote legislation by the Communistic bloc [who] are determined to take control of the Progressives in the Senate." The newspaper commented that Kannenberg "was referring to the fact that Biemiller belongs to the Farmer-Labor Progressive federation bloc in the Assembly which has been termed Communistic by various legislators"; and that Kannenberg indicated Evjue [Madison *Capital Times* editor] was a leader of the Communistic bloc and a "political prostitute." Kannenberg was later reported as saying his bill was the only one he would vote for; that he wouldn't vote for any bill bearing the socialist label; and that Biemiller was "not a true American."[31]

In the last stages of the legislative fight it was reported that "the Progressive coalition which had held firm in pushing the 'little TVA' bill to one step from passage, fell apart in the Senate this morning, and the measure was put over for final action until next Wednesday. Sen. Philip Nelson (R.) Maple and Arthur Zimny (D.) Milwaukee, voted with other Republicans and Democrats in delaying the passage of the bill until measures they were personally interested in had been satisfactorily disposed of. For the second time the absence of Sen. Michael Kresky (P.) Green Bay was partly responsible for the bill being put off. The 'Little TVA' bill could have been law today had Kresky voted with Progressives last week for a Saturday session to act on the measure. Kresky's vote was badly needed today as Nelson and Zimny switched but he did not appear in the Senate until after opposition forces had been solidified."[32]

Margins would doubtless have been greater and delays less, if some advocates of municipal ownership among Democrats and Republicans had not opposed the bill in the belief that it would harm municipal ownership rather than fulfill the professed purpose of promoting it. Republican Senator White, proponent of municipal ownership, took a determined stand against the bill. An early press comment was: "The position of Sen. White on the bill may have an important bearing on the Senate action. His father, Ferris M. White of River Falls, a public ownership advocate, is one of the incorporators of record of the Wisconsin Development Authority. It was Sen. White who introduced the four bills on municipal ownership, and regulation of municipally owned utilities, which were recently defeated in the upper house." And according to a later press comment, the fact that "at least some municipally owned utility commissions are opposed to the WDA bill is indicated by statements of Sen. Bolens (Port Washington) and Assemblymen Theisen (Sheboygan), Yindra (Manitowoc) and Bichler (Belgium) that the utility commissioners of Plymouth, Manitowoc and Cedarburg were opposed to the measure for fear that it might jeopardize instead of promote the future of their publicly owned plants."[33]

Still more potent a ground of opposition had been the oft-expressed view that the bill was a political sop to the Socialists for election support to the Progressives, and would permit realization of Socialist objectives through government entry into many fields of enterprise. More than one news story reflected the existence of this view. When the Assembly voted to engross its bill and rejected Assemblyman Catlin's [R., Outagamie, 1st.] amendment designed to insure that WDA's internal improvements activity supported by non-state funds should be confined to the utility field, the *Chicago Daily Tribune* commented: "Observers saw in today's action a significant concession by Governor La Follette and the Progressive Party in Wisconsin to the Socialists, who were 'adopted' two years ago into what was to be a big, happy family of radicals—the far-flung Farmer-Labor Progressive federation." Reference was made to the governor's "socialist secretary, Thomas Duncan" and "Socialist Biemiller." Earlier the *Milwaukee Journal* had observed: "Committee hearings have exhibited a widespread belief throughout the State that the measure's provisions can be expanded into fields other than state utility ownership. The belief appears to be based on WDA articles of incorporation and the prominence of 'production for use' in the last campaign. The bill redeems a pledge made by the Progressives when they caused the Farmer-Labor federation to drop the 'production for use' phrase from its platform. The thought then was that the plank would be replaced with something 'just as good.' " And later the *Sheboygan Press* quoted Republican Senator Coakley as saying: "This bill is the pay-off, the sop to the Milwaukee Socialists for their valiant efforts in behalf of the federation of the last election. You farmers are going to help them collect. You are going to put the State in the power business through the back door of a dummy corporation like that under the works bill [Governor La Follette's work relief measure defeated in the 1935 legislature]."[34]

True, the attorney general's opinion of May 11 had declared that WDA's powers under the bill and under its articles were restricted to the utility field, and the McDermid amendment to the Senate bill (like the Nehs amendment to the House bill) conditioned state-fund support on WDA's restricting itself to powers under the bill and existing articles. But comment after, as well as before, these events professed the same feelings expressed at the hearings: that WDA was intended to operate in many non-utility fields, and that language more specifically excluding that possibility should be inserted in the bill.

Editorializing in favor of an amendment specifically limiting WDA to the utility field, one newspaper referred to a conference between Governor La Follette and state chambers of commerce representatives, in which he disclaimed any intent of going beyond the utility field. One-third of his listeners, said the editorial, were of the type who won't concede a thing under any circumstances; another third, while pleased with his ideas, were skeptical of his absolute candor; only the final third "went away in a mood to accept the new scheme practically as it stands." On May 20, Assemblyman Shimek was quoted as saying he still thought that WDA could invade the non-utility field, and he pointed to the "any lawful purpose" language of the articles. Several days later the paper carrying Shimek's statement noted: "The error which its proponents undoubtedly made was not to make it more clear what the private agency can or cannot do. There remains a hazy opinion about this, hence the battle which is raging in the Senate . . . ." The same point was made (along with a vigorous protest against using public funds to "influence citizens to accept communistic and socialistic programs") in a statement by Senator Duel [R., 18th District] upon passage of the bill, in a front page story of the June 1937, *The Utilitarian,* monthly organ of the Wisconsin utilities.[35]

This suspicion of a Trojan-horse quality in the bill was probably helped along by the view that the administration was not being candid and straightforward in other respects. One newspaper reported the bill's opponents as insisting that the "little TVA" label was a misnomer, there being "little resemblance to the TVA aims and purposes"; and quoted Assemblyman Shimek's emphasis on the lack of governmental control compared to the executive and Congressional control over TVA operations. The eleven Senators who made the dramatic flight from the Senate on June 16 were quoted as defending their action in these terms: "After being subjected to gag rule through the use of the 'previous question,' a practice which for a period of some 20 years has seldom if ever been employed in choking off debate in the Wisconsin Senate, and being subjected to unfair and arbitrary rulings from the president pro tempore, and failure to secure recognition and obtain the floor to speak upon the questions involved, the only recourse left open to us was to leave the chamber, which we did, solely on our own initiative. It was the only way in which we could voice our protest against the arbitrary and unsavory methods employed in driving through the legislature a measure designed to accomplish by indirection what is expressly forbidden by the state constitution."[36]

It may be that not all, or perhaps none, of these grounds were crucial determinants of opposition as distinguished from convenient rallying points for opposition determined by other factors. Loyalties to political party, predilections toward a basically laissez faire economic philosophy, and pressures from the private utilities are also part of the total picture.

CHAPTER III

THE COURT FIGHT

Beginnings of the Litigation

On July 7, less than a week after the governor's approval of the WDA enactment, the "groundwork for an early court test of the validity of WDA was laid when the United Taxpayers Coop. Assoc. of Wis. served formal demand . . . on State Treasurer Solomon Levitan and Secretary of State Theodore Damman not to release any of the $60,000 annual appropriation to the corporation, on the ground it is operating unconstitutionally." The secretary of state asked the attorney general for an opinion on constitutionality, but the attorney general refused, referring the secretary to the opinion rendered during the legislative fight.[1]

WDA then itself set the stage for the court test by employing V. M. Murray, Norris Maloney, and H. I. Tuttle, Inc. for a few days in the beginning of August on projects it believed to be authorized by the WDA law and then presenting claims for three items of expenditure ($60, $40, and $9, respectively) to the secretary of state on August 6. On the same day, he refused to audit the claims, declaring that the WDA enactment was "never validly enacted into law in the manner required by law" and "if enacted in the manner required by law it is nevertheless unconstitutional." Whereupon WDA petitioned Dane County Circuit Judge Alvin C. Reis for the issuance of alternative writs of mandamus seeking to compel the secretary to audit the accounts. The petition emphasized that the appropriation made by the WDA law was for a public purpose, because it would further the existing state policy favoring municipal ownership and municipal power districts, and would help meet the public need for rural electrification and for research and education in these fields. The petition justified the expenditures made for Murray, Maloney, and Tuttle as outlays designed to further such policies and needs. Judge Reis ruled in favor of WDA.[2]

Judge Reis saw two "fundamental constitutional questions" involved in the law granting funds to WDA: (1) "whether the state thereby becomes engaged in works of internal improvement, contrary to express provision of the state constitution" [article VIII, section 10; text in Appendix B]; and (2) "whether the state is expending public money for a private purpose in violation of accepted constitutional principles."

(1) On the first question, he noted that there was no contention that the state's appropriation contracted a "debt" within the meaning of article VIII, section 10. Hence the only issue under that constitutional restriction was whether the state was here acting as a "party" to works of internal improvement. The WDA law, he emphasized, did not authorize the use of state funds to support WDA in itself actually engaging in utility operations, or rendering engineering, accounting, or other services to municipal and cooperative utilities (though the corporate charter would permit such operations, and the WDA law did not purport to prevent them when financed by non-state funds). Thus the state was not a party to the utility type of internal improvements in the sense of financing them. Would WDA's authorized use of state funds merely to "promote and encourage" utility operations by others make the state a party to internal improvements? No, said Judge Reis. The history of this constitutional provision as considered at the 1847 convention showed, he argued, that a distinct difference was understood between the concept of "encouraging" and the concept of being a "party."[3]

Moreover, the Wisconsin Supreme Court had held in the *Van Dyke* case that state funds covering 25 per cent of the labor cost on counties' and cities' public works for unemployment relief did not make the state a "party" to the public works. If the state can do this and not be a "party" to the public works, "because someone else made the work," argued Judge Reis, then how can "the state by encouraging the work before there ever is any work, become a party?"[4] At any rate, where the state does not bear the financial burden of the internal improvements themselves, there was case authority for saying the state was not a party.[5] Finally, Judge Reis refused to attach significance to the legislative defeat of the proposed constitutional amendment permitting the state to enter the power business. The state was not here doing what the defeated legislation had sought to let it do. It was not going into the power business; "by encouraging others to go in, it is keeping out."

(2) Nor did Judge Reis have difficulty in concluding that the "public purpose" requirement had been satisfied. If this were an issue of first impression, he said, it might well be concluded that a court is compelled to accept the legislative opinion on what is a "public purpose"—it being a matter of economic "opinion" or "philosophy" rather than law. But courts have already taken it upon themselves to scrutinize the purpose. Not closely, however. The principle of the Wisconsin cases was clear, he said, that the public purpose exists unless its absence is so clear as to be palpable to every mind at first blush—and on that basis, a public purpose was present here. The fact that for some purposes a municipal utility has been said to be operating in a "proprietary" rather than governmental capacity, did not mean the function was not "public" for the purpose of determining the permissible scope of legislative appropriation for a public purpose. The proprietary label was mere "nomenclature," useful mainly in cases involving the city's liability for negligence. Municipal operation of utilities, municipal bond issues and taxes for support of municipal utilities, were established practice, evidencing a weighty practical construction of the public purpose concept. "If it is good public policy to let cities and villages go into the electric business—and this has been their right since 1907—then we cannot conceive that there is a lack of public purpose in encouraging them."[6]

So, too, with cooperatives. True, the 1937 legislature had declared that cooperative utilities were not public utilities. But other cooperatives, also not public utilities, had been encouraged and assisted by the Department of Agriculture. "Who shall say—judicially—that it is not a public purpose to encourage cooperatives to organize to obtain electricity and to acquire utility facilities for production *or* transmission *or* distribution," ["We emphasize the disjunctive," he said, "because nowhere in the statute is there any suggestion that the privately owned utilities shall be put out of business. A new co-operative is conceivably a new wholesome customer for some existing utility. The co-op can tie on to the latter's high line, the co-operative engaging purely in distribution."][7] and that it *is* a public purpose to encourage carrying on agricultural activities cooperatively? The public benefit from increased use of electricity was clear; the *form* of organization to obtain it was a matter of legislative judgment primarily. The fact that the form used was that of a private corporation was inconclusive; no one doubted that appropriations to such private organizations as the Wisconsin Dairymen's Association were for a public purpose. The fact that cooperatives were *singled out* for beneficial treatment did not itself make the benefit private; a previous law making a bonus payment to ex-soldiers only had been sustained. Nor was the benefit private because WDA might seek to *localize* the use of its funds, for example, employ most of them north of a certain line in Wisconsin; the statute itself did not require such practice, and the statute itself was what was here attacked. Moreover, a prior case had sustained a statute which itself required the localized use of state money (to relieve distress from a cyclone in New Richmond).[8]

Judge Reis then disposed of miscellaneous lesser objections to the statute. He denied that such an appropriation of money involved a gift or loan of state "credit" in violation of the constitutional prohibition (article VIII, section 3; text in Appendix B). He further denied that there had been a violation of the constitutional prohibition (article IV, section 31; text in Appendix B), against "special or private laws . . . for granting corporate powers or privileges except to cities." (1) WDA had obtained its charter under the general corporation law. (2) The appropriation was not a special or private law granting corporate privileges. If it were, annual appropriations to many agricultural societies would be unconstitutional. It had been held in fact that the granting of *charters* by special act was what the constitutional provision prohibited.[9] (3) That the constitutional limitation was confined to grants of charter privileges also served to exclude from the prohibited area WDA's statutory privilege to call on state agencies for information. It had also been contended that the secretary of state's duty under the statute to audit disbursements constituted an invalid delegation of judicial power to determine constitutionality of expenditures. The court disposed of this by saying that this duty of the secretary would exist even without the statutory provision, and that the secretary's preliminary judgment was, of course, subject to judicial review.

Judge Reis then considered the argument that since Senator John A. Anderson and Assemblyman Charles B. Perry were members of the WDA corporation and members of the 1937 legislature, their compensation as public officers had been increased in violation of the constitution (article IV, section 26; text in Appendix B). The answer was, first, that the record revealed no compensation paid by WDA to these gentlemen, and second, that any such compensation would not increase their salaries *as public officers*. "If it [did], then the appropriation to the potato growers' association or to any one of the numerous agricultural societies would be void, should it turn out that a single one of the 133 legislators was an officer of said agricultural society or even a member."[10] Finally, Judge Reis saw no substance in the contention that the bill had not been passed by proper voting procedure. Since the bill ultimately passed with the required quorum present, that was enough for him. It was not the the court's concern that the Senate might have violated its own rules in the process.

Thus, the fact that the case had come before Judge Reis was for WDA a fortunate circumstance. Perhaps the judge's background gave some cause for anticipation of a favorable outcome. The opinion reminded its readers of his past association with the power problem. He acknowledged, however, his indebtedness to the voluminous briefs of counsel,[11] and the decision did not rest on any expressed opinion as to the desirability of municipal or cooperative utilities. On the contrary, such judicial predilections were declared to be irrelevant matters of economic "opinion" and "philosophy" which were primarily for legislative determination.

The decision did not go uncriticized. While a newspaper which had been politically sympathetic found it a "resounding opinion," one which had been generally hostile to WDA deplored it as another example of "subterfuge" in evading the constitution.[12]

The Case in the Supreme Court

The history of this litigation in the Wisconsin Supreme Court was unusual. The appeal from Judge Reis's decision was argued October 15, 1937. Four months later the Supreme Court reversed Judge Reis (January 11, 1938). Immediately requests were made for rehearing, and numerous additional parties filed briefs on rehearing. The argument on rehearing occurred April 15. On June 21 the Supreme Court repudiated the ground of the first decision, and adopted a different rationale which supported some of WDA's activities, but substantially frustrated its over-all effectiveness.

NATURE OF THE ARGUMENT

In the appeal to the Supreme Court, the course of WDA's and appellant's initial argument flowed in the grooves already established in the trial court: (1) the internal improvements issue, (2) the public purpose issue, and (3) the miscellaneous other contentions discussed by Judge Reis. WDA's argument for the most part was a more elaborate development of the analysis adopted by Judge Reis.

Briefs by the appellant secretary of state and various supporting *amici curiae* were largely concerned with the same issues. On the internal improvements question, it was urged mainly that state appropriations to WDA for promoting construction of utility plants made the state a "party" to the carrying on of internal improvements; that the state's constitution makers had not meant to bar state "encouragement" of economic growth, but in the contemporary view this had meant something distinct from being a "party" to economic undertakings—had meant only such measures for encouraging capitalists as liberal acts of incorporation; that the *Van Dyke* decision relied on by Judge Reis was based not on the validity of appropriations to others for carrying on internal improvements, but on the idea that the primary purpose of the appropriation was for unemployment relief.

On the public purpose question, the anti-WDA briefs argued that the WDA statute involved not general education in the public interest, but advocacy of only one side of a controversial public question—the work of a "paternalistic" and "European" form of government, contrary to the "genius of our institutions"; that the statute did not require WDA to make its studies available to the public; that aid to agricultural societies was different, because they were educational, aimed at advancing an industry upon which the whole public depended; that aid to electric cooperatives in particular constituted aid to private corporations; that while there had been statutes favoring farm cooperatives in the state, their constitutionality had not yet been definitely established (and possibly might be sustained on the special ground of a continuous, long-acquiesced-in construction).

Certain *amici curiae* briefs, however, injected a new major issue: the allegedly unconstitutional delegation of sovereign legislative power to a private corporation. Counsel for both WDA and defendant responded to this new contention in reply briefs and oral argument.[13] It became the ground of the first decision, reversing the lower court.

THE FIRST DECISION

The first decision was unanimous. Speaking through Justice Fritz, the court ruled (after rejecting the contention that the bill had been passed by improper procedure)[14] that the act invalidly used a private corporation as an instrumentality for the exercise of governmental functions. In the first place, the legislature had set out no substantial directions to control WDA's discretion in determining the circumstances and places in which it should spend its funds, or how it should allocate the monies among its different authorized functions. Nor did the statute make any provision for official supervision, beyond the annual report to the governor and the secretary of state's audit of expenditures. So unbounded a statutory grant was an attempt to confer full sovereign power.

In the second place, to confer such power as the act sought to give the Authority would, if validly done, constitute it a public officer—yet WDA could not qualify as a public officer. It could not meet the constitutional requirement (article IV, section 28; text in Appendix B) that a public officer must take an oath; nor could it satisfy the "fundamental principle of our government that a person not an elector of the state is ineligible to hold a public office therein, although our constitutions and statutes do not expressly so ordain"; nor did the general incorporation law under which WDA was organized authorize it to hold public office.

Therefore, the court found it unnecessary to decide the other "importan[t] and highly controversial" issues presented in "the excellent briefs filed herein." Thus, even though it be assumed, without deciding, that authority was conferred on WDA for a "public purpose," the "incapability of the WDA to receive the authority and to execute the act renders the provisions thereof invalid . . . ."[15]

True, some cases had decided that certain persons exercising functions conferred by the legislature—for example, the publisher of an official newspaper, one conducting a state-sponsored geological and agricultural survey, canal commissioners—were not public officers within the meaning of particular legislative or constitutional provisions. But, "there was not involved therein any such delegation of the governmental power to execute or administer a statute as is involved in the case at bar." For the same reason the court found not in point such cases as the *Industrial School* case (upholding appropriations to a private organization, for the care of helpless children), and the *Loomis* case (upholding the plan by which the University Building Corporation built the Fieldhouse and other structures on University lands, and received the Regents' pledge of operating revenue from the buildings toward rental and eventual ownership, as well as receiving loans from a state agency). "They did relate to services performed in the discharge of a public, governmental purpose, but the performance thereof by a private corporation was not the execution or administration of a statute in the exercise of governmental power." Thus "the state can have a private instrumentality construct a highway at public expense when the location, dimensions, and similar essential matters in relation thereto have been determined by or are under the control or supervision of an official vested with its governmental power in that regard. But the state cannot delegate the determination of such essential matters to an unofficial, private instrumentality with but the direction that it shall use appropriated state funds for the purpose of locating and constructing public highways of some kind, somewhere within the state."[16]

The press gave great prominence to the decision. Some expressed approval, some emphatic disapproval. One editorial complained

of legal hair-splitting. It could see no substantial difference between the WDA situation and the one in the case involving the
building of the Fieldhouse, or the case of the Industrial School
for Girls: "Perhaps these contradictions can be explained by calling attention to the fact that the Wisconsin Supreme Court is a
conservative court. Five of the seven members of the court were
originally appointed by Governor Kohler, and it is fair to pre-
sume they were appointed . . . because they reflected his point of
view. It is probably fair to say that the members of the court are
opposed to the entrance of the state into the field of private business. . . . You see—a Field House didn't matter so much. It didn't
compete with any fieldhouse in Madison owned by a private corporation . . . ." But apropos of the political complexion of the
court, another paper pointed out that the decision "was written
by Justice Oscar M. Fritz, a former circuit judge of Milwaukee,
and a so-called 'liberal' and progressive adherent . . . ."[17]

One story headlined the decision as a "jolt to the Governor,"
who was quoted as saying the decision was "one of the most serious, important, and far-reaching that has come down in the past
50 years." Some accounts reported general concern by the administration and by others over the impact the decision might have
on the State Historical Society, agricultural and veterans' associations and the recently established Wisconsin Agricultural Authority—though others found in such comments evidence of "scare"
and "smoke-screen" tactics by the administration. About the same
time, the administration was pictured as inspecting the "rusty
joints" of the neglected state utility corporation (referred to in
Chapter I) as a possible substitute for WDA. However, the administration's immediate next step was to seek a re-hearing.[18]

THE SECOND DECISION

THE GRANTING OF A REHEARING.—WDA supported its motion
for rehearing on January 25, 1938, by arguing that counsel had
not fully treated the delegation issue; that the importance of full
analysis was shown by the fact that "some three and a half months
after the passage of the Act in question, and after its constitutionality had been challenged by the Secretary of State, the legislature
enacted chapter 4, Laws of Special Session, 1937 which again util-
ized a private corporation (Wisconsin Agricultural Authority) as

recipient of a subsidy to be expended upon activities in the public interest"; that the "Secretary of State, correctly or incorrectly
has interpreted the opinion of this court as raising serious doubts
concerning the constitutionality of state appropriations amount-
ing to more than $200,000 per annum to numerous societies, as-
sociations, and corporations which for many years have been re-
cipients of funds awarded by the legislature for the promotion of
the public interest. Letters, of which this court may take judicial
notice, have been sent by the Secretary of State to these organizations notifying them that no further claims will be audited under
their appropriations unless and until these doubts have been dis-
pelled"; that it would be demonstrated that the functions bestowed on WDA were not sovereign, and the use of its funds sufficiently circumscribed by legislative and executive controls. The
potent political fact as to the claims of other private associations
had not been high-lighted as a "pressure" argument, but astutely
relegated to a footnote. It was there appended to the textual argument that the legal technique used in the WDA act was not "a
novel experiment or extension of authority, but is in the stream
of the law and life of this state as it has moved forward over three
generations."[19]

Also supporting the motion was a brief statement by three
members of the University of Wisconsin Law School faculty: Dean
Lloyd K. Garrison and Professors Ray A. Brown and Jacob H.
Beuscher. They regarded the decision as one of land-mark importance,[20] turning upon a legal ground which had not been fully
argued by counsel. They felt that the court should receive a full
presentation of (1) the history of the governmental use of private
agencies for public purposes and the economic, social, and governmental factors producing a trend in that direction; (2) the question whether appropriations to private agencies for carrying out
specified functions constituted a "delegation" at all; and, if so,
(3) whether the functions delegated to WDA were in fact of a
non-sovereign variety which need not be vested in public officers;
(4) the extent of discretion, free from governmental controls,
which may properly be lodged in such private agencies discharging public functions.

Counsel for the defendant secretary of state, of course, opposed
the motion for rehearing, claiming the Supreme Court had thor-

oughly analyzed the controlling issue. He asserted that uncertainties in the application of the decision to other societies or in the dividing line between sovereign and other powers should be resolved not by an overall generalization to be discovered through a rehearing but by the normal process of case-by-case adjudication; that the corporations used by the federal government were subject to closer governmental ties than were present in WDA's case; that the judiciary must be wary of assaults on our Constitutional form of government through "novel experiments in governmental affairs."[21]

The other, and more strenuous, opposition to rehearing came from the *amici curiae* representing certain utility and other business interests. They objected to the scanty presentation made in the request for rehearing. And they denied that the controlling ground of the Supreme Court's decision had been insufficiently discussed by counsel prior to the oral argument: *they* had analyzed the problem in their brief made available to WDA's counsel two weeks prior to the oral argument, and WDA's subsequent reply brief filed prior to oral argument discussed the issue at length (as did the secretary of state's reply brief filed after oral argument).[22]

On March 1, 1938, the court granted the motion for rehearing and also included an invitation to other private corporations receiving state aid to file briefs *amici curiae,* if they were so advised or deemed themselves affected.[23]

The court's invitation opened up the gates to a Niagara of argument. The printed pages of briefs on the first hearing had already reached the five-hundred mark; the briefs at rehearing added about eight hundred more. There were briefs not only by the previous *amici curiae* but also by new ones.[24] All concentrated on the delegation issue deemed determinative in the court's first opinion. There was much repetition, but there were also differences worth noting.

REHEARING ARGUMENTS AGAINST THE FIRST DECISION.—The two major briefs attacking the court's first decision were by WDA and the *amici curiae* law professors. The following summary of the latter brief also represents, with some variation in emphasis and detail, the substance of the other.[25]

The argument began by stressing that the decision impaired

the capacity of government to deal with the increasingly complicated tasks confronting it. Among the techniques devised for dealing with increasing pressures and complexity were not only government corporations (that is, corporations wholly or largely controlled by government), but also the governmental use of wholly private corporations for public purposes. On the federal level, the latter device had been used for the "handling of the country's finances and the issuance of its currency, the custody and the discipline of prisoners, the construction of canals, railroads, and other works of internal improvement, the development of educational institutions, the assistance of unfortunates, the eradication of certain diseases, the improvement of agriculture and so on." On the state level, there had been Wisconsin grants relating to "custody and treatment of prisoners, the encouragement (through municipalities) of railroad, bridge, canal, and road construction, the putting out of fires, the care of orphans and the sick, the reformation of juvenile delinquents, the training and education of the young, the advancement of agriculture in its manifold forms, the conduct of research and dissemination of information, and so on" (p. 4).

There was no adverse legal significance in the fact that the WDA statute used the word "instrumentality" and provided that no funds be used for activities that would be unconstitutional if carried on by the state and bestowed "duties and functions" and permitted discretion in the exercise thereof. All this made the WDA law no different from numerous similar laws which had either gone unchallenged or been upheld. Outstanding among federal examples was the Second Bank of the United States. Here was a privately controlled corporation upon which Congress bestowed many duties, including that of acting as depository for federal government funds; and Marshall's famous opinion upholding the bank act had declared a Maryland tax on the bank unconstitutional as a tax on "an instrument employed by the Government of the Union to carry its powers into execution."[26]

Prominent among Wisconsin illustrations were the *Industrial School* case, upholding a state grant to a private organization for the execution of statutory powers to care for helpless children; the *LaCrosse Public Library* case, sustaining a city appropriation to a privately controlled public library; statutes which since the early

1850's had made grants to the State Historical Society and to various agricultural associations, such as the Potato Growers' Association, Cheese Makers' Association, Horticultural Society, with no more, and often fewer, controls over disposition of the money than were present in the WDA law. Nor was WDA to be differentiated on the ground of its adverse impact on other legitimate interests, such as the private utilities. The Second Bank of the United States adversely affected private banking groups. Aid to railroads adversely affected competing transportation agencies. Indeed, aid to almost any institution may adversely affect those who are not aided. And the decisions have been clear that there is no legal right to be immune from government-sponsored competition which injures the complaining party but which is otherwise lawful (that is, free from such elements as fraud or malice).[27]

In making these arguments, the professors' brief urged that the WDA law be viewed as a measure which merely made an appropriation to a corporation's pre-existing functions, because the public had an interest therein. Especially should the court so construe the law, if the court felt that to designate a private corporation an instrumentality for the execution of state law would be unconstitutional. For where alternative constructions are equally possible, that which does not impugn the statute's constitutionality is to be preferred. However, the argument ran, even under the view that WDA was here given authority to execute and administer a statute delegating sovereign powers, the statute was not unconstitutional. Thus, it was precisely because the Second Bank of the United States was invested with sovereign power that the United States Supreme Court had held it immune from state taxation and regulation. More sovereign power was involved in the *Industrial School* case than in WDA's limited promotional and educational functions. And the latter case, it was asserted, had not been tenably distinguished when the court in its first WDA decision said that the Industrial School was not engaged in the "execution or administration of a statute in the exercise of governmental power."[28]

Further, the Wisconsin court had sustained statutes involving delegation of other governmental powers, for example, the power to make the initial selections from which an appointment is made to public office or the power of eminent domain. Authorities from other jurisdictions were also invoked, sustaining the private execution of public functions, under statutes dealing with care of children and animals, education, public improvements, and police powers. That a broad scope of delegated administrative discretion was often demanded by the subject matter of public regulation had been the doctrine of the well-known Wisconsin case which sustained the broad discretion over rates lodged in the insurance commissioner; in the case of WDA and its functions of promotion and education, it was argued, the subject matter did not lend itself to any detailed, fixed rules. Moreover, the past decisions already referred to had upheld delegations to private agencies involving a broader exercise of discretion than that involved in WDA's limited functions.[29]

Nor could it be said, the brief contended, that by designating WDA for performance of these functions, the statute usurped the executive appointing power. This kind of appointive designation had been made in other cases too without being invalidated, and at any rate under the Wisconsin constitution the appointive power was not lodged exclusively in the executive.[30]

Finally, it was argued that the court's first opinion erred when it asserted that WDA would exercise the kind of governmental function that might be conferred only on public officers. The mere fact that these functions might have been given to public officers did not mean that the agency to which they were given was a public officer. Cases from Wisconsin and other jurisdictions showed that persons appointed to discharge functions of investigation and recommendation, or even more executive functions, were not necessarily "officers" within the meaning of constitutional or statutory requirements. And the present case was distinguished from certain past cases since they had invalidated statutes which went much further. Those statutes had allowed private organizations to determine whether a tax should be levied, or whether there should be a state law directly affecting people's rights, and what such a law should contain.[31]

Arguments similar to those just summarized, though with some variations, were made in the other *amici curiae* briefs opposed to the decision. These consisted of a brief by six veterans' organizations, one by seventeen corporations receiving state aid (the same six veterans' associations plus eleven other groups), and another by the Wisconsin Agricultural Authority.

REHEARING ARGUMENTS SUPPORTING THE FIRST DECISION.—The appellant secretary of state reasserted some of the conclusions of the first decision: a private corporation could not be a public officer; the incorporation laws did not authorize a private corporation to be a public officer; WDA would be exercising a public officer's sovereign power. The secretary developed the latter theme with an imaginative list of WDA's implied powers and added the contention that by making an "appointment" to public office the WDA law usurped an executive function.[32]

Other arguments were designed to refute those made by WDA and its supporters. Thus, while the eminent domain power had admittedly been delegated to private corporations, this power, it was argued, was not so sovereign in nature as WDA's powers. Nor was the enactment a "mere appropriation" act. "Without the Act, [WDA] is not exercising its powers in the execution of a statute. The Act itself creates the statute which is executed by the WDA." True, many corporations had been used by the federal government, but these either were "public" corporations (like TVA or RFC, where the government controlled the stock or the directors) or they were private corporations (such as the national banks) used merely for "furnishing services" to the government; whereas WDA was "really a Governmental department endowed with sovereign power." Wisconsin, too, had examples of "public" corporations, such as the Regents of the University, where the executive appointed the controlling personnel. But the private corporations used and subsidized by the state (such as agricultural societies, the State Historical Society, educational institutions) did not exercise discretion of sufficient breadth to constitute them public officers, and did not exercise sovereign power.

This was not contradicted, said the secretary of state, by the reference in the *Industrial School* opinion to delegation of the "sovereign" power over education. That statement was made to justify the use of state funds as being for a public purpose, not to show that the school was exercising sovereign power. Further, the court there said that the delegation of a government function to a private body would be improper if the function had been "ex-

pressly or by necessary implication restricted to public agencies."
And, as WDA conceded, the fact that the function of maintaining
dependent children might be delegated to a private corporation
did not mean that all government functions might be; thus the
question, which functions are delegable, was "still left open."[33]

In behalf of business and taxpayer interests an *amicus* brief
contended that WDA had been given extremely broad discretion
in the exercise of a type of authority more clearly governmental
than in the case of the cited precedents supporting public use of
private agencies. Another brief, submitted by county fair associations, attempted to differentiate WDA from agricultural societies.
Still another brief, by W. G. Ryan, on his own behalf, argued
that while there were precedents for public aid to private institutions, none of the latter had involved functions like those of WDA,
and some alleged precedents did not involve private corporations
at all. He stressed the invalidity of public promotion of a particular method of furnishing power, as distinguished from promotion
of a greater use of power in general.[34]

THE COURT'S MAJORITY OPINION.—*(1) There was no invalid
delegation.* When the court's second opinion came down on June
21, 1938—eight months after the original argument and two
months after the reargument—it presented a rare legal phenomenon: the court frankly admitted recent error. "We were in error
in holding [that the WDA provisions] constituted an invalid delegation of executive power to a private corporation and designation of such corporation as a public officer." In "centering our
attention upon this very large question [of the extent to which
governmental power may be vested in private hands] we failed
to give adequate weight to the extent of the pre-existing corporate
powers of the Wisconsin Development Authority. When these are
considered in relation to the act, the act must be held to constitute a mere appropriation measure and not to confer sovereign
power upon the corporation, or indeed any power at all except to
spend the allotted money for purposes defined in the act."

Even the statutory provisions regarding WDA's access to governmental information did not confer substantially new power
and at any rate did not confer "sovereign" power. The intent to
confer sovereign power could not be deduced from the statutory
grant of authority "for the execution of certain duties and func-

tions provided"; such language was generally associated with appropriations to private corporations for public purposes (as in the case of the State Historical Society, or the Wisconsin Agricultural Authority) and was generally used in appropriation bills to limit appropriations to specified public purposes rather than to confer sovereign power. The same was true of the statute's use of the word "instrumentality."

Moreover, the new-found conclusion that whatever power might have been conferred was not sovereign in character, was reinforced, the court thought, by its concurrent disposition of the "state purpose" issue: "[I]n view of the fact that an important group of purposes under the act is later in this opinion held not to constitute a proper state purpose, it is clear to us that the discretion and responsibility referred to in the original opinion has been so far diminished [when confined to purposes held to be proper state purposes] that what remains could not constitute a power sovereign in character, if it were held to be a power at all." Since the court now found that the act did not seek to delegate sovereign power, the rehearing opinion declared that the "rule" previously laid down against delegating sovereign power to a private corporation "has no further materiality in this case," and that "it is unnecessary to re-examine the soundness" of it.

What of the agricultural and other societies whose "appropriations are thought to have been put in jeopardy" by the first decision? "While we have not discovered any such peril as is asserted even if our original position had been adhered to, it is obvious that, if it existed, it has disappeared with the abandonment of the position."[35]

(2) *WDA activities of a generalized nature were for a public purpose; but the granting of power to promote the formation, acquisition, or other development, of any particular enterprise violated the "state purpose" requirement, though this activity might be for a "public purpose."* — Turning to the other issues, the court began with a general statement of the "public purpose" requirement applicable to appropriations as well as to taxes. "The validity of an appropriation must be judged by the validity of any tax which might be levied to support it, and . . . for the state to appropriate for a private purpose money raised or to be raised by taxation would be to take the property of one citizen or group of

citizens without compensation and to pay it to others, which would constitute a violation of the equality clause as well as a taking of property without due process of law." The court recognized that this doctrine did not exclude payment "to or through a private corporation or agency," where the appropriation "is solely for a public purpose and is under proper governmental control and supervision." This general test, borrowed from equivalent language in the *Industrial School* case quoted by the court, was deemed to explain not only that case but also the unfavorable decisions in *Curtis' Adm'r. v. Whipple* and *Whiting v. Sheboygan and F.D.L. R.R.*, which two generations before had invalidated subsidies to a private educational institution and to a railroad; in those instances the appropriations "contained no continuing limitation or control to insure that the funds would be used solely for a public purpose." Moreover, "practical construction sanctioning appropriations to privately... controlled organizations ... for public purposes is afforded by" the many statutory appropriations beginning in the 1850's to agricultural societies, the State Historical Society, and veterans' organizations.[36]

The opinion touched other facets of the public purpose problem by reference to principles announced by Wisconsin and United States Supreme Court cases: "If a public purpose can be conceived which might rationally be deemed to justify the act, the court cannot further weigh the adequacy of the need or the wisdom of the method"; "the fact that an expenditure of public funds benefits certain individuals or one class more immediately than it does other individuals or another class does not necessarily deprive the expenditure of its public character"; the "course or usage of the government, the objects for which taxes have been customarily... levied" are "material considerations, as well as the rule that to sustain a public purpose the advantage to the public must be direct and not merely indirect or remote."[37]

After these general considerations, the court referred to situations which had been "held to fall on one side or the other of the line," citing cases in Wisconsin and elsewhere illustrating what had been held to be public purposes;[38] and cases in Wisconsin and elsewhere illustrating what had been held to be private purposes.[39] But "these cases give no comfort to one who seeks a rule of thumb that will easily dispose of all questions in this field," though "the tendency of later cases is toward greater liberality in characterizing taxes or appropriations as public in purpose."[40]

However, there was another constitutional principle limiting the validity of appropriations: there was "the general rule applicable to appropriations that a tax must be spent at the level at which it is raised. Applied to an appropriation by the legislature, this means that the appropriation must not merely be for a public purpose but for a state purpose."[41]

The court then took stock of the provisions of the WDA statute on the basis of the criteria of public and state purpose. (a) The opinion concluded that the survey and research provisions in Section 199.03 (5) aimed at an abundant and cheap supply of utility services throughout the state, authorized "state-wide expenditures for a clearly public purpose." And it could fairly be inferred, the court thought, that the information obtained was intended not for WDA's sole benefit but to be state property, available to all citizens—a conclusion required by the ordinary presumption of constitutionality. (b) The provisions of Section 199.03 (1) and (2) (when "construed to authorize encouragement of cooperatives and power districts by general educational activities of the sort permitted in the case of agricultural cooperatives but not to authorize agitation for, or organizational activities directed to, the creation of any particular power district or cooperative") authorized funds for "public and state purposes." (c) The provisions of Section 199.03 (6) (authorizing collection and dissemination of information, and necessary research, planning, and educational activities) the court thought were "properly ancillary to Section 199.03 (1) and (2)," and hence "for a public and state purpose."

However, under Section 199.03 (3) and (4), WDA might promote the acquisition, construction, or other development of any particular plant or part thereof by any particular cooperative, municipality, power district or non-profit corporation. The court found this grant of power invalid, because it was not for a *state* purpose, though possibly it was for a public purpose. "We pass the question whether it is a public purpose. Certainly the acquisition of a plant by a municipality is a public purpose viewed from the standpoint of a particular municipality, and if the state may authorize the acquisition of plants by municipalities, its encouragement of such acquisition by general educational means might at least be argued to constitute a public purpose. But [these sub-sections authorize] the WDA to urge and assist a particular group or municipality to construct or acquire a particular plant, and . . . this is a private, local and proprietary matter with which the state has no concern. The appropriation is not for a state purpose within the rule of the *Froehlich* and *New Richmond* cases."[42]

The court felt that enforcement of the state purpose limitation had point particularly regarding municipalities; for it was established state policy that municipal ownership must be determined by local referendum, and the general policy of the home-rule constitutional amendment (article XI, section 3; text in Appendix B) re-enforced this. But also the same state purpose requirement barred encouragement of particular municipal power districts, co-operatives or other non-profit corporations to acquire, construct, or otherwise develop particular plants.

The situation, the court thought, was unlike that involved in "aids to local communities for the promotion of education and public health." In the latter situations the "state is dealing with matters concededly affecting the whole state and being properly state functions, namely health and education." So, too, the 1937 law which created the Wisconsin Agricultural Authority to make studies and offer assistance in promoting agricultural prosperity, contemplated promotion in behalf of the state at large, rather than "particularized activity of a purely private, local or proprietary character."[43]

(3) *There was no merit in the "internal improvements" objection and miscellaneous other constitutional objections.*—The argument that the statute violated the constitutional ban (article VIII, section 10; text in Appendix B) on state participation in works of internal improvement did not impress the court. The constitution drafted by the first constitutional convention ("rejected by the electorate largely because of objections to other provisions") had coupled with this prohibitory clause a provision that the state "shall encourage" internal improvements by individuals, associations, and corporations. This "demonstrates convincingly that there was deemed to be and is such a material distinction between those two activities that the mere encouragement of others to engage in such works was not considered to constitute the carrying on, or being a party in the carrying on, of such work." And the

point was sustained, said the court, by Wisconsin authorities: the *Jensen* case, upholding the state's power to provide for state roads and impose the cost thereof upon counties and towns; the *New Richmond* case, upholding a state appropriation to defray a city's costs of rehabilitation after a cyclone; and the *Van Dyke* case, sustaining state reimbursement of part of the cost of local public works programs undertaken for unemployment relief.[44]

As with the internal improvements issue, the Supreme Court adopted substantially the analysis used by the court below in dealing with lesser constitutional contentions: (a) there was no violation of the prohibition (article IV, section 31) against special or private laws granting corporate powers or privileges; (b) there was no invalid delegation of judicial power to the secretary of state; (c) there was no violation of the prohibition (article VIII, section 3) against giving or loaning the state's credit in aid of any individual, association, or corporation; and no violation of the restriction (article IV, section 26) on changing a public officer's compensation during his term of office.[45]

(4) The valid portion of the act was separable.— Finally, since the court had invalidated part of the statute, it had to consider whether the rest could stand by itself, under the broad "separability clause." Although the court recognized that such a clause was not conclusive, it felt that "the portions of the act held to be proper and valid constitute a substantial part thereof" and come within the requirement of "a complete law in some reasonable aspect."[46]

Accordingly, applying the foregoing principles to the three specific applications before it, the court affirmed the mandamus in the Murray case, to compel payment for services in making a survey of energy resources; and affirmed the mandamus in the Tuttle case to compel payment of the claim for multigraphing 585 copies of the form letter informing municipal officers of services available from WDA. The court so held in the Tuttle case even though the letter not only called attention to the services which WDA might, under the instant opinion, legitimately perform, but also offered to perform promotional services in the particular community or to determine the feasibility of municipal ownership in particular municipalities. This over-statement of its services should not make the expenditure improper. Bringing its services to the attention of those to be served was a matter of "mere detail," and it would be "harsh doctrine" to rule out the expenditure because the statement of services was not completely correct.[47] But the court reversed the mandamus in the Maloney case, involving payment for services in promoting the organization of an electric cooperative in Crawford County. "The account for this activity should not be audited. The people of the state at large have no interest in the question whether a cooperative organization is organized in Crawford County. That is a local and not a state problem, and the money of the state may not be devoted to its solution."[48]

JUSTICE FRITZ'S CONCURRING OPINION.—Justice Fritz, who had written the first opinion, concurred in the second, "except insofar as it is stated in effect that the WDA was empowered by its articles . . . to do everything that it could do after the enactment of ch. 334, L. 1937 and that . . . it must be held to constitute a mere appropriation measure which does not confer any power at all except to spend the appropriation for the purposes defined in the act." Whether the act conferred governmental power must be determined not by the articles, but by what the act itself provided. Section 199.04 (text in Appendix B) giving access to government agencies' information, was intended to confer powers which its articles might not give WDA, and the presence of this provision was some evidence of an intent to confer governmental power, when considered with other WDA functions involving the exercise of discretion and responsiblity. "However, the discretion and responsibility . . . and the consequences thereof . . . have been diminished to such an extent by holding that an important group of purposes under the act do not constitute proper state purposes . . . that what now remains to be performed . . . does not constitute the exercise of governmental power."[49]

JUSTICE FOWLER'S DISSENTING OPINION.—While he agreed with the majority's position that the statutory authority to promote particular projects was invalid for want of a state-wide public purpose, Justice Fowler would go much further: none of WDA's purposes was constitutional and no state funds could be expended for them.

(1) The favoritism to power districts and to cooperative and non-profit utilities violated the principle of "equality of inherent

rights" as embodied in article I, section 1 of the Wisconsin Constitution (text in Appendix B).⁵⁰ (2) The provisions for surveys, and for collecting and disseminating information, were not linked to a public purpose since the statute did not require the information and the survey results to be made available to the public generally. (3) On the basis of the majority opinion's principle against aiding particular projects, the provision concerning cooperation with the federal government was invalid insofar as it involved aiding the federal government to extend electric service to particular communities. (4) Even the generalized educational activity approved in the majority opinion was not a proper function of government. To preach the advantages of these alternatives to private ownership of utilities was propaganda, rather than the dissemination of information. It was not the proper function of government to advocate principles of any particular political party, and advocacy of electric cooperatives or public ownership was part of the platforms of the Socialist, Farmer-Labor-Progressive, and Progressive parties. (5) The implication in the majority opinion that it was constitutional to "favor" cooperatives over ordinary corporations was unsound. The Wisconsin statutes on cooperatives cited by the majority had not been judicially construed, and the case authorities did not establish validity of the favoritism involved in the present statute. (6) Finally, the majority opinion erred on the issue of separability. The main purpose of the statute was embodied in the provisions held by the majority to violate the state-purpose requirement, hence the whole act should be invalidated.⁵¹

JUSTICE FAIRCHILD'S DISSENTING OPINION.—Justice Fairchild agreed substantially with the Fowler dissent, and asserted further that the argument of the original opinion on the delegation issue was still sound. By giving WDA power to commandeer information and assistance from other agencies, the statute gave it more power than it had by its articles. The general educational functions permitted under the majority opinion could not have been intended by the legislature, and at any rate, "education in a democratic government must necessarily be non-partisan, presenting the merits of both sides of a question." While public funds had "been appropriated to various societies to enable them to promote and encourage projects of public interest . . . this has never been done where the effect would be to influence the minds of voters on matters of public controversy. There has been no opposition to horticulture, to cranberry growing, to cheesemaking or to the preservation of historical records .... There comes to mind but one instance in which there may have been a detriment to a particular group of interests, namely the use of public money to encourage and promote the formation of cooperatives. One such instance does not constitute a course and usage of government."

Moreover, the majority's attempt to draw a line between general education and assistance to particular projects led it, in effect, to add to the statute a requirement that information gathered must be made generally available. The majority position was beset with many impracticalities: "How is it possible to encourage the formation of municipal power districts *in general* without encouraging the formation of particular power districts? .... Sec. 198.03 provides for an election to determine in a particular locality whether a municipal power district shall be formed .... Is it proper for the state government to influence a local election? .... Must WDA foresee the holding of an election in a particular community and thereafter refrain from sending its ... encouragement into that area?" The majority had sustained the Tuttle claim for the multigraphing of a form letter informing of WDA's general education function and offering particularized aid as well. Did this, asked Fairchild, "make it possible for public money to be used for the private purposes of WDA whenever the private purpose is coupled with a public use?" Finally, "the doctrine of severability does not save the law," for the functions upheld by the majority were never intended by the legislature to stand by themselves or in that form. The legislature intended "to place in the field a militant agency, aggressively devoted to the building up of organizations to compete with privately owned utilities, bus and interurban operators. The result of the present decision is that the agency cannot operate as intended by the legislature but that in its stead there may be an educational institution to benefit all concerned, including the very privately owned companies it was calculated to oppose."[52]

REACTION TO THE DECISION.—According to the press, the immediate reaction of the governor was that the decision was gratifying. It was never "contemplated by WDA sponsors," he said, "that the State's $60,000 appropriation should be spent to propagandize in any particular city for passage of referendums to acquire local utilities." A friendly newspaper account declared that the "most important phase of the decision, according to the Governor, is the fact that the court recognizes that the state is warranted in the present complex economic period in finding new and better methods of administration. In other words, the high court approved such quasi-public corporations as the WDA and WAA as a means of carrying out state functions, the Governor believes."[53]

Less sympathetic comment was that the governor was whistling in the dark. "Has the Governor read the decision?" asked one editorial. On the basis of what the court said, "how . . . does the Governor expect [WDA] to 'promote' the building of REA cooperatives? How, when the 'authority' is limited to 'general educational activities' does he think it can give technical advice or services to specific operating plants? How, when it can do nothing but educate, does he expect it to accomplish the 'prudent' development of electric power in Wisconsin?" Sharing this skeptical view of WDA's remaining powers was another press comment: "The State Supreme Court which six months ago took away an ax—The Wisconsin Development Authority—with which the La Follette administration hoped to cut a way to public ownership of utilities, today handed it back in a five-to-two decision but the blade was made of rubber." As we shall later see, the skeptical view was the correct one.[54]

CHAPTER IV

WDA OPERATIONS

AFTER THE LITIGATION

Operations with Public Funds, to 1939

Since its public operations were held in abeyance pending the Supreme Court's final decision of June 21, 1938, WDA did not begin such operations until more than a year after passage of the WDA law: it opened its office on August 1, 1938. And since its authority to use public funds was repealed as of March 22, 1939, this left only about eight months for its public operations.[1]

Basic operational data appear in its 1939 report to Governor Heil. Out of its $60,000 appropriation, it was entitled to spend $45,000 for the period of its operation, but it spent only $31,412.61. In furtherance of what it termed "education and promotional assistance," it had given general advice on the organization of electric cooperatives and the procedure for obtaining benefits under the federal REA act, at the request of interested groups in the counties of Adams, Marquette, St. Croix, Washburn, Waupaca, Rusk, Wood, and Shawano. And it had "cooperated," on power problems with municipalities, cooperatives, and federal agencies. The Authority felt it had thus facilitated the progress of rural electrification in Wisconsin, though it disclaimed complete credit for the fact that during its eight months of operation over $4,000,000 in REA funds were allocated to Wisconsin electric cooperatives, to finance construction of over three thousand miles of line. Also, in furtherance of this same "education[al] and promotional" function, WDA had printed and distributed a pamphlet,

"Wisconsin Gets a Power Program," giving some brief history of rural electrification in Wisconsin, the development of WDA, the scope of its functions under the Supreme Court decision, and other miscellaneous data. The pamphlet expounded the benefits flowing from wider use of electricity, the important work done by the REC, whose general educational activities were now absorbed by WDA, the rate-advantage being offered by municipal utilities in Wisconsin compared with private utilities, and some analogous data on TVA rates compared with private rates. Reference was also made to a current study of existing and potential electrical facilities in Wisconsin, "with a view of forming a statewide plan for their integration and coordination." In this connection the pamphlet reprinted a map entitled "Wisconsin-Fox Rivers Development Plan," prepared by the Wisconsin State Planning Board and showing, according to the pamphlet, "the proposed development of the Wisconsin and Fox Rivers sought by the state . . . through the Wisconsin Hydro-Authority"—a project which would "harness latent hydro-electric power, control floods, improve sanitation and navigation on the two rivers, create a great recreational region for Wisconsin and provide useful emergency and permanent employment."[2]

The pamphlet was enthusiastic about the agency's form of organization, stating that WDA's objective of a "coordinated and intelligent power development of Wisconsin" would be "impossible through utilization of a state department," whereas the state's use of a private non-profit corporation like WDA permits the "elasticity of private business methods" and "eliminates any profit evil." No great concern was shown in the pamphlet over the limitations placed on the Authority by the Supreme Court decision. "The door has been left open," it declared, "for general promotional and educational action. The Authority is proceeding carefully but persistently . . . and is pledged to abide strictly by both the letter and the spirit of the decision . . . ." Its discussion of its permissible functions revealed that it was not in fact adopting a latitudinarian construction of the quite narrow powers to which the court had confined it.[3]

In its report to the governor on its eight months of activity, WDA referred, in addition to its "educational" or "promotional" function, to a second major function: "research." Here it could point to a comparative study of the taxes paid by various power units (cooperatives, municipalities, private utilities); to studies of electric rates, both residential and rural; to a pamphlet on the procedure to be followed in organizing municipal power districts; and to miscellaneous other studies which there had not been time to complete. The report indicated that at the close of WDA's operations as a public instrumentality on March 21, 1939, it was using for such operations, seven full-time and three part-time employees, and fifteen employees who divided their time between the public and private activities of the corporation.[4]

Repeal of the statutory basis for WDA's public operations in 1939 did not mean the end of state sponsorship for such activities. Some five months after the repeal, the legislature established within the Department of Agriculture and Markets, a "Wisconsin Rural Electrification Coordination Division," which was authorized to engage in activities rather similar to the public activities of WDA, but with a substantially reduced budget, and the duty to cooperate with "private" as well as municipal companies and cooperatives.[5]

In 1945, coupled with a still further reduction in budget, these functions were transferred to a simultaneously created rural electrification division in the University of Wisconsin College of Agriculture, as part of "a postwar program for . . . rural electrification on an area coverage basis . . . to the end that electricity at reasonable rates shall be made available to all Wisconsin farmers desiring central station electric service and not now receiving such service." In 1951 the $5,500 appropriation was repealed, but the statutes still bestowed these functions on the College of Agriculture.[6]

Private Operations, to Dissolution in 1954

Since WDA was organized as a private, though non-profit, corporation, and included within its powers the rendering of engineering and other services pertinent to its general electrification purposes, the 1939 repeal of state support did not automatically kill the corporation. It continued to render technical services, almost exclusively in the area of rural electrification, on a non-profit basis until 1944, and did not dissolve until 1954.

Some idea of the nature and scope of its functioning in this period may be learned from a manuscript pamphlet prepared by WDA in early 1941 for the purpose of interesting federal officials in using WDA on defense work. The corporate resources as of December 1, 1940, were stated to be $40,000 (in cash and in fees earned and due); available bank credit was stated as $20,000; and there were no liabilities beyond "current payroll and bills." A wide variety of engineering services, for electrification and for other purposes, was listed; services currently being performed were described as "designing, receiving bids, awarding contracts and supervising construction of 13 electric distribution systems totalling 1626 miles and costing approximately $1,336,000." The current payroll totalled forty-two persons, and there were five officers and five directors, all serving without pay. A list of clients, and the work done for them was given, including numerous electric cooperatives and the Bangor municipal utility. Some of the work had been done by WDA and some by WREC ("Statewide"), an organization referred to in Chap. I.[7]

But the corporate outlook grew progressively gloomy. Partly this was because, as General Manager Davlin reported to the membership meeting of August 6, 1941, the "rural electrification program [was passing] from the construction to the utilization stage." Partly it was because the requirements of national defense in the pre-Pearl Harbor days and the requirements of war thereafter had an impact both on personnel and on the availability of materials necessary for WDA-serviced projects. While some work was accomplished in 1941, the necessity for obtaining defense work and expanding the type of service offered was repeatedly recognized.[8]

On the 1941 work accomplished, the chief Engineer reported in November 1941 that among other things, three projects (Polk-Burnett, Grant, and Adams) were recently completed, seven were in process, bids had been taken on three more, eleven had been submitted to REA for allotment, and plans for the Washington Island project had been submitted to REA. But John Becker, the General Manager on leave, who took a special trip to Washington seeking defense business had reported lack of success to the membership meeting of February 7, 1941. And General Manager Davlin reported to the membership meeting of August 6, 1941, as follows: "We have made a determined effort to obtain engineering work outside of the REA program. A connection has been made with an architectural firm, and some work is being performed for the cooperatives along this line but the actual profit is very small and some may actually result in a loss, but the contacts with the co-operatives are being retained, which may lead to more work in the future.... WDA has also retained some consultants for use outside of the regular electrical engineering work. It is hoped that with these connections new work can be obtained to retain the personnel we now have, and diversify the experience of the organization. The effort to obtain defense work has led to no actual contracts ...."[8]

A board resolution of Nov. 7, 1941, called for a "program of retrenchment," and in 1942 things came to a virtual standstill. The chief engineer reported to a special board meeting on March 27, 1942, that stop-orders had been placed against some projects, and "right now there is no work available and none immediately in sight. There seems to be no opportunity for sub-contracting work, and no success ... in obtaining new work. Defense work is all that is available now and that is hard to get without the proper connections. These connections have not been made." For the year ending June 30, 1942, the corporation showed, for the first time, a net loss.[9]

At a membership meeting of August 4, 1943, the inevitable suggestion was made, that in view of the lack of work and lack of personnel, WDA should consider disbanding or joining with some other engineering concern; and a committee was appointed to investigate. This ultimately resulted in passage of a motion at a special membership meeting of January 6, 1944, that WDA discontinue engineering services from March 1, 1944, or sooner if outstanding contracts were completed; the President together with John Becker and Carl Fries were empowered to settle engineering contracts before completion; office fixtures and equipment were to be liquidated; records were to be stored until WDA again offered engineering services; the President, in cooperation with Becker and Fries, was authorized to contact Wisconsin Electric Cooperative or anyone else that might be interested in taking over the engineering services, and to turn over engineering contracts and data to them. Shortly thereafter, on February 1, 1944, WDA entered into an agreement with Wisconsin Electric Cooperative to turn over to the latter WDA's engineering contracts (active and inactive), equipment and files (with some exceptions), for a consideration of $2,000. For almost nine years thereafter, the corporate records reveal no activity—just the gradual diminution of surplus, largely for payment of the part-time employee acting as secretary and custodian of the records.[10]

During this time the feeling grew, according to Secretary Thomas Davlin's 1954 conversation with the writer, that the diminishing funds should be put to some use consistent with the informational purposes for which this non-profit corporation had been organized. There was discussion of a history of rural electrification in Wisconsin. Some incomplete efforts had been made in that direction some years before, particularly by William Thomas, currently in charge of Wisconsin Electric Cooperative and connected with rural electrification since the early days of Governor Philip La Follette's Rural Electrification Coordination agency. WDA succeeded in interesting both WEC and the University of Wisconsin. At a WDA membership meeting of December 1, 1952, there was reported a memorandum of agreement between WDA, WEC, and the University of Wisconsin, for the preparation by the University of a history of rural electrification in the state. The agreement provided for a $6,000 contribution from WDA (which was voted at this WDA meeting) and $3,500 from WEC. There were to be representatives of each of the three groups on a committee to aid in planning and for consultation. The project was to begin July 1, 1953, and be completed by June 30, 1957. WEC, which was to publish the manuscript without revision except as approved by the authors, was to make proper acknowledgment of the contributions of WDA and the University. And the University reserved the right to publish if WEC had not published within twelve months of delivery of the manuscript.[11]

There was nothing left for WDA now but the final dissolution. At a meeting of August 5, 1953, the balance of its funds was voted to the Wisconsin Association of Cooperatives in order to pay the expenses of Kenneth Hones, the WDA representative on the three-man committee, and to buy copies of the history when completed. At a special meeting of April 28, 1954, the corporation formally dissolved. Unlike its birth, the death of WDA escaped public notice. When the history of Wisconsin rural electrification was ultimately published in 1961, but 5 pages out of 150 were devoted —not unfairly—to the study in frustration which was WDA's story.[12]

CHAPTER V

THE WDA DECISION

VIEWED IN RELATION

TO SOME CONTINUING

PROBLEMS OF STATECRAFT

IN WISCONSIN

In assessing the total social contribution of WDA, one is inclined to think first of the benefits from increased rural electrification. Yet, as we have seen, WDA functioned fitfully for only eight months with public funds, and for a few lean years with private funds. It could only lend a helping, and apparently not indispensable, hand to the rural electrification movement. It had been semi-paralyzed by a court decision.

It is that decision, rather than the contribution to rural electrification, which constitutes the main legacy of WDA. For the decision bears importantly on basic and continuing political-economic problems in Wisconsin.

Proper Use of Public Funds: The General Problem

The public purpose doctrine (including the ancillary state purpose principle) is obviously a basic one for governmental administration. A glance at the issues treated in the cases of Appendix A partially reveals the breadth of application of the principle: May public funds be used to aid railroads by stock subscriptions? by donations? May a manufacturing company be similarly aided, by tax concessions or other aid, in return for its coming to a Wisconsin city and agreeing to meet certain payroll requirements? May the state, instead of aiding individual companies, promote particular forms of economic enterprise—the cooperative form? other forms? May the state itself engage in economic enterprise normally engaged in by private individuals? And may it authorize muncipalities to contract to build private roads? May it retroactively grant an exemption from taxes already due and not yet paid? May state funds be used to increase the pensions of already retired teachers? to pay veterans a bonus? to assist in a veteran's housing program? to finance the bringing and holding of an American Legion convention here? May state funds be given to a free public library run by a non-profit corporation? to a non-profit corporation which cares for abandoned or wayward girls? to a locality which has suffered a natural calamity? This sampling of major issues leaves altogether out of account the many other problems which do not reach the court or even the attorney general for decision, but are handled, in a day-to-day government administration, in the light of the court doctrines.

A doctrine which is adhered to in spite of its creation of so formidable a progeny of problems must have powerful policy bases. (1) one clear policy objective is avoidance of the discrimination against particular individuals, groups, or localities which comes from giving more favored treatment to others in the use of public funds. The *WDA* opinion expressed this when it said that taking "the property of one citizen or group of citizens without compensation and [paying] it to others" would violate the "equality clause."[1]

(2) That opinion further stated that a departure from the public purpose doctrine would involve a violation of the policy of "due process of law." In other words, such governmental conduct would have an arbitrary quality, quite apart from its discriminatory effect. Perhaps reference was here being made to the idea often expressed in Wisconsin cases, that the taxpayer must receive some clear benefit in return for the taking of his property by taxation—an idea also embodied in the "taking" clause of article I, section 13 of the state constitution (text in Appendix B). Perhaps this, as well as the non-discrimination idea, also lies behind the invocation in the *Heimerl* case of article IV, section 4,

of the federal constitution, guaranteeing to every state a "republican form of government."[2]

(3) The latter case also reveals another of the roots of the public purpose doctrine, a policy favoring laissez faire—the general idea that governmental interference with the free play of competitive economic forces must be kept to a minimum. It is this which led the *Heimerl* court to restrict the use of municipal taxes as a means of carrying on a municipal business to those businesses involving a "public function" or "some element of public utility"—and this attitude towards municipal enterprise was responsible, even before the *Heimerl* case, for executive invocation of the public purpose principle to block proposed legislation. Again, it was a laissez faire philosophy which made the *Curtis* court say that using public funds to aid any useful trade or employment is "obviously incompatible with the genius and institutions of a free people; and the practice of all liberal governments as well as judicial authority is against it." This was merely a less elaborate statement of the laissez faire doctrine articulated quite specifically the following year in a leading public purpose decision by Judge Cooley in Michigan.[3]

(4) Policy roots may be found also in the desire to avoid the financial instability and official corruption which would come from the permissible use of public money for "private" purposes. Chief Justice Dixon's observation in the *Whiting* case that "certainly the consequences of upholding such subscriptions have been most sad and disastrous to many cities, towns and counties throughout the country,"[4] represented a sentiment which doubtless had influence in other cases.

In the application of these policies to the types of problems previously listed, what was the contribution of the *WDA* case? This might be measured by the use made of the *WDA* decision in later cases. Ignoring the numerous citations of the decision on other issues (for example, state debt) we find that in addition to being invoked for (a) the general public purpose doctrine and (b) for its summary of cases on each side of the line, and (c) for the general state purpose doctrine, *WDA* was later cited for (d) the proposition that a private corporation may properly have a public purpose, and (e) the proposition that the purpose is not necessarily made private by the fact that some individual or class is benefited more than others; that among the relevant considerations are (f) the "course and usage of government" and (g) the relative "directness" of the advantage to the public; that (h) the determination of purpose is to be made in the light of a strong presumption favoring the legislative judgment; that (i) aids to local communities for public health and education are for a state purpose; that (j) state funds should not be thrown into the scales to influence elections on local matters; that (k) state funds may be given to a private corporation for only those educational activities that the state itself could engage in; that (l) the state may spend money to promote sale of dairy products.[5] The list is not exhaustive.

In other words, the *WDA* case has served later opinion-writers as a rich storehouse of general principles clustering around the public and state purpose problem—rather than as a precise precedent on it facts. Factually similar cases were almost non-existent. Perhaps the most closely analogous cases were those determining that the state Department of Veterans' affairs or the state Veterans' Housing Authority in giving educational assistance to local housing authorities might not give specific assistance on specific projects without violating the state purpose requirement.[6] Perhaps the explanation for the richness of doctrine afforded by the *WDA* case lies in the unusual range and quality of argument at the bar, and in the unusual job of research and analysis done by Justice Wickhem. His gathering together of diverse bits of principle from the precedents and his attempt to present a truly comprehensive statement of the public and state purpose doctrines produced a fertile opinion, which has served as a kind of doctrinal plateau from which subsequent disputation upon these issues seems to start. This is not to say that every subsequent case on such issues has mentioned the *WDA* case. Nor do we suggest that a subsequent court's invocation of the case necessarily showed that the case was the decisive factor in the court's decision. Nonetheless, in this area of the law, the *WDA* decision has become, as much as any decision can become, the "leading case."

As for the future of the public purpose doctrine, it may well be rather different from its past, in Wisconsin as well as elsewhere. It is true that the policy basis of the doctrine is so strong that courts have applied the doctrine even where, as in a majority of the states, it is not specifically in the constitution. It has been derived generally from the "due process" clause or equivalent clauses, from the "organic" law of the Constitution as a whole, from the constitutional clause against a state's loan of its credit, or from "common law" principles. There is also a slight possibility that even where a state amends its constitution, to overcome the public purpose requirement for specified purpose, the state may run afoul of the due process clause of the Fourteenth Amendment. This result seems unlikely, however, in the case of recent state constitutional amendments permitting promotion of industrial development.[7]

Indeed the growing strength of the movement for municipal or state promotion of industry is the primary force eating away at the public purpose doctrine. The movement has not been without criticism—from bankers, municipal finance officers and others. However, it is significant that the National Municipal League included in its 1948 edition of a Model State Constitution a stringent public purpose clause, yet in its 1961 publication, "Salient Issues of Constitutional Revision," observed: "In these post-World War II years, when states have begun to assume greater responsibility for the economic well-being of the various communities within its [sic] borders, the constitutional prohibitions against aiding private undertakings must be re-evaluated in the light of present needs. The current impact of these limitations has received little or no study anywhere in the nation. Forward-looking state economic development schemes might very well run counter to these long-standing prohibitions."[8]

The economic-promotion pressures exist in Wisconsin, too. Their history and current status are examined in the course of the discussion in the next section below.

Economic Promotion by State or Municipality

The specific activity of economic promotion by the state may be discovered at many points in Wisconsin's history prior to WDA. Conservation of the state's own resources—fish, game, water, forests, wildlife—is a special kind of promotion with which we are not here concerned.[9] What of promotion of the development of private economic resources? The extensive aid to private agricultural societies and fostering of farm cooperatives we have already encountered—in addition to which there were various other examples of agricultural aids, including loans and tax advantages.[10] Analogous efforts in the industrial field were urged from time to time by the state's governors[11] and some other suggestions found their way into legislative enactments. Most prominent, of course, was railroad aid, taking the form of favorable state tax treatment and local aid authorized under both general and special enactments. In 1875 a specific limit to railroad aid in terms of 5 per cent of the locality's taxable property was imposed (the constitution had in 1874 placed such a limit on a local government's debt), and in the seventies and eighties some special railroad aid provisions for particular situations were still being passed.[12]

For non-railroad industry, aid was considerably smaller. In the last quarter of the nineteenth century there was aid authorized for "industrial" as well as agricultural fairs and expositions; a reward was offered for invention of a "satisfactory steam-wagon"; the corporation laws were amended to permit organization of a promotional type of corporation (namely "for the purpose of locating, building, encouraging and establishing . . . manufacturing establishments in cities and towns within this state"). Congress was memoralized for tariff reform to help Wisconsin industry. The most common form of state aid, in view of constitutional limitations, was through state-wide tax exemptions or tax preferences for depressed industries—particularly agriculture and forestry.[13]

It was not until the mid-depression year of 1935 that promotional advertising by the state came to the fore, in provisions for state advertising of dairy products throughout the United States, for advertising and promoting the sale of Wisconsin potatoes, and for activity by the Conservation Commission in collecting and distributing information about the state's recreational facilities, and coordinating similar efforts of other organizations. Two years later came not only the promotion of the cooperative form of private electrification in the WDA legislation, but also the enactment of Governor La Follette's request for a special Department of Commerce. This was repealed in 1939, and nothing substantial was done along such lines until 1953 saw the creation of a joint interim committee for 1953–55 to study industrial development and to propose a sound program of industrial promotion.[14]

A staff report of this committee revealed that state advertising (for which a coordinating committee representing agriculture, conservation, and the executive was created in 1951) and industrial as well as agricultural promotion were then being conducted by a number of official and non-official agencies of the state. Such functions were continued by the Division of Industrial Development in the Executive Department, created in 1955 upon recommendation of the interim committee and approval by the Legislative Council. The next significant development was the 1959 law consolidating this division's functions with those of the Planning Division of the Bureau of Engineering, into a new Department of Resource Development. Its Division of Industrial Development has pursued a vigorous program in four fields, which it has described as "(1) economic research; (2) assisting Wisconsin communities in obtaining new industry and encouraging the growth of existing industry; (3) plant location service; (4) promotion." Another and lesser form of state expenditure promoting industrial development is illustrated by recent small appropriations made until 1960 to the Wisconsin Development Credit Corporation, which had been formed under a 1955 law authorizing formation of corporations to aid business development by extension of credit when credit is not elsewhere readily available.[15]

There is also a record of considerable aid to industry by municipalities. In the third quarter of the nineteenth century, there were scattered enactments generally falling into this pattern: an authorization to a particular municipality to issue bonds (generally subject to a maximum limit and subject to ratification by local referendum) so as to obtain stock in a named private economic enterprise within the municipality.[16] Disappearance of this type of enactment is traceable to the 1874 constitutional amendment limiting local debt to 5 per cent of the locality's taxable property. Occasionally came an authorization like one given to Portage in 1889 to use half of its funds from licenses and ordinance-violation penalties for "promoting the commerce and manufactures of the city"—and sometimes there was a specific *caveat* as to constitutional limits. A broader authorization occurred in the statute of 1915 declaring that upon a local referendum adoption of the plan, cities "shall annually appropriate" from $2,000 to $4,000, depending on the class of city, "for the purpose of aiding and encouraging the location of manufacturing, industrial and

commercial plants therein and for other purposes designed to increase the population, taxable property and business prosperity
of such city, and for the purpose of defraying the necessary incidental expenses incurred in relation thereto . . . ." After slight revision in 1921, this was repealed in 1953, evidently at the instance
of the League of Wisconsin Municipalities which regarded the
provision as a limitation rather than a grant of powers. Four years
later, however, there appeared on the statute book an authorization to cities and villages (extended in 1961 to towns) "to borrow
for the reservation and development of industrial sites," and "the
expenditure of funds therefor [was] determined to be a public
purpose." Sites thus purchased could be developed by installation
of utilities and roadways but not by building construction; and
while sites could be sold or leased for industrial purposes, this
could be "only for a fair consideration to be determined by the
governing body."[17]

This supplemented the authorization which had existed since
1937 to appropriate up to one-tenth of 1 per cent of the local
assessed property valuation for "advertising the advantages, attrac-
tions and natural resources" of the locality, and "to develop and
improve the same," and which provided that the municipality
might "cooperate with any private agency or organization in such
work." This particular authority, orginally applicable to cities,
villages, and towns, was restricted to towns in 1953.[18]

Local aid had its heyday in the nineteenth century period of
railroad promotion; it is not the major source of public aid today, if the state-wide tax exemptions or tax preferences for agriculture and forestry are taken into account. It is primarily because of these latter factors that a 1956 study found a shift, in
twentieth-century Wisconsin, from local aid to state aid.[19]

How does the *WDA* case bear upon the promise of these and
future attempts at promotion? In the first place, insofar as future
schemes for economic promotion by the state may use the device
of an intermediate private corporation or may involve construction of some undertaking that may be denominated an "internal
improvement," the *WDA* case will be influential in the ways we
shall indicate in the next two sections. Secondly, insofar as the
doctrines of public and state purpose will be invoked to challenge
state promotion, the *WDA* opinion is likely, as we have seen, to

be treated as the leading authority. When applied to the contemporary state promotional efforts outlined above, the case would seem to sanction the generalized promotions of agriculture and of industry, but cast doubt on the validity of particularized aids— at least where a substantial segment of industry or agriculture is left outside the area of benefit. This suggests that the appropriations to the Wisconsin Development Credit Corporation, which in turn would extend credit to particular companies, were as vulnerable under the state purpose standard as were the appropriations to WDA. It suggests further that the authorization since 1957 for local borrowing and spending for site purchases and development for later sale or lease is probably saved by the requirement of a "fair consideration" in the sale or transfer.

Finally, it seems that insofar as particularized industrial benefits by municipalities were given a general state sanction in the 1915 statute repealed in 1953, this was *unconstitutional* (and will continue to be unconstitutional if extended by municipalities on the basis of their claimed general municipal powers as distinct from specific statutory sanction). The *Suring, Wendlandt, Kiel* and *Lake Mills* cases of 1926, 1936, 1942, and 1957 respectively, dealing specifically with municipal subsidies, seem to make this quite plain, if it had not been plain enough under the pre-existing public purpose principle.[20]

But here is an instance where the "law in action" may markedly diverge from the "law in books." We have already seen that particularized subsidies have persisted in Wisconsin from an early date. And a 1947 study of 130 cases of industrial subsidization in Wisconsin during 1930–46 shows that in the great majority of cases, the source of the subsidy was municipal rather than private funds. In short, although the principles of the *WDA* case will doubtless figure in any constitutional litigation over such municipal subsidies, the litigation may not materialize at all, because of general community support for the subsidization.[21]

Assuming that the litigation does materialize, and the Wisconsin Supreme Court, because of a change in its concept of public purpose or because of a constitutional amendment making the change, is ready to uphold at least some of these particularized aids, some suggestions are perhaps in order. The court must avoid the facile assumption of automatic public benefit from aid to a particular industry. There should be an appropriate court record on the basis of which the court can be articulate—as other state courts have generally not been, in upholding particularized aids—on such factors as the economic need for the project, its likelihood of success, the consequences for local labor conditions, community industry and commerce, and the impact on certain non-economic values. And initial judgment on these matters would properly be lodged by the legislature in an appropriate administrative agency acting pursuant to standards expressed in the legislation.[22]

Internal Improvements: The General Problem

We have seen that the public purpose and state purpose limitations were not set out as such in the Wisconsin constitution, but were judicially derived from particular language of the constitution. On the other hand, the constitution is explicit in its ban on internal improvements by the state—just as are the constitutions of almost a score of other states.[23] In spite of some opposition to this restriction, it was generally supported at both the 1846[24] and 1848[25] constitutional conventions on the ground that, as experience in other states had recently shown, state participation in internal improvements invited financial ruin, inefficiency, and corruption, as well as being not a proper "object of a state government."[26]

This policy against internal improvements, like the related general policy of the constitution against state indebtedness, may need serious reconsideration, as has been suggested from time to time.[27] Over the years, judicial construction added to the difficulties; for in the *Froehlich* case, which barred the state from improving the Portage levee (a decision which seems to have been nullified by the state's practice) a definition of internal improvements was announced which proved a source of uncertainty and dissatisfaction.[28] Whether desirable or not, the internal improvements ban has been a substantial barrier to prompt legislative action on a variety of important public problems. When years of effort in constitutional amendment are necessary, as they were in Wisconsin, to give the state authority to engage in such improvements as highways, forests, airports, veterans' housing, or port facilities, it is clear that the constitutional clause is one of no narrow impact. It was the clause which, as we have seen in Chapter I, was the immediate provocation for use of the peculiar legal device by which the WDA promotional program was launched.

The WDA device, approved by the court, by which state funds were used in encouraging others to engage in internal improvements was an extension of some of the devices hitherto used to avoid the constitutional ban. The courts had approved almost a century ago the device of state authorization to governmental subdivisions to incur debts for internal improvements, and had approved even some compulsion upon them to incur such debts or expenses.[29] Sanctioning the use of state funds to encourage others is, of course, a considerable step beyond the sanctioning of a program involving the others' use of their own funds.

But the *WDA* court went further. It viewed the *New Richmond* case (App. A #29) as upholding (though it had said nothing about internal improvements) state encouragement in the form of state financing of local improvements made after a cyclone hit the city; and it viewed the *Van Dyke* case (App. A #72) as upholding state encouragement in the form of partial state financing of local public works undertaken for unemployment relief. These cases involved more than encouragement through education. They involved encouragement through defraying some of the cost of the internal improvements engaged in by others. While the 1948 veterans' housing case (App. A #74) refused to recognize the validity of this concrete form of encouragement for veterans' housing construction, it failed to come to grips with the *New Richmond* and *Van Dyke* holdings as construed in the *WDA* opinion. It is true that the *WDA* case itself had sanctioned, for WDA's operations, only the educational form of encouragement. However, its frowning on the concrete form was based not on the internal improvements ground but on the state purpose ground. Its view of the internal improvements precedents was that they permitted the state to encourage, by helping to finance, internal improvements engaged in by others. This view was first clearly suggested in the *WDA* opinion. If the potentialities of the suggestion are fully appreciated,[30] it might leave the internal improvements ban no longer a significant limitation in state legislative action. (Of course, the constitutional restrictions on state indebtedness and the public and state purpose doctrines would still be important hurdles to be met by a state internal improvements program utilizing governmental subdivisions or private corporations analogous to WDA).

Whether the 1960 shopping center case (App. A #80) is to be construed as going far toward realizing this potential significance of the *WDA* decision remains unclear. The case involved the University of Wisconsin's use of non-profit corporate instrumentalities organized by its friends to develop a shopping center on what had been university lands. Under traditional criteria, the shopping center would have been an internal improvement if engaged in directly by the state or state university. But the Supreme Court of Wisconsin said: "This Court has repeatedly held that nonstock, nonprofit corporations organized by friends of the university for its benefit, could do things which neither the state nor the university could do directly, that such corporation is not an arm or agency of the state and does not engage the state in work of internal improvement or create a state debt." This rationale did not accurately reflect the rationale of the university building corporation cases of 1928 and 1955 (*Loomis*, App. A #41, and *Giessel*, App. A #77). There the internal improvement ban had been held inapplicable because university buildings were deemed *not internal improvements* (just as the state office building was held not an internal improvement in the 1954 building corporation case, App. A #76). In the 1960 case, where the shopping center clearly was an internal improvement, the Court's rationale seemed to be different: the immediate or direct participation in the internal improvement having been by the nonprofit building corporations, the participation was *not by the state*.

Yet the scope of the rationale is still in doubt. For example, is it to be restricted to *university* building corporations? Does it legitimize the use of *state funds* (or other property) to encourage or subsidize the nonprofit corporation's activities that would be barred to the state as an internal improvement if undertaken directly?

Perhaps an affirmative answer to the latter question is rendered doubtful by the fact that the Court opinion concerned itself seriously with the question whether the university had received a *fair price* for its lands from the friendly non-profit corporation which leased them to the friendly non-profit development corporation. However, the majority seemed to be considering this "fair price" question only in connection with the public purpose issue.

It was the dissenting justice who specifically raised the point that if the state received less than a fair price for its lands, it would to that extent have subsidized an internal improvement contrary to the constitutional ban. (He assumed, *arguendo*, that the university regents' "anonymous funds," unlike the lands, were of such a special nature that they could be donated to the first corporation, for purposes of the land purchase, without the donation's being considered a prohibited use of state funds for an internal improvement.) Thus it may be that the court majority in the shopping center case has implicitly followed the broad "encouragement of others" principle of the *WDA* case, at least where the "others" are non-profit building corporations friendly to the university. If so, the Court has walked through a large gap in the constitutional barrier—a gap which constituted the major contribution of the *WDA* case on the internal improvements problem.

What makes this gap more likely of doubt-free recognition in the future is the fact that, as we have noted, the internal improvements prohibition is being subjected to serious criticism. The Model State Constitution drafted by the National Municipal League contains no such prohibition. As students of the problem have pointed out, state planning and coordinating of improvements is a more efficient procedure than leaving it to the localities to make improvements on their own. Moreover, if the federal government, in making funds available for improvements, deals directly with the localities, this aggravates the problem of disappearing "states' rights" and advancing federal encroachment.[31] Probably considerations of this sort influenced the Wisconsin Governor's Commission on Constitutional Revision in 1960. While its Report omitted a change in the internal improvements provision from its list of "highest priority" revisions, it recommended as a "substantial question deserving consideration," a "relaxation" of the provision "insofar as it excludes by specific reference to matters stated therein other public purposes for which public money may be spent."[32]

Use of an Intermediate Corporate Instrumentality
The state's use of an intermediate agency of a private corporation was, as we have had occasion to note, not original with the WDA legislation—though court decisions on the validity of the practice

did not come until some fifty years after the practice had started. In 1899 in the *Industrial School* case (App. A #28) and in 1916 in the *LaCrosse Public Library* case (App. A #34) the use of private educational institutions in the fulfillment of legislative purposes was deemed proper. The court's major attention was devoted to the fact that public funds were involved; and it felt that so long as the purpose of the expenditures was public, and the instrumentality was subject to reasonable public controls, then the private character of the instrumentality was immaterial.

Neither in these cases nor in the longstanding practice of such public grants as those to agricultural societies or veterans associations, was there any legislative desire to avoid some constitutional restraint on direct state action. Such a desire did appear in the 1923 legislation upheld in the *Loomis* case (App. A #41), where the state by its use of the University Building Corporation sought primarily to free the University of Wisconsin building program from the constitutional ban on state indebtedness.[34] The device was used in later building programs of the state as well.[35] Although the 1954 state office building case (App. A #76) held that the mortgaging of a leasehold interest in state property by a building corporation violated the provision of the constitution limiting state debt, the court found no such violation in the basic device by which the state leased land to the corporation, which would construct buildings for lease to the state, which would pay "rentals" and eventually own the building. Analogous devices in the use of "dummy" building corporations were upheld in a 1955 case (App. A #77)—involving no mortgaging of a state property interest—even against the state-debt objection. And in the 1960 shopping center case (App. A #80), as we have noted, the Supreme Court observed that a nonprofit university building corporation "could do things which neither the state nor the university could do directly, that such corporation is not an arm or agency of the state and does not engage the state in work of internal improvement or create a state debt."

Thus far, then, we are justified in concluding that: (1) As far as the public purpose doctrine is concerned, this restriction is not violated by the mere use of an intermediary private corporation, when subject to appropriate public controls. And since the public purpose restriction applies to governmental appropriations, the restriction can hardly be *avoided* by the use of such a corporation after the funds have been appropriated. (2) As for the internal improvements ban, this restriction can, to some still uncertain extent, be avoided by use of the intermediate corporate instrumentality.

There is, however, still another respect in which the *WDA* case and related cases have a bearing on the problem of the corporate intermediary: they make pertinent the basic constitutional doctrine against undue "delegation" of sovereign power. In the *WDA* case, for the first time in the line of cases involving state aid to private corporations, the issue of invalid delegation of sovereign power to private parties was squarely treated (perhaps because of the new emphasis which had just been given to this issue by the United States Supreme Court in invalidating some New Deal legislation).[36] The court's first opinion, it will be recalled, declared that sovereign power was being delegated to a private corporation without guiding standards or adequate supervision, and that to confer sovereign power would constitute the instrumentality a public officer, whereas (in view of constitutional requirements that a public officer be an elector and take an oath) WDA could not qualify as a public officer. Upon rehearing, the court concluded that there was no invalid delegation after all. The WDA legislation conferred no powers which the corporate articles did not already give to the corporation; and if any such new powers were conferred, they were (in light of the limited functions held permissible under the state purpose doctrine) not sovereign in character. Thus the court thought it "unnecessary to re-examine the soundness of our original conclusions based upon the assumption that the act delegated sovereign power . . . . " The first opinion, therefore, remains as a possible judicial block to future state attempts to use private corporations in the administration of public functions.

However, the second *WDA* opinion exerts a strong contrary force. In addition to re-emphasizing the proposition of the *Industrial School* case, that the private nature of the instrumentality does not disqualify its use on public purpose grounds, the *WDA* court indicated the means to successful avoidance of the delegation objection. The legislation might grant funds to a corporation whose articles already legitimately endowed it with the powers for whose exercise the funds were given; the legislation might provide for segregation of the corporation's public and private funds, with auditing of the public fund expenditures by the secretary of state, and an annual report of its public fund expenditures by the corporation to the governor; might declare that none of the public funds should be used for activities which would be repugnant to the constitution, if carried on by the state, and might further hedge off the state's role by stipulating that the state should not be liable for any corporate debts or obligations. This was a pattern which was faithfully adopted in the legislative session following the *WDA* decision, in the plan for state support of the national American Legion convention in Wisconsin, upheld in the *American Legion* case (App. A #48). It was objected in that case that the statute set insufficient standards to guide the exercise of discretion in expenditure of funds by the state's corporate delegate. The court replied that the authorization to spend the appropriated funds, "to assist in the holding and the operating" of the convention, was "substantially in the same form and as definite in prescribing standards as the terms which were held sufficiently definite for that purpose in making the appropriations which were held valid by the court in" the *WDA* case, and substantially similar also to the terms used in making appropriations over the years to the various private agricultural societies and veterans' associations referred to in the *WDA* case.

Thus the *WDA* case was influential here as well as in the later turnpike corporation case (App. A #75) in dispelling objections in terms of improper delegation to private parties.[37] This objection is still to be reckoned with, however, in situations outside of the indicated WDA legislative pattern, as shown in one aspect of the *American Legion* case and other leading Wisconsin cases involving alleged delegation to private parties—some of which cases have been more stringent than others.[38]

No good reason appears why the law should condemn out of hand the device of the corporate instrumentality, which affords greater flexibility in the attainment of legislative objectives. Wisely, the Wisconsin Supreme Court has sanctioned the device, against public purpose and delegation objections, if the corporation is subject to sufficient public controls and standards, and the purposes fulfilled by the public funds are otherwise public and statewide purposes. And it is consistent with the spirit of modern administrative law that the Court should not insist on rigid or detailed legislative standards and controls in this connection.

But should the device be sanctioned when used as a means of enabling the state to do indirectly what the constitution prohibits it from doing directly—such as incurring a debt or engaging in internal improvements? On the issue of state debt (with which we have in this study been only tangentially concerned) the Court was apparently winking at the realities in allowing the state to insulate itself against the debt restriction by means of a corporation bearing close ties to the state. Here the wiser course may have been, by adverse decision, to have forced the state to a constitutional amendment, especially since the consequent savings in debt financing charges would be substantial. In the area of internal improvements, the Court was again permitting indirect accomplishment of what was prohibited when undertaken directly —though there was somewhat more basis here for the judicial view that the constitution itself contemplated this permission, at least with respect to state encouragement of others to engage in internal improvements. Thus, though the internal improvements prohibition may be something of an anachronism in the modern state, it presents no serious barrier to Wisconsin improvement programs if the encouragement-of-others rationale of the *WDA* decision, and what is probably the rationale of some more recent decisions, will prevail in the future.

CHAPTER VI

JURISPRUDENTIAL

PERSPECTIVES

From the narrative of WDA's origins, its legislative and judicial vicissitudes, its post-litigation experience, and its posing of statecraft issues, we turn now to consider some more strictly jurisprudential implications of its history.

The Problem of Predictability

Predictability is one of the much mooted issues in jurisprudential literature. Although there are other facets of the issue, the one with which we are here concerned is the matter of unpredictability of judicial decision—a subject much emphasized by Jerome Frank. We shall present below, (a) an analysis of the extent to which the participants in this litigation were correct in anticipating the grounds of decision, (b) a delineation (on the basis of illustrations from the major lines of precedent invoked in the court arguments) of the various areas of judicial freedom which make for unpredictability on the basis of doctrine alone, and (c) an over-all analysis of the factors affecting predictability of decision.[1]

EXTENT TO WHICH PARTICIPANTS ERRED
IN ANTICIPATING THE GROUNDS OF DECISION

At the stage of legislative hearings on WDA in spite of the bitter opposition from numerous sources and the representation of contending positions by lawyers, there were practically no warnings of unconstitutionality. Press reports of the first hearing reveal only one person as possibly referring to a constitutional defect. William Ryan, who was later to file an *amicus curiae* brief in the litigation attacking constitutionality of the statute, was reported to have deplored the "delegation of public authority to a private corporation."[2] Even if this were intended as a constitutional argument, it was given substance only by the first court opinion, not by the ultimate ground of decision. The transcript of the second and more extensive hearing reveals no one who came even that close to anticipating that the fate of WDA would turn on its constitutionality. Closest perhaps was the question we have seen put by a representative of telephone companies: Why should sixty thousand dollars be spent in propaganda for public ownership only; why not educate the public on both sides of the issue? But even this thought—which would be one strand in the public purpose objection voiced by the dissenting judges—was advanced at this legislative stage as a policy argument rather than as a constitutional one.

When the bill was on the floor of the legislature, again, despite the intense opposition, there was little objection on constitutional grounds. Such as there was seemed directed either at passage of the bill without a constitutional quorum, or at indirectly accomplishing through the use of a private corporation the constitutionally forbidden state participation in internal improvements. Neither objection was adopted by the trial court or by any judge of the Supreme Court, either in the first decision or in the majority, concurring or dissenting opinions of the second decision.

Finally, did the lawyers in the litigation succeed in anticipating the way in which the judges would dispose of WDA's future? (1) Consider first the delegation issue—which was the basis of the first decision. We have seen that this issue had been subordinated in the trial court, and was not treated squarely or fully in that court's opinion. It was not raised at all in the main briefs of the two principal parties in the Supreme Court; and was discussed by them in reply briefs and oral argument only after the issue had been injected into the case by briefs of *amici curiae*. And though this ground was adopted by the court in the first opinion, it was repudiated in the second.

(2) Not a single judge took the position on the internal improvements issue so elaborately urged by all participants opposing

WDA, or the position so urged on the miscellaneous minor constitutional objections.

(3) Regarding the public purpose issue—which was the most extensively argued point in the briefs prior to the rehearing arguments on delegation—the whole court in the first opinion felt it unnecessary to treat the question, and the majority in the second opinion saw a public purpose in WDA's generalized activities, and possibly even a public purpose in its particularized activities, though, again, the latter point was not decided.

(4) The ground upon which the most important (i.e., the particularized) activities were invalidated—the state purpose concept —was virtually a "sleeper" in this litigation. As we shall elaborate below, the concept was buried with the most tangential kind of reference in the trial court's opinion, in the brief of the main party opposing WDA, in the brief of WDA, and in the various briefs of *amici curiae,* except that one of the latter gave it moderate emphasis.

Thus, trial judge Reis, answering an objection that WDA might choose to restrict its services to only part of the state, e.g., the northern counties, said the statute itself did not require such a choice. He was evidently not talking about the kind of particularized activity represented by promotion of a particular plant as part of a state-wide offering of services. He referred to no state purpose doctrine. He cited the New Richmond cyclone case to show that the Supreme Court had upheld even a statute which required the spending of state money on a localized basis.

In appellant's brief opposing WDA the state purpose idea was not treated separately from that of *public* purpose. In a long discussion of public purpose in appellant's brief (pp. 51–63), only two short sentences were connected with the state purpose idea: "The benefit derived from the enactment is not of state-wide application. The people in one part of the state are not interested in the promotion or encouragement of municipal ownership of a public utility situated in another portion of the state" (p. 58). This occurred at the end of a paragraph devoted to showing that the agency was promotional rather than educational. It was unaccompanied by citation. It was clearly not stated as a separate legal doctrine directly applicable to the issue of validity of the appropriation.

The WDA brief, as a short part of the discussion of the *public*

purpose doctrine, made the point that the fact that an appropriation benefited certain individuals or one class more immediately
than others did not rob it of its public purpose (pp. 96–7). And
in the course of the argument on *internal improvements,* the
brief observed: "The activities of WDA are not directed to the
promotion or encouragement of any *particular* utility or utilities
but rather to education in the particular fields involved, and use
which may be made of particular municipalities, non-profit corporations and cooperatives is the means to the end rather than the
end itself" (p. 86). In neither instance was there any reference to
an explicit legal doctrine on state purpose. Understandably, counsel for WDA would not wish to highlight such a doctrine.

The brief of the business and taxpayer interests, in the course
of its lengthy discussion of the delegation issue, illustrated the
allegedly uncontrolled discretion involved by saying that WDA
didn't promote cooperatives and municipal utilities in general,
but had discretion to encourage "specific or particular ventures
within the state" and to determine which ones and where, including which plants to encourage acquisition of (pp. 11, 29). The
brief of the veterans' associations argued the *public* purpose doctrine (pp. 16–49) with copious quotations but none of the cases
or other authorities mentioned the criterion of state-wide effect
or action. A few times, however, the adjective "state-wide" was
added to the phrase "public purpose," and this also occurred in
the reference to public purpose in the outline of argument. A
similar statement can be made about the brief of the Wisconsin
Agricultural Authority.

Only the *amicus* brief of William Ryan specifically invoked the
requirement of a state-wide purpose as separate from the public
purpose requirement; Ryan said that Mr. Maloney's promotion of
a co-operative in Crawford county was a "local" matter that didn't
"subserve the common interest and well-being of the state as a
whole." The brief cited article VIII, section 5 of the state constitution as establishing the requirement that state tax funds are to
be spent only for "state," i.e., state-wide, expenses, and cited case
authority for this interpretation (pp. 34 *et seq.*).

Let this be clear: We have not been—nor could we practically be
—concerned with predictive estimates that remained unexpressed,
e.g., on the part of lawyers who felt their anti-WDA contentions

would not prevail, or legislators who voted either for or against the bill with silent conviction as to its unconstitutionality. Nor do we suggest that any sound generalization on predictability can be made without analyses of numerous other litigations, and involving many different types of subject matter. And above all, it should be clear that we are not here concerned with predictability of result—i.e., judgment for one party or the other. The latter is doubtless greater than predictability of grounds of decision. Even Jerome Frank has said that Cardozo was "perhaps not too wide of the mark" in saying that at least nine-tenths of the cases coming to the New York Court of Appeals could reasonably be decided by that court in only one way. At another point Cardozo had put his estimate in terms of a "majority" of the cases coming to that court. Llewellyn's estimate is 80 per cent or more, based in part upon a study of the cases decided on a particular day by the same New York court. Federal circuit court judge Charles E. Clark, who said he agreed with Prof. Edwin Patterson's judgment that Cardozo's nine-tenths figure was too high, declared that the "majority" figure was a "fair" statement. It should be noted that the vague "majority" estimate is not helpful, particularly since pure guess work will predict close to half the cases accurately—one difficulty being the occasional occurrence of a third alternative, the in-between judgment not fully satisfying either party.[3]

What we are warranted in saying is this: Here is a case, much more elaborately argued than most, involving issues of broad socio-economic significance, threatening the status of powerful economic interests. Yet those who expressed themselves—at hearings, in the legislature, and in the court—goaded as they were by partisan interest to muster all relevant legal doctrine, failed almost completely to anticipate the grounds of decision.

EXTENT TO WHICH THE VARIOUS PRECEDENTS
PERMITTED A JUDICIAL FREEDOM TO DECIDE EITHER WAY

One of the virtues of the Anglo-American legal system, as against the Continental system, is said to be the stability which comes from reliance on precedent. But there has been exaggeration, not only of the alleged instability of the Continental system, but also of the restraint which the Anglo-American system puts on the judge. Particularly since Cardozo's speculations in the 1920's on

the nature of judicial process, and the "realist" movement of the
1930's, Americans have been more and more prone to question
the "slot-machine theory" according to which the judicial process
is akin to feeding precedents into a machine which then produces
the "correct" decision, or the related theory that the judge is a
mere conduit for transmitting the law—which he has "discovered"
or "found" rather than "created" or "made." There is still controversy on whether judges do "legislate," i.e., "make" law. But
this debate ultimately reduces to controversies over how much the
judges make law, rather than whether they do it. The question
becomes: To what extent, and through what techniques, does the
appellate judge have freedom of action in his decision in spite of
the existence of prior judicial decisions urged as controlling precedent? This question cannot be answered by one study alone—
just as the aspect of predictability previously discussed cannot be
so answered. But here, as there, a case study in a particular area
makes some contribution to a partial understanding of the whole.
This analysis is presented with that limited objective in mind.[4]

The following catalogue of techniques by which judges may
achieve freedom from the restraint of precedent has been constructed from an analysis not only of the *WDA* opinions but also
of the Wisconsin precedents on the two leading problems in the
second *WDA* opinion: (1) the problem of public and state purpose; (2) the issue of state participation in internal improvements.

Determining what a particular precedent stands for.—(1) In
determining what a particular precedent stands for, the court is
said to be seeking a rule, rationale, or principle (the *"ratio
decidendi"* or rule of the case) bearing some relation to the "material" facts of the precedent. But how close this relation must be,
and how materiality is to be determined, are areas of controversy
sufficiently respectable to give courts ample freedom of action.

For example: in constructing the categories of material fact that
go into the rule of the case, the later court may conceive of these
categories as *very narrow or very broad or somewhere in between.*
Thus a very narrow statement of the *New Richmond* decision
(App. A #29) might be this: A state appropriation is for a public
and state purpose if it consists of $21,400 to discharge a city's
indebtedness incurred when a tornado hit the city and the city
relieved the distress occasioned by destruction of the entire business section, 100 homes, city hall, utility plants, bridges, churches,

and the deaths of 115 and injuries to 500 out of a total 1900 population, requiring burial of dead and measures for prevention of suffering, disease, and crime. A later court unwilling to uphold the appropriation in the case before it might be slow to read broader fact-categories into the holding of the prior case so as to extend its precedent value. But the opposite view may be taken by a later court which does wish to uphold the appropriation in its case—where, for example, the later case involves a very different amount of money, or a man-made calamity or a calamity of very different proportions, or no element of prior municipal indebtedness, or no danger of disease and crime or some combination of these factors. The broader category might then run in terms of: relief of distress from any substantial calamity or emergency.

The point is well illustrated by the treatment in the *WDA* opinion of the *Van Dyke* decision on internal improvements (App. A #72). Viewed narrowly, *Van Dyke* stood for the proposition that a state does not become a party to a public works internal improvement when, for the primary purpose of aiding employment, it reimburses counties and cities to the extent of 25 per cent of their labor cost on public works undertaken for unemployment relief. A much broader reading—apparently adopted by the *WDA* opinion—was that *regardless* of the purpose and amount of state expenditures which go into building internal improvements, such expenditures don't make the state a party to the improvements whenever some one other than the state conducts the improvement operations, using the money supplied by the state.

To be sure, the later court's choice of a narrower or broader reading of the precedent is not completely free from limitations. We shall say something of these limitations later. But the permissible extent of expansion in the fact-categories of a precedent constitutes a major source of judicial freedom.[5]

(2) In the course of thus choosing at what level of generality it should view the precedent's fact-categories, the court has certain supplementary means of achieving freedom of action. One of these consists in *ignoring* a clear rationale or principle stated in the precedent. Thus, as indicated above the 1935 *Van Dyke* case had used a primary purpose rationale to solve the internal improvements issue: "the primary purpose of the state was not to become a party to carrying on works of internal improvement but

to reimburse the counties and cities which had made work simply for the purpose of providing employment to the unemployed." Yet in the 1948 veterans' housing case (App. A #74), such a rationale was completely ignored by the court when it declared that the state made itself a party to internal improvements by contributing funds to help defray the cost of a veterans' housing project constructed by a local housing authority. This occurred in spite of the argument vigorously pressed in the state's brief (pp. 34–38), buttressed by specific reference to the rationale of the *Van Dyke* decision and other precedents, that the "dominant purpose" was the long-sanctioned one of aiding veterans rather than becoming party to an internal improvement in the form of housing. Indeed, the veterans' housing case sinned doubly, for it also ignored the possibilities inherent in the encouragement-of-others rationale of the *WDA* case, though quoting approvingly an attorney general opinion which in its unquoted portion had invoked a narrow construction of the encouragement rationale.

Instead of being ignored, the rationale or principle of a precedent may be subjected to *violent handling or distortion*. This is what happened in the instance previously cited, where the *WDA* opinion described the *Van Dyke* case as having "held" that it was constitutionally permissible for the state to encourage internal improvements by others. This broad reading of the precedent was a distorted one; in the *Van Dyke* opinion the Court characterized the challenged statute as one under which the state did not have the primary purpose of engaging in or encouraging internal improvements. Again, the reader will recall from the discussion of the internal improvements problem in the preceding chapter, how the Court in the 1960 shopping center case (App. A #80) did violence to the rationale of the prior university building corporation cases relied on as precedents.

A more subtle exercise of judicial freedom of action ascribes to a precedent a holding on a *point to which the prior court had never addressed itself*, though it would have had to decide the point in the ascribed way if the decision for the victorious party were to stand. The usual judicial attitude is that such *"sub silentio"* rulings—particularly when even counsel did not raise the point—have no binding force as precedent. Yet there is some freedom here, and the opinion in the *WDA* case exercised it. The

Court there said that the *New Richmond* case, by sustaining the state aid to the city of New Richmond, had "held" the encouragement of internal improvements by others to be not within the ban of the constitutional prohibition against internal improvements by the state. Actually the *New Richmond* opinion concerned itself only with the public purpose issue, and said nothing about internal improvements.[6]

A court may still further expand the area from which it may derive an authoritative principle: it may cite from a prior case a proposition which had not been necessary to the decision because the proposition dealt with a *type of factual situation not before that court.* Such a statement in an opinion is usually referred to as *"dictum."* It may occur separately. Or it may occur as part of a broad generalization addressed to the facts before the court and to other types of facts as well, in which case the proposition is often said to be *dictum* as to the latter facts. (Exactly when these facts are to be regarded as of a different type as distinguished from being closely similar to the precise facts of the case is a difficult problem we shall later discuss. Obviously a case must be regarded as going to *some* extent beyond its precise facts, else it could not serve at all as a precedent for a later case involving parties of different identity, events occurring at different times, etc.)[7]

A *dictum* is not part of the authoritative holding of the case. This is the official dogma. Yet no attentive student of judicial opinions can fail to observe that reliance on *dictum* is part of the judicial folkways. Thus, the first *WDA* opinion supported the view that WDA's functions must be exercised by public officers by quoting with approval the broad generalization from *People v. Salem* that "the money of the people belongs in the custody of the agents of the people."[8] Not only did this language come from a concurring opinion; not only was it directed in that opinion at the public purpose issue rather than the delegation issue for which the *WDA* court was citing it; but it covered a far wider range of situations than had been presented to the *Salem* court for decision (validity of public aid to railroads), and would scotch any conceivable use of a private corporation for a public purpose. The *WDA* court was clearly quoting a proposition that was at least partly *dictum.*

Still more loose a use of precedent is illustrated by the practice of going beyond the four corners of the precedent itself, to rely upon *what other cases or other authorities have said about it.* In one of the public employee pension cases (App. A #50) the court was concerned whether the granting of a certain pension violated the public purpose doctrine as evolved in the Wisconsin cases. Instead of directly relating those precedents to the case before it, the court simply fell back on the exact language which had been used in the *WDA* opinion to analyze those precedents. This is, of course, not a deviation from the precedent system itself; it utilizes language in a precedent as a means of interpreting other precedents. Sometimes this technique of going outside the precedents involves a reliance on authorities other than the cases Thus, what the treatise writers have stated as the rules emerging from the cases has often been cited in the opinions we are considering.[9]

(3) We have argued that in the course of determining how broad or how narrow it should conceive the rule of a precedent to be, a court may use a number of devices, e.g., ignoring a rationale or principle stated in the opinion, distorting it, emphasizing a point which the prior court had not even mentioned or had made in relation to hypothetical rather than to actual facts of the case, or going beyond the opinion to rely on what other authorities have said of the case. Analogous devices may be seen in the cases when we focus on the flexible handling not of prior rationales but of particular facts of the prior case. Consider first the *violent handling or distortion* of facts. The court in the *Keeley Institute* case (App. A #27), invalidated county payments to private institutions for treatment of impecunious habitual drunkards. Taking account of a Maryland precedent upholding a statute authorizing such payments, the court said merely that "the Maryland act was broadly distinguishable from the one at bar." And yet in every respect deemed significant in the court's analysis of the Wisconsin statute, the Maryland statute seemed the same. Both involved a private corporation—in fact the same one; both required that the patient be unable to pay for treatment (the Maryland court described its statute as requiring "financial inability," and the Wisconsin statute said in one place, "pecuniarily unable," and in another place, "has not the means"); and the

malady, habitual drunkenness, was the same in each. An unexplained and evidently inaccurate assertion about the facts of a precedent (here the "facts" as to the actual provisions of a statute) was the court's dubious means of circumventing the precedent.

Again, as we have seen the court do in dealing with non-factual aspects, the court may *ignore* troublesome aspects of the facts rather than characterize them in an inaccurate or highly questionable way. Thus, in the *WDA* case, in evaluating legislative precedents for public aids to private corporations, Justice Fairchild's dissent declared that there was only one prior instance where appropriations were used so as to be "detrimental to a particular group of interests"—the "use of public money to encourage and promote the formation of cooperatives." One such instance, argued Fairchild, "does not constitute a course and usage of government." This analysis, however, ignored the range of ways in which aid to any particular groups might involve detriment to those not aided. Aid to veterans created an inequality with non-veterans; aid to agricultural groups (many were not cooperatives) created an inequality with industrial groups.

Sometimes construing or misconstruing the facts of precedents may consist neither of ignoring facts, nor of stating them in an apparently inaccurate way, but in treating as highly significant some facts which (though stated accurately enough) had not been treated as crucial in the prior court's opinion. The *Whiting* decision (App. A #4), in invalidating a municipal donation of aid to a railroad, explained that prior decisions had upheld aid to railroads only where the municipality obtained stock in the railroad. To this the dissenting Justice Paine was able to state that "among all the cases where the validity of legislation authorizing such aid has been contested and sustained, I think not one can be found which has made the fact of such stock subscriptions material to the validity of the law. On the contrary, the struggle has uniformly been upon the very question made here, whether the purpose for which the tax was to be raised was a public or a private purpose. And the laws have been sustained not upon the ground that the stock subscriptions made the enterprise public, but upon the higher and broader ground that the nature and character of the works themselves made them so." Shortly thereafter, the United States Supreme Court made a similar criticism of the *Whiting* decision's treatment of the facts of the precedents.[10]

Thus far we have been illustrating the areas of freedom in the process of determining what a precedent stands for. But even after this determination has been made, there arises as we shall see below, a second broad area of choice: the freedom of choice between different precedents, each of which may seem applicable but which lead to contrary decisions.

Choosing between competing precedents.—A court may find itself in the position of choosing between two quite broad principles which have emerged out of different lines of cases that developed independently of each other. The case being presently decided may merge the two doctrinal lines by qualifying one or the other principle. Thus, there are authorities for the broad proposition that government power may be exercised only by public officers. There is also the proposition (clearly enunciated in the *Industrial School* case [App. A #28]) that as long as the purpose is public, the agency effectuating the purpose may be a private one, assuming there is reasonable accountability to the public. The first *WDA* opinion rested on the former proposition, the second on the latter. In choosing the latter, the second *WDA* opinion merged the independently arising lines of doctrines by qualifying the one by the other.

This situation involves the reconciliation of inconsistent rules which are so broadly phrased that no substantial question arises as to whether the facts of the immediate case easily come under both rules; they do. The situation is somewhat different where the competing rules are stated with a greater particularization of the determinative facts, so that the issue becomes whether the facts in the case before the court are more analogous to the material facts categorized in one precedent's rule than to those in another. This is the typical problem—for the orthodox view is that a decision should be rationalized in a rule that is closely patterned to its facts. The point may be illustrated by the *WDA* case. The court in dealing with the public purpose issue may be regarded as asking, among other things, this question: Is granting of public funds to a private, non-profit corporation for promotion and education in cooperative and public ownership of utilities under the conditions involved in the *WDA* statute, *more analogous* to (a) granting public funds to a private, non-profit corporation for education of wayward or abandoned girls under the conditions involved in the *Industrial School* case (App. A #28), where the grant was upheld, or more analogous to (b) granting public funds to a private corporation engaged in general educational work under the conditions involved in the *Curtis* case (App. A #21), where the grant was invalidated?

Thus, whether a choice is being made between two broadly phrased rules that lead in opposite directions, or between two sets of facts, each of which bears some similarity to the facts in hand, it is clear that precedents are in genuine competition with each other for choice. (Factors affecting the making of the choice will be discussed at a later point.)

The role of ambiguous language.—Obviously, in the cases we are considering, the constitutional directives themselves are full of ambiguous language: the rule that the purpose must be "public" rather than "private," that it be a "state-wide" rather than a "local" purpose, that the state not be a "party" to an "internal improvement." Further, in the application of these directives through fairly specific rules of law derived from precedents, judicial flexibility could be honestly exercised because the language of precedent opinions was often ambiguous. For example, an ambiguity as to the breadth of fact-categories in the rationale of the case typically leaves unclear whether the precedent court intended to have its rule apply to the facts of the later situation as a "similar" or "analogous" situation.

In addition to these basic and pervasive forms of ambiguity are some lesser ones. In the application of the fundamental constitutional directives, subsidiary concepts were introduced, which were also full of ambiguity. In the public purpose cases, the requirement that the benefit to the public be "direct" rather than "remote" falls far short of a clear bench-mark. How inevitable was the conclusion of the *Curtis* case (App. A #21), that while aid to ex-soldiers produced a "direct" public benefit, aid to an educational institution did not? Reference, in these same cases, to the "past course or usage of government" involves a counting and a weighing with no explicit standard by which to evaluate the number and weight. So, too, in some of the "internal improvements" cases, a subsidiary concept of "dominant" or "primary" purpose left considerable room for legitimate difference of interpretation.

A special contextural type of ambiguity still further enlarges the area of arguable doctrine: the same word may be given different meaning in different contexts. If a railroad enterprise has enough of a "public" character to justify the legislature in giving the railroad the eminent domain power (the power to condemn property for a *public use*) it may seem natural to conclude that the legislature's giving the railroad financial aid would be using funds for a *public purpose*. But this would reckon without the contextual ambiguity of "public." It was the recognition and application of this kind of ambiguity that led the *Whiting* majority opinion to conclude that public donations might not be made to railroads; and the failure to recognize this type of ambiguity that underlay the dissent in that case.[11] Similarly, while a non-profit building corporation was treated in some cases (*Loomis*, App. A #28; *Giessel*, App. A #77) as separate from the state for purposes of determining whether it was violating the state debt provision of the constitution, it was in the 1950 *Bareis* case (257 Wis. 497) treated like the state itself, for purposes of determining whether the corporation might enjoy the realty tax exemption for state property.

In conclusion, it should be noted that the particular cases we are analyzing rarely turned on ambiguity in the language of statutes—though that is another large source of judicial freedom of movement. Statutory ambiguity was well illustrated by a few of the railroad aid cases.[12]

Ignoring some precedents.—We have referred to instances where the court ignores a particular rationale in a precedent. We here consider the ignoring of the precedent itself.

In permitting recovery on town bonds issued in return for railroad stock, *Bushnell* v. *Beloit* (App. A #2) had declared that under the constitution, (article XI, section 3), the legislature might confer power on municipalities for other than strictly "municipal purposes." Yet the court held exactly the contrary in the very same year. In *Foster* v. *Kenosha* (App. A #3) the court enjoined collection of a city tax designed to pay for a railroad stock subscription. The city charter had authorized special taxes deemed to be in the city's interest and approved by the voters. The court ruled that in this respect the statutory charter violated the constitution, particularly the "municipal purpose" provision of article XI, section 3. Neither court nor counsel cited the *Bushnell* case.

Again, the much-cited *Whiting* case (App. A #4) had ruled in 1870 that public aid to railroads in the form of donations, as distinct from stock subscriptions, violated the public purpose standard; yet the *Lynch* case of 1883 (App. A #13) treated a town subscription to railroad stock as enforceable whether or not, as it was alleged, the stock was worthless. The court ignored the *Whiting* precedent—though counsel and the dissenting opinion invoked it as being in effect contrary to the court's position.

Cutting loose from the cases for a fresh start.—Occasionally a court makes short shrift of precedent by saying that the decisions have created such confusion as to warrant beginning all over again. This is the court's view in the *Donald* case (App. A #33, 61): "It may well be admitted that courts have been quite, and perhaps too, resourceful in discovering methods of so construing the terms 'debts' and 'indebtedness' as to restrict the meaning thereof so as to meet the exigencies of particular cases. The safest way is to cut quite loose from case law and look to the fair meaning of the Constitution itself. To study the many judicial sayings and endeavor to evolve a rule of unwritten law therefrom would be liable to impair the constitutional mandate and add to the confusion which I think already exists."

Overruling or disparaging a particular precedent.—This represents one step beyond the preceding category. It is a last-ditch stand which courts normally avoid taking. While not inconsistent with the theory of a precedent system—since the theory does recognize the legitimacy of occasional overruling for the most compelling reasons—it does represent a departure from the norm. We have seen that such departures may be made through decisional techniques that make no avowal of departure. Sometimes a court goes a step further by taking cognizance of the troublesome precedent and declaring that it is being confined to its particular facts; or, more forthrightly still, that it is being overruled. Within the boundaries of the Wisconsin cases we have been analyzing, examples of this phenomenon are the overruling of *Loomis* v. *Callahan* in the 1954 state office building case (App. A #76); the *WDA* court's overruling itself upon rehearing; and the Wisconsin case referred to in the latter opinion (App. A #46, 194–95) as overruling an earlier one on the scope of the constitutional prohibition against special laws granting corporate powers. There was more than one instance where a court expressed frank dissatisfaction over the rule permitting municipal subscriptions to railroad stock—but felt impelled (a) to adhere to the precedents because of the "vast pecuniary interests" which had grown upon the basis thereof and (b) to avoid expanding the permission.[13]

Reliance on a standard not derived from the specific language of decisions or documents.—In choosing to ignore or reject precedents, a court may, instead of invoking other precedents, simply go to a different source for its standard: the "unwritten" law, the "natural" or "inherent" or "implied" rights. In construing a contract, a court may imply from the express language what the parties intended but did not say, and may also imply, as a matter of policy or justice, what they did not intend. So too, in the construction of a constitutional document, standards from outside its language have sometimes been applied.

Thus, Justice Fowler's dissenting opinion in the *WDA* case (App. A #46, 205) observed: "There is no provision of the constitution that expressly declares that appropriations shall be for a public purpose. There is no express provision in the constitution probihiting the legislature from enacting statutes infringing on the inalienable or inherent rights of individuals, but any act of the legislature so infringing is unconstitutional." This as well as other observations in the Wisconsin public purpose cases, like those in some public purpose cases outside of Wisconsin, are reminders of the influence of a natural-rights philosophy in this area. The dominant tendency in the Wisconsin cases was to invoke particular constitutional clauses (one of which itself referred to "inherent rights") as embodying the substance of a public purpose limitation. But, as in the case of most states, there was no clause specifically stating a public purpose doctrine. The state purpose doctrine, too, is not specifically stated as such, though it has been judicially derived from particular language.[14]

Interpreting and categorizing the facts of the case before the court.—Just as there is judicial freedom in construing the facts of the precedent, there is some freedom in interpreting the facts of the case before the court. This may play a vital role in determining whether the case is to be fitted into one prior rule rather than another.

In the first opinion in the *WDA* case, the court ignored the fact that the WDA powers stated in the statute were in large measure the same as those already contained in WDA's articles of incorporation. On rehearing, this fact became a central feature of the analysis rejecting the court's previous position on the delegation issue. In the *Hamman* case (App. A #71) the court was able to bring the Horicon Marsh wildlife refuge project within constitutional boundaries by calling it a "park,"—although as a Wisconsin attorney general was later to remark, "concededly . . . [it] did not come within any ordinary meaning of the term." This was so unusual a characterization of the facts before the court that the thorough briefs of counsel had not argued the "parks" question at all, and only when the court itself asked for briefs on the matter, did counsel consider it.[15] Finally, in the teachers' pension case (App. A #51), a major difference underlying the cleavage between the majority and dissent was on this factual aspect of the case: whether the law liberalizing pensions for already retired teachers would actually induce existing teachers to remain in the profession. Thus, not only the finding and characterization of existing facts, but the determination of presumed factual consequences of a particular law or a particular decision may be an important source of divergence in judicial conclusions. Since evidence on factual consequences is not normally presented in the case, the court relies on "common sense" intuition, and the like, sometimes explicitly invoking a doctrine of "judicial notice," according to which facts that are self-evident, widely accepted, or officially established are accepted without evidence.

In characterizing the facts of the case before it, a court sometimes takes a considerable leap from reality through the use of "legal fictions." Such palpably untrue assertions of fact may serve a number of argumentative purposes, concealing legal innovation or softening the shock of innovation. Some of the cases we have analyzed came close to this technique, if they did not actually illustrate it.[16]

FACTORS AFFECTING JUDICIAL DECISION AND ITS PREDICTABILITY

It is easy to be misled by this sampling of judicial techniques for achieving freedom-within-the-precedents. That judicial decisions are virtually unpredictable would be a fallacious inference. The fact that the weapons exist that enable a court to defend whatever result it arrives at (i.e., for plaintiff or for defendant) does not itself make the result unpredictable. Factors may exist which influence the court strongly in the direction of one result rather than another, no matter which techniques or grounds of decisions are selected in the court's opinion to defend that result. Indeed, factors may exist which also influence the court in the direction of some techniques and grounds of defense rather than others. Predictability on the appellate court level may be said to be a function of at least three major variables: (a) the kind of case; (b) the kind of court; (c) the kind of lawyers on each side. The range and variety of the influences which may work upon decision through these variables reach beyond what may be illustrated by the lines of precedent involved in the *WDA* case. To some extent, therefore, the analysis in this section and other sections on judicial process goes beyond the borders of these precedents.

The kind of case.—The first variable encompasses, among other things, differences in the emotional impact of different cases. Prominent in the facts of some cases may be circumstances which would appeal rather powerfully to the emotions of most people (including judges), and hence tend to push the judges in a particular direction. Judge Cardozo reminded us in 1921 of "the likes and dislikes, the predilections and the prejudices, the complex of instincts and emotions and habits and convictions, which make the man, whether he be litigant or judge . . . . The great tides and currents which engulf the rest of men do not turn aside in their course and pass the judges by." Human reaction to the catastrophe suffered by the city of New Richmond perhaps had something to do with the strained decision (App. A #29) that state funds to relieve the city's distress were for a state-wide purpose.[17]

Again, one precedent may have more compelling force because it clearly rests upon some common sense or otherwise appealing policy that makes sense for the situation before the court, as distinct from a rival precedent whose policy basis is not so clear or so obviously sensible or so clearly applicable. Consider the *Consolidated Stone* case (App. A #31) invalidating an appropriation to pay sub-contractors on the State Historical Society building the balance due them from the contractor after the latter's bankruptcy. The rationale of the prior public purpose cases had recognized the propriety of appropriations for claims founded on "moral obligation" or on "equity and justice" where a strong enough public interest was involved, as in the case of bounties to war veterans (App. A #20 and 36). Was that policy applicable here so as to justify the state's payment of one private party's debt to another? And was it applicable in spite of prior decisions like *Froehlich* (App. A #30) which found *insufficient* equity in the claim of an innocent purchaser of a county obligation issued for treatment of drunkards in a private institution under a law held unconstitutional (App. A #27) after issuance of the obligation? This decision had stressed that the appeal of prior opinions to concepts of equity, justice, and morality had not been intended "to justify a tax for every claim which one private party may have against another . . . though founded in equity and justice . . . or in gratitude or charity." Surely the broad, sensible policy against using public funds for predominately private benefit, and the narrow scope of the "equity" exception made prediction of the *Consolidated Stone* decision fairly easy.[18]

Indeed, it seems reasonable to believe that this factor of trying to do justice by applying a "sensible" or "fair" policy to the type of situation presented to the court is a most powerful factor in determining the result, and in determining which of the available techniques we have surveyed will be selected for achieving the result. This reasonable supposition seems corroborated by Llewellyn's elaborate studies in the common-law tradition. The more clearly the kind of case before the court fits into a situation-type for which a particular precedent rule makes good sense, the more predictable the result should be. Hence one reason for the importance of the "kind of case" variable. This much can be said even though we offer no clearly defined criteria for determining the existence and boundaries of a situation-type. Neither Llewellyn nor other students of the judicial process have made bold to suggest such criteria.[19]

The kind of court.—This variable has a number of facets. It is no secret that there are variations in the predispositions, value preferences and philosophies of individual judges. Familiar dichotomies, for instance, are the humane judge vs. the "hanging judge"; the "liberal" vs. the "conservative"; the protector of "property rights" vs. the protector of "human rights"; the believers in "activism" vs. the believers in "self-restraint"; the judicial "technician" vs. the judicial "statesman." Though these categories are ambiguous, are not mutually exclusive in their application to many judges, and may even apply in opposite fashions in different cases decided by the same judge, they do point to significant variations that may influence decision and affect predictability.

Their significance in these respects is reduced to some extent by the fact that the appellate decision is generally a *group* decision. Moreover, some unifying effect stems from the fact that all members of the group have been subjected to roughly similar professional training (which is not to belittle the important differences in attitudes inculcated by different law schools)—training in what Pound called "a taught tradition of logically interdependent precepts and of referring cases to principles." This common background means that particular conglomerations of facts may *tend* to suggest to all members of the craft particular concepts and precepts that help point the way to decision: for example, that a party seemed to be acting as an "agent" of another; that a person's conduct may be such as to "estop" him from making his claim; that a document may be said to contain an "implied warranty"; that a man shouldn't profit from his own wrong; that one shouldn't be allowed to do indirectly what he must not do directly; that a statute, except in certain special situations, should be regarded as presumptively valid. Judges, as Pound and Llewellyn have emphasized, are members of a *craft*, and the lawyer member of the craft who engages in prediction is aided by the conceptual predispositions he shares with the jurist members.[20]

On the other hand, the "group" quality of an appellate court exerts some influence in the direction of diversity and unpredictability rather than unity and certainty. This is not merely because of the variety of human beings who may constitute the group. It is also because human beings' behavior in groups may differ from their behavior as lone individuals. One need not subscribe to all that has been written about "small group dynamics" to recognize that an appellate judge's process of decision-making is subjected to a set of peculiar pressures from other judges in the group: their personalities and intellects, bargaining strategies, and other tactics of persuasion within a conference discussion or in a post-conference attempt to win agreement on a particular opinion. Studies by Professor Walter Murphy in the papers of United States Supreme Court justices show many instances of such pressures actually or probably at work. Thus, for example, Mr. Justice Jackson acknowledged his change of mind after reading the draft opinions of his colleagues; and in another case, Chief Justice Stone's draft dissent led the majority to modify their position by adopting a paragraph from his analysis. Pressure on the majority opinion may come from the very possibility that a dissenting or concurring opinion may be filed; such an apprehension may produce compromise or dilution in the majority position. A chief justice on the United States Supreme Court and on the highest court of some states is in a special position to influence the votes of his colleagues because of the power to award "plums"—the writing of opinions in the more interesting or more important cases. And he may exercise this opinion-assigning power in strategic ways, for example, he may assign an opinion to a moderate justice, whose draft opinion is likely to keep uncertain members of the majority from falling away and may gain recruits from the tentative dissenters. It seems true that a judge in an appellate court, unlike a lone judge, is inevitably under some pressure to bargain. This may lead, in the interest of greater bargaining strength, to formation of voting "blocs" within the court; thus, there is evidence of "rump conferences" by Taft and by Stone at their respective homes. Finally, there are the miscellaneous ways in which an individual judge may be consciously or unconsciously influenced by the personality of a colleague—his charm, his leadership quality, his intellectual persuasiveness, his friendliness, perhaps even his having urged one's appointment on the chief executive (as Taft did for Butler and Sanford, and Stone did for Cardozo).[21]

Important also, as part of the "kind of court" variable, are the customary attitudes or approaches that may characterize the court in a particular historical period—whether or not this is linked with the influence of great judicial leaders of the period such as Cardozo of the New York Court of Appeals, or Lemuel Shaw in Massachusetts or Gibson in Pennsylvania. Llewellyn has argued, for instance, that the period 1820 to 1850 or somewhat beyond was a period in which the American judicial tradition exhibited more freedom of movement, more concern for, and open discussion of, principles purporting to give fair results, than the more "formal" period covering roughly 1880–1910; and that a trend toward the spirit of the earlier period began about 1920.[22] We have not found that the court opinions surveyed in this study clearly support this generalization for Wisconsin; indeed, since the relevant Wisconsin cases began in 1859, they do not offer full opportunity to test the thesis.

A more familiar kind of historical thesis is that in a particular era some social claims press more heavily upon courts for recognition than other claims or than in other periods. Knowledge of such pressures in a particular case may, of course, make the decision more predictable. For example, might it not have been anticipated, in the light of the declining social need for railroad building that the court in the 1923 *Herreid* case (App. A #17) would not display nineteenth-century acceptance of railroad subsidies? There, narrowly construing a statute which on its face appeared to apply both to railroads already built and to those being planned, the court refused to apply the act to a road already constructed. Since 1859 the court had upheld municipal aid to railroads through subscriptions to railroad securities. Even in the nineteenth century, however, later decisions accepted this doctrine with reluctance; and now, in a twentieth-century context, the judges seized an opportunity to reduce the impact of the questioned doctrine. Still, the impress of historic context is not sharply defined, and we have not found it possible to spell out firm patterns in the public purpose cases from an analysis solely in terms of historical periods. One fact (confirmed by the case-digests in Appendix A) is that the affirmations and negations of public purpose usually came in bunches, ranging from two to five in number, rather than in alternating fashion, but the bunches covered widely disparate time periods, namely, from two to seventeen years.

Variation in the performance of courts may flow also from the mechanics of their operations. This is a factor which may affect the substance and the predictability of decision. Suppose the practice is that at some stage before the court confers and votes on the case the chief justice assigns the case to a *single* judge whose charge it is to report to the conference an analysis and proposed decision. And suppose the practice is to vote on the case not many days after oral argument. Both practices enhance the possibility that one man will dominate the decision; at least such practices reduce the advantages obtainable from group decision. For they tend to mean that there is no substantial study by *every* judge of the briefs and record prior to the voting conference. Wiener has unearthed disquieting data on the extent of these practices in both state and federal courts—including the Wisconsin Supreme Court.[23]

Other mechanical features of possible significance are the extent to which law clerks are used for research and decisional ideas; the extent to which the court sits not as a whole group but in panels of, say, three judges; the extent to which a court makes a practice of *per curiam* decisions in which the court is wholly or almost wholly silent on the specific reasoning by which it arrived at decisions; the extent to which dissenting views (often the "voice of the future") are, in the practice of the particular court, smothered in the interest of a fictitious harmony, being voiced only on rare occasions; the extent to which the particular court, because of a crowded docket, cuts unduly the time it spends on consideration of a case.

The kind of lawyers.—A distinguished lawyer has sadly observed: "The influence of powerful counsel on courts, and the unequal chances of success which follow from this alone, irrespective of the merits of a cause, are so far a result of that partiality in distributing talents for which nature is responsible that it can hardly be considered as any other than an unavoidable disturbance in the cause of justice."[24] This variable may reflect not only unequal talents but also differences in argumentative techniques that might be chosen by different lawyers of quite equal talent.

Why did the argument on delegation in the *WDA* first opinion ignore the important prior instances of analogous use of private corporations? Probably because the delegation issue had not been fully argued by counsel; it was injected into the case for the first time by an *amicus curiae,* then treated in the parties' reply briefs. Were it not for the *amicus curiae,* the issue might not have been in the case at all. Again, in the opinion on rehearing, the critical argument on state purpose which ultimately crippled WDA's operations might not have appeared had it not been for one of the *amici curiae*—for the argument as we have seen earlier in this chapter, had been ignored by the major parties to the litigation. The *WDA* opinion further evidenced an important type of advocate's influence when it made word-for-word adoptions of material from the briefs.[25]

Doubtless the variables we have discussed are not a complete catalogue of the factors affecting judicial decision. But they are surely enough to give pause to one who surmises that prediction of judicial decision depends solely on a careful and complete survey of existing rules and doctrines. They give pause also to one who is asked to believe, as has recently been urged, that success in prediction of judicial decisions will attend the use of a quantitative analysis of judicial behavior—e.g., through "bloc analysis," "game theory," "scalogram analysis," or "content analysis," and even the use of mechanical computers. The future may indeed bring a refinement in predictive methods, but the present state of the *science* of predicting an appellate decision in a particular case is still pre-Copernican.[26]

Legal "Logic" vs. "Policy"

In discussing the "nature of the case" variable, we noted that the court's aim of applying a sensible policy to the type of situation before it is a signally important factor in determining the result, and in determining which of the judicial techniques we have surveyed will be selected for achieving the result. But since this idea of judicial freedom to make policy choices is not easy to reconcile with orthodox views of the relation of policy to the demands of legal logic, some further discussion seems necessary.

The orthodox view runs along these lines: Precedents, which establish the "law," are restraining influences on subsequent judges. The restraint is necessary; the judicial system must have the stability reflected in the ideal of a "government of laws and not of men." The law must be free from human caprice and decide cases in the light of "principle." This is to be done in a "logical" way, on the basis of "analogy" to prior cases. Considerations of "policy" and "experience" on the other hand, are properly in a state of flux—but they are for the legislature rather than the court.

Exemplifying this orthodox theory is the statement of Chief Justice Ryan in the *Bound* railroad aid case (App. A #12) that court judgments must not "proceed upon policy rather than upon principle.... Courts have nothing to do with the consequences of judgments rendered on settled principles of law." The quoted sentiment is not unusual, even past mid-twentieth century.

Indeed one can find in the works of outstanding legal scholars examples of the same sentiment: that the method of legal "logic" is primary, and "policy" is a thing apart, which may only occasionally be allowed to supplement the primary method. So Wigmore and Williston were sometimes prepared to leave the matter.[27] Cardozo too gave this impression, by treating "analogy" or "logical progression" as the *usual* judicial technique (which he also called the method of philosophy), as compared with *alternative* methods: the method of evolution (consideration of "historical development") or tradition (consideration of community customs) or sociology (consideration of "justice, morals, and social welfare, the mores of the day"). The impression, however, becomes a misleading one, when his analysis is considered in the context of his supplementary remarks.[28]

Our study has suggested that this apparent dichotomy between the demands of legal logic on the one hand and the allegedly lesser demands of "policy" on the other is seriously misleading. First, it errs insofar as it assumes that two alternative processes are involved. That is, it errs in assuming that the process resulting in a decision which is described as "logically consistent" with, or "analogous" to, a precedent is a process which is and should be *alternative* to rather than *inclusive* of, the process of determining what decision represents desirable policy. Second, it is an untenable assumption that conscious judicial inquiry into, or unconscious judicial reaction to, matters of desirable policy is an illegitimate or second-best or occasional or minor approach. Let us see, in some greater detail, why these assumptions are errors.

The conclusion emerging from the syllogism of judicial logic depends, as in the case of other syllogisms, upon the premises. That there is generally a choice of premises we have already seen from our analysis of the areas of judicial freedom within the precedent system. We have further seen that the choice will importantly depend upon the policy objectives of the chooser, and the policies he sees embodied in alternative precedents. We may take this one step further: the policy basis *should* be the central and conscious basis for the choice. This is so because legal rules or decisions cannot sensibly be regarded as ends in themselves. They are means. They are made by man for man's purposes. They are a means of solving human problems, in accordance with the policies deemed most appropriate for the production of certain consequences deemed desirable.

Conceivably, this doing of justice can be accomplished without prior rules. But our system uses the rule form, primarily in order that the policy which does justice can be followed again in future similar cases (i.e., those cases to which the same policy is deemed appropriate) thereby achieving an economy of thought and time,[29] and helping attain a certain limited amount of legal stability and equality of treatment of litigants in different cases. The formulae of the rules must be constantly revised, through expansions, contractions, exceptions or explicit modifications, or overrulings, in the light of the policy that will do justice for the fact pattern facing the court—rather than to let the policy be shaped by the supposedly rigid character of a formula which in fact always contains some ambiguity as to scope of its application to new facts, and which always is tentative.[30]

Does this over-emphasize the creative element in the process? Is it, for instance, inconsistent with this analysis to say, as Cardozo did, that in a majority of cases coming before a particular appellate court the law and its application to the facts are clear, and in another substantial percentage the law is clear and merely the application is unclear? We believe there is no inconsistency. It remains true that every time an existing legal rule is being "applied," there is involved a set of facts different in *some* respect from those which gave rise to the rule, and the appellate court must determine (a) whether the difference is so unimportant in the light of the purpose of the rule, i.e., the cases are so closely "analogous," that the rule should be held to apply to the new set of facts, and (b) whether this purpose of the rule is still so defensible (and perhaps also whether reliance on the rule has been so substantial) that overthrow of the rule is unjustified. The "application" of the rule is thus a clarification of the rule, through a value-judgment determining whether the rule should be regarded as covering the new facts; and it is an evaluation of the rule, through a value-judgment determining whether it should be retained.[31] Cardozo was surely aware of this non-mechanical nature of rule "application." Perhaps however his attitude toward those cases which involved the *small* extensions, contractions or exceptions to rules (as against those involving either larger ones or wholly new rules) underestimated their contribution to unpredictability of decision, or unduly depreciated the importance of their cumulative effect, or underestimated the need for constant re-evaluation (in addition to clarification) of the established rule even in the apparently routine case. Llewellyn's discussion of what is and should be the appellate judge's creative role in the routine case suggests this.[32]

Some further exposition of the relation of our view to the judicial syllogism may be helpful. Suppose that the disposition of the internal improvements issue in the *WDA* case is stated in the following syllogism:

1. The state's encouragement of others to engage in internal improvements does not make the state a "party" to the internal improvement.
2. The state's appropriation to the WDA corporation for the latter's promotion of cooperative and public ownership of utilities constituted an encouragement of others to engage in internal improvements. Therefore,
3. The state's appropriation did not make the state a party to an internal improvement.

The major premise had to be derived from the express and implied *policies* of the prior cases by a process which, as we have seen, is by no means inevitable in its result, and which in this instance represented a considerably elastic or "broad" reading (though there was an equally permissible "narrow" reading) of the prior internal improvement cases.[33] The minor premise uses the same "encouragement of others" language. It thus regards the facts in this case as coming within the *policy* applicable in the prior cases to "encouragement" of "others." Again, there was no inevitability about this construction: only some of those prior cases involved encouragement by money grant, and none of them involved a private corporation in the "others" category. Policy judgments had to be made in fashioning both premises, if the court was to operate intelligently, that is, was not to be guilty of what a philosopher has called the greatest stupidity, namely, forgetting what we are trying to do.

Of course, judicial opinions are not usually written in clearly syllogistic form. But they can be schematized into that form. The court's determination of some underlying principle from the precedents may be viewed as the formulation of the major premise. And the determination of whether the essential features of the case before it are "analogous" or "similar" to those embodied in the underlying principle may be viewed as a determination of whether the minor premise shall be so formulated as to bring it within the categories of the major premise.

It is further true that the policy problem involved may not be actually discussed in the opinion—a fact which may give a misleadingly mechanical or impersonal flavor to the opinion. This is what led Holmes to the criticism that "the judges themselves have failed adequately to recognize their duty of weighing considerations of social advantage. The duty is inevitable, and the result of the often proclaimed judicial aversion to deal with such considerations is simply to leave the very ground and foundation of judgments inarticulate, and often unconscious . . . ." The criticism is not so applicable however to constitutional law opinions, since constitutional clauses and doctrines on their face generally embody broad policy directives (policies against state participation in internal improvements and against use of public funds for private purposes are examples, along with "equal protection of the laws" "due process," and the like).[34]

Is there no sense, then, to the "law vs. policy" dichotomy? The answer is that there may be some sense, if the distinction is given a meaning other than the one we have been considering. Thus, the distinction could be reconciled in part at least, with the analysis we have presented, by recognizing an ambiguity in the word "policy." He who urges the traditional dichotomy may be viewed as saying: the judge must not be swayed by policy considerations *other than those* apparently underlying the rules in the precedents. That is to say, the policy manifested in a precedent is directly relevant in determining whether the facts of the instant case are so analogous to those of particular precedents as to make the policy of those precedents applicable; but the judge cannot and generally does not embark on a "legislative" role, i.e., fashioning policy beyond this *policy-within-the-precedents.*

This distinction seems to point in the right direction, though it is not an easy distinction to deal with. When would a court's policy be regarded as going beyond those of any precedents? When it overrules? But overruling when there are strong policy reasons for doing so, is a bona fide technique of the American precedent system itself (and often in doing so the court invokes some *other* precedent of another jurisdiction or other era). Hence we are left with this indefinite limitation imposed by the theory that a court should not go beyond the policy of the precedents: it should not depart from earlier policy *except for strong reasons.* This limitation is not so powerful in constitutional cases. For where other than constitutional issues are involved, a legislature may change policies declared by judges in common law or in statutory interpretation; but a court's interpretation of constitutional language cannot be changed by the legislature. The only avenue of change—if it is not to be the court itself—is the cumbersome process of constitutional amendment. This has led the Supreme Court to recognize that there may be greater propriety in judicial overruling in constitutional cases than in others.[35] Moreover, the primary reason for requiring "strong" reasons for overruling—avoiding the harsh impact upon those who have relied on the earlier rule—is undermined if the court gives only prospective effect to an overruling decision.[36]

Other limitations on courts may also be linked with the policy-within-the-precedents analysis. Implicit in the effective operation of such a judicial approach are the requirements that the court consider its own case situation primarily in terms of a sensible policy for that situation, and that the prior opinions it canvasses should exhibit clearly defined policies for clearly defined situations. This would facilitate the court's task of intelligent choice as well as the job of prediction on the part of others. Also implicit in the effective operation of the approach we are considering is a basic candor not only in the court's communication of its own policies but in its identification and characterization of precedents. This would mean that *some* of the techniques we have seen used in the public purpose and internal improvement cases would be *improper*; e.g., ignoring pertinent precedents, or violently handling or distorting the situation before the court or the factual and non-factual aspects of the precedents. In this way, the previously surveyed freedom-giving techniques of handling precedents would properly allow less freedom than they seem to permit.

Miscellaneous Misconceptions of Judicial Process

THE EITHER-OR FALLACY

Perhaps the most persistent misconception of judicial process is the notion last considered: the view that opposite poles or mutually exclusive alternatives are represented by "law" or legal "logic" on the one hand and "policy" or "experience" on the other. Always, we have urged, the process is, or may be put, in deductive logical form; always some policy or experience is being effectuated, and should be.

This erroneous "logic *and not* policy" view is related to another, embodied in the adjuration that courts must remember that ours is a "government of laws and not of men." Clearly the "not" introduces an erroneous notion. In the judicial process it is "men," the judges, with all their variant views on what constitutes good policy, who give life to the "laws"—the legislative and prior judicial rules. The rules are indeed necessary, but they require "men" for interpretation, evaluation, and reinterpretation and re-evaluation.

POLICY DECISIONS AS ARBITRARY DECISIONS

But it is argued that this alleged misconception has some kernel of truth in it nonetheless; that it expresses a proper concern about *arbitrariness*. An analysis of the court's policy role along the lines we have presented is said to be dangerous nonsense, because it amounts to saying that the court can, and does, and should, decide any case any way it pleases. The logic of the court opinion becomes a mere "rationalization"—a facade that is intended to conceal or is capable of concealing from others the arbitrariness of the actual process of decision.

This position harbors more than one misconception. In the first place, it errs to the extent that it assumes that we view a court as deliberately concealing its actual process of decision. The less sophisticated judge, the judge less self-conscious about the decisional process, may indeed have nothing to conceal; he may be unaware of the difference between his preliminary thought processes and the deductive thinking followed in setting forth his opinion. There seems to be a human tendency to forget these preliminary stages in one's thinking—a tendency for which Llewellyn has given some interesting speculative reasons.[37] But even if the judge is quite persistently aware of his preliminary policy "hunches" or "policy thinking" and of the difference between that early stage and the later deductive process, there is still no basis for a charge of concealment. The fact that the opinion has the form of deductive logic is not a representation by the court that this was the form of its entire process of decision. Rather, the validity of the court's suggested deductive justification of the decision must be judged independently of the inductive process which preceded it. The Court is offering for critical examination: (1) the policy choice embodied in the conclusion; (2) a major premise which purports accurately to embody in legal-rule form, the policies of the precedents deemed pertinent (unless, in the unusual case, precedent is being repudiated); (3) a minor premise which purports to categorize the facts of the present case in a manner which brings it within the fact categories of the major premise. By this rational procedure, the court attempts to persuade others that its conclusion is just, and is reasonably consonant with prior principle, if prior principle is being followed. It is also the procedure by which the Court has persuaded itself that its tentative conclusion—whether selected by an amorphous kind of hunch or, as it should be, by a careful weighing of competing policies—is rationally justified as a principled conclusion.

Such a procedure for appellate judges is what the rest of us would generally view as normal and legitimate decision-making procedure for ourselves. For, as Max Radin once put it: "We may say with complete assurance that thoughtful men have never entered on a course of action of major or even minor importance without weighing the reasons for and against it . . . . This weighing of reasons is nothing more than seeking major premises under which either contradictory alternative may be subsumed. The fact that it is done at all implies that various major premises can be found."[38] The judge is in a similar position, though the availability of alternative major premises is limited to some extent by the requirements of a precedent system, in spite of the techniques of judicial freedom we have discussed.

This leads us to a second misconception in the argument on arbitrariness: it assumes that our analysis fails to recognize any *limits* on the choice of conclusion and choice among alternative premises to fit the conclusion. Nowhere have we asserted that the road to judicial arbitrariness is a broad highway free from obstacles or tolls. We shall canvass some of them below.

One barrier to undue judicial freedom comes from language. That is, *some* words of prior judicial rules, of statutes, and of the constitution strike in most of us a common chord of meaning, so that judicial repudiation of that meaning without solid basis in context or current need would strike most of us as arbitrary, and no judge wants to be considered arbitrary.

We must remember also the check on arbitrariness which comes from the *group* process of decision. If a judge holds capricious or ill-considered views, these must run the gauntlet of colleagues' critical reactions; if a court majority is inclined to arbitrary judgment, the judges must brook the critical reactions of the profession as a whole. Even when the maverick judge is unpersuaded by his colleagues, the tradition is for him to go along with the majority, except where strong convictions compel that he register dissent.

Efficacy of the group process of deliberation in influencing the individual case determinations of United States Supreme Court justices has been questioned by Thurman Arnold. But, however apt his skepticism may be as applied to some individuals and some issues of fundamental judicial philosophy, those who have participated in meetings of corporate boards of directors; of committees of unions, university faculties, churches, fraternal societies; of law partners; of government commissions; of parole boards, or other groups charged with decisions, can surely attest to occasions when group discussion moderated, modified, or reversed the views of participants. More than one Supreme Court justice indeed, has acknowledged that such changes of mind have occurred even after draft majority and minority opinions have circulated within the court.[39]

Moreover, a tradition embodied in Canons 20 and 21 of the

Canons of Judicial Ethics counsels suppressing the expression of personal value judgments that are opposed to community value judgments, and suppressing a personal approach to decision that is not "the usual and expected method of doing justice." "Justice," says Canon 21, "should not be molded by the individual idiosyncrasies of those who administer it." Cardozo's observation in this connection was that the judge "is to regulate his estimate of values by objective rather than subjective standards, by the thought and will of the community rather than by his own idiosyncrasies of conduct and belief."[40]

True, judges do not always adhere to traditions. But these traditions of responsible decision are coupled with another—the judicial duty and desire to do justice—and with the tendency for relatively disinterested minds to agree on the just policy for the situation in hand. That courts do not usually depart from all these traditions and tendencies is perhaps suggested by the fact that predictability of the result of the case is as high as we have seen it to be.

Pressures against arbitrariness are probably even greater when the case involves the requirements of a statute or constitution. Here the original policy choice is not that of the court. The court is asking, with respect to a statute, what was the actual or implied legislative policy for the case in hand. In most constitutional cases, it is asking whether the choice of values represented in the challenged statute is consistent with the actual or implied policy choice of the constitution. The well known presumption (relaxed to some uncertain extent in civil liberties cases) favoring such consistency between the choices in statute and constitution embodies a basic tradition of restraint on the court in constitutional cases. It is, of course, true that there are many rules available for construing statutes; perhaps the range of judicial techniques for dealing with the meaning of statutes is even greater than the range of techniques for dealing with common-law precedents. There are also rules (not free from ambiguity or exceptions) for construing constitutions. And the precedent system applies, although with somewhat different force, to prior judicial constructions of statutes and constitutions. In other words, in the statutory or constitutional case, too, there is considerable judicial freedom, including the illegitimate freedom to be arbitrary. But some curbing of freedom stems from the fact that the court's initial focus is not on its own policy views but on those of legislators and constitution makers. In addition to this consideration, the restraining judicial traditions we have seen applicable in common-law cases apply here too.[41]

Criticism of "activist" tendencies of some members of the Supreme Court of the United States amounts to the criticism that these judges have departed too much or too often from these general restraining traditions, or from the special restraining traditions in statutory and constitutional cases (including some in addition to the special constitutional tradition mentioned above). The restraints being ambiguous, it is understandable that there should be disagreement about their scope. And it has been argued with some force that the judicial critics of "activism" as against "self-restraint" are themselves "activist" when they feel strongly enough about the policy judgment involved.[42]

SINGLE CORRECT RULE OF A PRECEDENT
AS FOCUS FOR PRESENT DECISION

A popular view has been that in determining the rule of a precedent, the appellate judge focused on those facts deemed material by the prior court, that this approach would arrive at *the* correct *ratio decidendi* of the precedent, and that the rule so derived from the precedent would then be examined to see if it excluded or included the situation now before the court. Our analysis of the factors in the judicial process refutes the assumption of a single correct *ratio* for a precedent, as well as the assumption that the prior court's view of the breadth of its rule (even if more readily ascertainable from the opinion than it usually is) should be the primary focus of the later court's decision of its own case. The focus, we have suggested, should be on a just policy for the case before the court, and a determination of whether the policies underlying any given prior decision should be regarded as equally applicable to the present case. If so, the prior case becomes an applicable precedent, and its rule can, within limits, be given the necessary breadth by the later court. The legitimate techniques for accomplishing this are ample, though limits do exist, primarily in the form of the judicial traditions we have previously discussed.[43]

RESULT-ORIENTED DECISIONS AS DEVIATIONS
FROM DISINTERESTEDNESS AND NEUTRALITY

Dean Griswold of the Harvard Law School criticized the Supreme Court of the United States in 1960 for being sometimes too "result-oriented." The charge may embody another misconception. The Dean argued that the judge must strive for "intellectual disinterestedness." He must seek hard "to be guided by an outside frame of reference, called for convenience 'the law', in arriving at his conclusion, rather than focusing his intellectual effort, perhaps unawares, on justifying his conclusion arrived at somehow or other in some other way.... The scope of individual decision is properly narrow, and the place for individual decision is not reached until the guides of the law have been thoroughly explored and evaluated, with detachment, as well as skill."[44]

If our previous analysis of judicial process is sound, then the emphasis in Dean Griswold's statement is misplaced. We have argued that because the law is not an end in itself but a means for doing justice, judges must focus on the policy consequences of their decisions. This is to say, they *should* be "result-oriented." We have argued further that there are ample respectable judicial techniques for expounding from precedents a principled justification for choosing one result over another; but that there are limiting factors in the form of certain general and special traditions. When Dean Griswold asked that the judge be "guided by an outside frame of reference, called for convenience 'the law' ... rather than focusing ... on justifying his conclusion arrived at ... in some other way," was he not glossing over (1) this instrumental character of law, and (2) the fact that in light of the numerous judicial techniques we have explored, doctrinal "guidance" speaks with a forked tongue?

The Dean's criticism might be expressed less controversially. Perhaps he was particularly troubled by decisions which are *merely* result-oriented. That is, the opinions lack justification of the result by sufficiently clear exposition of sufficiently general principle, sufficiently integrated into the precedents. The criticism would then be similar to that expressed by Professor Wechsler, of Columbia, in his 1959 Holmes lectures.[45] But needless confusion was created by the language of the critics: the attack on "result-oriented" decisions that are not "disinterested" was matched by

Professor Wechsler's attack on decisions that are not based on "neutral" principles. The language was inept; both distinguished critics were aware that courts inevitably face policy choices, and more openly in constitutional cases. Their criticism, we think, is seen in its best light as we have above re-stated it. It can then be viewed, as we have viewed the criticism concerning judicial "activism," as asserting that the general and special traditions we have discussed as curbing judicial arbitrariness are too much or too often departed from.

One difficulty with the criticism is that the traditions in question suffer from ambiguity and vagueness of boundary. Another is that insofar as the criticism emphasizes that judicial decision should follow some sufficiently general principle, it is curbed by the counter criticism that for wise decision the principle must not be *too* general. Indeed the contemporary Supreme Court which has been criticized for insufficiently principled decision has also been criticized on the ground that many decisions lack the careful, cautious workmanship of narrow formulations. The latter are of course particularly desirable in relatively unexplored areas of decision.[46]

MYSTICISM

One final *caveat*. Our stress on wise policy making as the central element of ideal judicial decision carries with it a danger encountered by any theory stressing the ethical or "ought" element: the danger of an attempted "natural-law" sanctification of particular policy choices. The policy choice which to Judge X seems persuasively defensible as being in accord with *the* "correct" law which is "natural" to or "immanent" in the case situation, may to Judge Y, who sees no such natural or immanent law, seem unpersuasive or persuasive for other reasons. Llewellyn mars his stimulating study of the common law tradition by subscribing to Goldschmidt's statement that, "Every fact-pattern of common life, so far as the legal order can take it in, carries within itself its appropriate, natural rules, its right law .... The highest task of law-giving consists in uncovering and implementing this immanent law."[47] This smacks unnecessarily of mysticism. One can refrain from embracing Goldschmidt's Law and at the same time concede that in a given American appellate court today, upon a full canvassing of the policy problem and the applicable precedents, the decision of the judges is likely to be, and should be, primarily guided by their conception of justice, wise policy, or, in Goldschmidt's language, "right law" for the "fact pattern" before the court. Note that we have said "their conception" of justice. By this phrase (which is intended as an elliptical reference to the judges' conception of the sober second thoughts of the community on the matter, as Chief Justice Stone would put it) we intend to emphasize the diversity of reasonable views that judges may hold regarding the "appropriate, natural rules" for given fact patterns. This diversity may exist in large part because in the given state of our knowledge we find it enormously difficult to verify (a) the purported consequences of decision, or (b) the value judgments prompting the decision. This is why faith in *the* correct or "natural" or "appropriate" rule seems a misplaced, mystical faith.

The seemingly mystical strain in another thinker of great analytical power and creativity, Lon Fuller, is as puzzling as in the case of Llewellyn. In Fuller's view, the development of the rule of a case through a series of subsequent cases, results in fulfilling, in the last case, a purpose which the courts in the preceding cases really contemplated, even if unconsciously. Ernest Nagel's characterization of this assumption as "myth" seems just—unless Fuller were to define "purpose" so broadly as to make his thesis trivial.[48]

The Promotional Role of Law— A Comparative Approach

To round out this survey of jurisprudential implications, we shall take a perspective look at some aspects of the promotional role of law not specifically considered in our discussion of promotion in Chapter V. We are here concerned particularly with a comparison of legal and non-legal factors in WDA's history and with the functioning of legal institutions in this twentieth-century project compared with their functioning in certain nineteenth-century promotional projects.

RELATIVE ROLE OF LAW IN WDA

In the story of this particular legal promotion, how did the role of the strictly legal compare with the role of other factors?

The interacting variables in the complex of pertinent forces present no simple answers. Thus in the origin and passage of the WDA legislation an important factor was the long-standing pressure within the state for public power (an ideological factor as well as one of alleged economic need); there had been a favorable attitude within the state towards cooperatives (ideological) augmented by the favorable attitude of the federal government and the attractive financial assistance it was giving for development of rural electric cooperatives (economic) as well as the existing favorable Wisconsin legislation for the organization of cooperatives (legal); there was the vigorous promotion being given, particularly to public power, by Governor La Follette and his party (personal; political); and there was the imaginative use of the corporate instrumentality device for avoidance of the "internal improvements" obstacle in the constitution (legal). It was not surprising that the legislative institution creaked and groaned when these forces converged upon those who stood to lose directly and those whose economic ideas were in the mold of existing institutions—but the legislature's role as representative of the majority will was eventually fulfilled.

In the litigation the unusual array of able lawyers as well as the outstanding ability of the Justice who wrote the opinion on rehearing (personal) affected the substance and form of the final opinion; and the precedents presented to the court (legal) were so varied and so malleable as to suggest strongly that they became the instruments of judicial policy views (ideological), some expressed, some not. It cannot be said, of course, that because the legislation was substantially thwarted, judicial institutions had functioned contrary to their role in a democracy—for one of the established jobs of the American judiciary under the doctrine of judicial review (legal) is to determine, irrespective of majority opinion, whether the policies of the constitution itself stand in the way of the disputed legislation.

We have been discussing factors operating upon the statute and decision. What of the reverse? The statute and decision had this social consequence: the growth of rural electric cooperatives in Wisconsin was somewhat speeded, and the development of a strong public power program, the main purpose of WDA, was thwarted. In addition, future promotional programs of the state were likely to reflect the fact that there had been a WDA—in their avoidance of local favoritism and in their use of intermediaries for the spending of state funds.

PROMOTIONAL ROLE OF LAW IN TWO CENTURIES

Is there anything distinctive about this twentieth-century project in legal promotion compared with promotional projects of the nineteenth century in the same state? Can any historical generalizations be made about the promotional role of law and legal institutions in these two centuries?

The question is sharpened if it is viewed in relation to two nineteenth-century promotions in Wisconsin—the Milwaukee-Rock River Canal of the latter thirties and early forties, and the Fox-Wisconsin Rivers Improvement of the late forties, fifties, and sixties. Each of these two projects had its own complex history, too detailed for recitation here. However, we can profitably make some comparative examination of them, to throw into sharper relief various aspects of the WDA story.[49]

Structural similarities and differences in projects.—All three projects had some things in common. All had direct public subsidies, through land or cash; in none was there government representation on the board of directors; in none did the government own stock in the aided enterprise (though it was contemplated that government might own the Milwaukee-Rock River Canal after statehood, and the state reserved the right to purchase the Fox-Wisconsin Improvement after twenty years, for the price of the private company's expenditure). Yet certain differences are clear. (1) In each nineteenth-century project, aid was being extended to a private-profit corporation, whereas WDA and the organizations ultimately aided (cooperatives, municipalities, power districts) were non-profit organizations. (2) In the nineteenth-century projects, public funds defrayed the actual construction costs of the works; public money defrayed only an educational cost in the case of WDA. (3) WDA served as a corporate intermediary between the state and the aided groups; there was no such intermediary in the two earlier projects, for there had been no corresponding motivation to avoid an internal improvements prohibition. (4) The nineteenth-century projects embodied substantial regulatory restraints on the operations of the aided enterprises (though they were indulgent in some respects, such as not requiring full and regular company reports or government participation in original company decisions). The restraints were absent in the case of WDA. The omission was understandable in view of the limited nature of the projected activity; moreover, WDA's expenditures of public funds were subjected to a reporting requirement and to a government audit. (5) In the case of the nineteenth century projects, the state aid, though given to individual companies, was for projects deemed to affect the welfare of the state as a whole. The WDA aid was of a more particularized nature—so much so that the Wisconsin Supreme Court found that it violated the state purpose standard for expenditure of public funds.

On the whole, then, the twentieth-century promotion represented a *more indirect and a narrower* participation in, regulation of, or assistance to, the aided enterprise. Nor was it aiding a profit enterprise at all.

Attitudes toward state enterprise and promotion.—This difference in pattern of state activity suggests the possibility of a general difference in pattern of prevailing attitudes, during the two periods, toward state enterprise and promotion. Attitudes in territorial Wisconsin towards government enterprise and promotion cannot be described as hostile. There was a generally favorable attitude toward the "cooperation" represented by public aid to the Rock River Canal; such aid was viewed as preferable to government enterprise. Only after years of failure and fruitless inquiry and negotiation did a committee of the 1848 legislature ruefully declare "an alliance between a State and a private company . . . always more or less embarrassing." There was settler opposition to the Rock River Canal project, but based on hostility to the terms of land disposal rather than to mixed enterprise; the opposing promoters of rival projects had wanted the bounty of mixed enterprise for themselves. The rival Fox-Wisconsin project in the pre-constitution period had strong initial support as a governmental enterprise—perhaps partly as a result of disillusion with "cooperation" between the Territory and the Rock canal company. Largely because of the intervening disastrous experience of other states in the prosecution of internal improvements, sentiment at the time of Wisconsin's 1848 constitution had veered enough away from government enterprise to ban state prosecution of improvements. Even so, the constitution framers of 1848 had been willing to lift this ban to the extent of the avails of land granted to the state for particular work and revenues from such works. The Fox-Wisconsin project did start as a state enterprise and entered in 1853 upon a long period of state-aided, and in some ways state-restrained, private enterprise.

On the other hand, attitudes toward the twentieth-century mixed enterprise had not been favorable. WDA met immediate strong opposition in the legislature and in the courts. This opposition was based not only upon constitutional doctrine but upon claims of the impropriety of mixed enterprise as a matter of public policy.

Insofar as this apparent contrast between the centuries highlights interventionist or anti-laissez faire practices and attitudes in mid-nineteenth-century Wisconsin, the result is consistent with historical studies of the pattern of public policy in the first half of the nineteenth century in a number of other states, though the techniques of government assistance showed some variation.[50]

This is not to suggest, however, that there was an across-the-board contrast in policy between centuries. The two nineteenth-century projects and WDA are not necessarily representative of other enterprises involved in public aids, or of the range of legal issues dealt with in such matters. We have seen that case-law developing in *both* the latter nineteenth century and the twentieth century set limits, in the form of the public purpose and state purpose doctrines, to public promotion of private enterprise, though the limits were sometimes honored in the breach. Also, our prior discussion showed that outside of our particular projects, a considerable variety of public aids was offered in *both* centuries. Thus, nineteenth-century promotion included agricultural aids, railroad aids, and some industrial promotion; industrial promotion became prominent in the latter nineteenth century through state-authorized municipal investment in private enterprises deemed important to the growth of the locality. The twentieth century saw a continuation of agricultural aids, continued industrial promotion by municipalities (with freer use of outright subsidies to induce the particular location of plants), a spurt in state-wide promotional efforts in the thirties, and a resurgence of interest therein in the fifties and sixties. Hence, the hostile attitude toward mixed enterprise manifested in the battle over WDA cannot be made the basis of a century-broad generalization on attitudes and practices in the field of promotion. Perhaps most significant in setting WDA apart was the fact that of all twentieth-century promotions, WDA probably most clearly involved a strong threat to the economic status of a powerful industrial group, and government's alignment on one side of an issue already in sharp controversy between private groups.

Roles of legal agencies.—Another point of comparison is the roles of the legal agencies, that is, the courts, legislatures, executives and administrators. The courts clearly were a crucial factor in the fate of the twentieth-century project, because of the constitutional issue raised. There was no such judicial impact on the nineteenth-century projects; courts can affect a situation only if litigants bring them to the arena of action. Both the nineteenth-century projects went through their most controversial phases in years before the development of a lively tradition of judicial review of legislative action, and neither stirred the kind of ideological differences calculated to shape a justiciable issue of constitutional law.

There are various aspects from which we may appraise the legislative role. The two nineteenth-century projects reflect a much greater legislative willingness to make *delegations* of power to private corporations. The broad powers to invoke eminent domain, charge tolls, and regulate traffic with which the nineteenth-century companies were endowed, and the broad powers given the Fox-Wisconsin Company even during its more confined trusteeship period of 1856-63, contrast with the delegation made by charter and statute to WDA of the functions of research, education, and promotion, subject to control by report and audit. Even the limited delegation to WDA encountered serious opposition; and the hostile attitude of the Supreme Court's first opinion was not completely erased by the opinion on rehearing. The conclusion that the twentieth century showed more jealous care against putting legislative prerogative into private hands would harmonize with the case-law we have mentioned in discussing the place of the WDA case in the history of Wisconsin delegation cases: the decisions striking down delegations were twentieth-century decisions.

Frequent and influential reports by *legislative committees* marked the treatment of both nineteenth-century projects, particularly the Rock River Canal, but not of the WDA. The contrast is illusory, however, since WDA, unlike the earlier projects had not stretched out over the years so as to afford an opportunity for periodic committee investigation. Moreover, committee reports and such recommended bills as accompanied them concerning the canal and the Fox-Wisconsin projects emanated generally from special investigating committees rather than from standing committees to which an introduced bill had been referred for report. Thus, legislative procedure affecting these earlier projects did not deviate substantially from the practice of twentieth-century Wisconsin legislative committees; such committees typically made little published comment on referred bills, except for the occasional bill of outstanding public concern.

Legislative promotion by *memorializing* the Congress for land grants was a persistent feature of both nineteenth-century projects. Absence of this technique from the WDA history is not significant, for by this time, of course, the public-land source of nineteenth-century federal largesse had dried up. Perhaps some equivalent of the ad hoc legislative memorial to Congress may be seen, as in the case of other twentieth-century federal aids, in the regularized availability of federal REA funds. WDA aided in the acquisition and effective utilization of such funds.

A greater legislative tendency to *depart from the letter of the law* had been exhibited by the nineteenth-century projects. In the case of the Rock River Canal, the Wisconsin legislature flouted federal requirements by reducing the federally established minimum land price, and diverting canal land proceeds to non-canal purposes; and there were some lesser illustrations of such behavior in the case of the Fox-Wisconsin at mid-century. These deviations had no counterpart in the later project. Rather, WDA represented an attempt at legitimate legal avoidance of a constitutional limitation. Again, however, one must take note of evidence we have encountered beyond these projects. For example, we noted that many municipal promotions of particular industries in the twentiety century ignored the established legal standard of public purpose; and the state's flouting of the *Froelich* decision on internal improvements, though related to the Fox-Wisconsin project, had occurred in the twentieth century.[51]

We must expect the twentieth century to build on experience and to show a more imaginative *experimentalism in the use of legal techniques* to accomplish social objectives. WDA was indeed described by its sponsors as an adaptation of the modern federal technique of a government corporation, exemplified by TVA. However, the WDA program did not involve the strong governmental control characteristic of a federal government corporation. Further, we must recognize that the device of a corporate intermediary for receipt and expenditure of public funds had been much used in the earlier century. Moreover, the two nineteenth-century projects had revealed no stolid rigidity in the use of legal forms. In the case of the Rock River canal, there were varied applications of the trusteeship concept to the relations created by the land grant, and the government-company relations established by law were dynamic, including the possibility of partial and eventually complete stock ownership by the state. In the case of the Fox-Wisconsin improvement, the legislature showed imaginative flexibility in use of legal forms, variously involving state enterprise, private enterprise under specified legal obligations, private enterprise under a state-imposed trusteeship, and foreclosure and reorganization into another private enterprise with specified legal obligations.

Careful *planning, with safeguards of the public interest,* was by no means lacking in the case of the Rock River Canal and Fox-Wisconsin legislation. Yet there were serious defects. The legislature was apathetic about demanding fuller information from the canal company and did not delineate the company's obligations to the project as precisely as the Territory's obligations had been. The legislature failed to require full reports to it by the Fox-Wisconsin improvement company. The critical 1853 law transferring the improvement from state to private hands failed to make the company itself rather than its incorporators alone, guarantee the obligations imposed by the law. The WDA project was not subject to criticism along these lines. The shortcoming here was not in the area of protecting the public interest, but in gauging the constitutionality of the legal forms adopted.

Poor legislative technique, and especially recurrent haste which required recurrent amendments, created *complexity* in the nineteenth-century statutes which led to many errors, both by participants and by historians in their references to applicable legal requirements. The WDA project, charter and statute, were not without some necessary complexity, but they represented a level of professional competence often lacking in nineteenth-century legislative operations, and there was no indication in its short career that WDA would have suffered from defects in the craftsmanship of its organic documents.

Complexity of statutes is one reason for their *ambiguity*. The legislature had been at fault in the nineteenth-century projects, in creating ambiguities which produced disputes that might have been avoided. In the case of the Rock River Canal, the fault was not always that of the legislature, for some of the disputes had stemmed from attempts to flout or distort clear legislative meanings. The legislature was free of any such fault in the case of WDA; the ambiguities at the heart of the twentieth-century controversy were not those of the legislature but of the constitution. Parenthetically it seems proper to observe that an assessment of fault upon the constitution-makers would be questionable. In a broad charter of government designed to endure through varied centuries, the presence of ambiguities (or, in this case, a lack of explicit delineation of a doctrine deemed by later courts implicit in a constitutional policy which includes such concepts as "due process" and "equality") is more readily defensible than ambiguity in a statute designed for prosecution of a specific project.

Executive influence had been strong in the projects of both centuries. In the two nineteenth-century enterprises, the governor sometimes acted as administrative agent for the legislature, and sometimes offered resistance to the legislative will. For the most part, he actively and persistently promoted the projects, largely through information, advice, and exhortation to the legislature. So, too, Governor La Follette was responsible for initiating the twentieth-century WDA project, and pushing the fight in the legislature. The state's attorney general did not importantly affect the course of any of these projects, though Attorney General Estabrook's opinions in the early 1850's had considerable temporary influence on the Fox-Wisconsin project. Government *administrators* played no significant role in the structure of WDA, except in connection with the report and audit requirements. In the Rock River Canal project, canal commissioners and the territorial engineer exercised their surveillance functions efficiently. An objective investigation disclosed no serious shortcomings in the operations of the Board of Public Works, which operated the Fox-Wisconsin Improvement in its initial period of state enterprise; a trusteeship set up in 1856 for the latter project failed, but the failure could not be ascribed to any inadequate discharge of the trustees' limited duties. We deal here with an apparently atypical contrast, for it is the twentieth century which has witnessed the greatest development of the administrative arm of government.

Legal vs. non-legal factors.—What can be said of the relative significance of legal and extra-legal factors in each of the two periods? We have indicated at the outset of this section on the promotional role of law, that the legal component in the career of WDA was prominent in the complex of other (economic, personal, ideological, political) factors interacting to shape the history of the project, particularly since what had killed WDA in the end was litigation. In the nineteenth-century enterprises (though we have seen some contrary evidence outside these particular projects) the legal factor seems to have had a more subordinate position. True, legal controversy had been a persistent feature of the canal's protracted history, due largely to legislative ambiguities; and the ultimate termination of that project in 1842 had been through legislative action. So, too, the Fox-Wisconsin history had been marked by a parade of legal measures—some giving rise to disputes over legislative and constitutional ambiguities; some of them aiding the enterprise and some tending to retard it. But the above-mentioned non-legal factors, particularly the economic were not only prominent throughout the course of each nineteenth-century project, they were crucial in the failure of each. Neither failure could properly be ascribed to specifically legal elements. Indeed, even the death of the twentieth-century project need not as a matter of law have been decreed by the court; the legal factor harbored a pervasive ambiguity (in such principles as public and state purpose, and in the very concept of *stare decisis* itself) which robbed the specifically legal element of any *necessary* force in a particular direction. In all three projects law had, for the most part, acted as a channel for the operation of other forces.

A reminder is in order: the suggested similarities and contrasts between the centuries have been presented as highly tentative; they must be supplemented by other studies before generalized hypotheses about government-internal improvement relations may be ventured. In particular, conclusions that stretch across the continent as well as across the centuries will hardly be reliable until those on a smaller geographical and time scale have been buttressed by scholarship.

CHAPTER VII

RETROSPECT

The literature of jurisprudence notoriously abounds in dreary abstractions. They float far above the social realities, in what Jhering called a heaven of juristic concepts (*Begriffshimmel*). The present study proceeds on the assumption that legal theoreticians can more fruitfully turn their energies to earthbound facts. What, in brief, can a legal theorist accomplish in dealing with historical events which have legal as well as political-economic dimensions?

Some of his possible avenues of analysis are illustrated by the kinds of inquiries pursued in the foregoing pages. He may, to set the stage for such inquiries, explore the pertinent facts surrounding the political-economic events involved. For us this meant focussing upon the origins and purposes of WDA, the political struggle engendered in the legislature, the battle in the courts, and the post-litigation denouement.

He may pursue the implications of his facts in a number of directions. He may examine the relative role of legal and non-legal factors in his story. He is likely to find some evidence supporting each of the emphases in the traditional historical "schools": e.g., the role of economic and political forces, of ideas, of the "great man." We have in Chapter VI noted the mutual interaction of all these factors.

He may choose another line of attack. Jurisprudence has tended to blur the distinctive roles of legislative, executive, and judicial offices and officers by resort to over-generalized and vague concepts of "law." He may therefore wish to explore the relative role of the different legal agencies among themselves, and may test historical generalizations about their relative roles in different periods. In following such a course, we discovered some basis for doubting commonly held assumptions on the role of law and of legal agencies in two centuries.

He may choose to subject one or more of these legal agencies to particularly close scrutiny. Thus, recent detailed studies of the passage of particular federal statutes have illumined the theory of legislative process. Although we surveyed at some length the WDA legislative happenings and the apparent forces behind them, we chose to devote particular detail to the court litigation and to the nature of other pertinent court cases. The wealth of concrete fact thereby made available served to contribute far more clarity to the subsequent analysis of judicial process than any amount of abstract theorizing alone could have done. The significance of these illustrations of judicial techniques was enhanced by the fact that they existed in such full panoply in spite of having been drawn exclusively from a narrowly confined area of law in a single state. It is more common to propound generalizations about judicial technique each of which may have to rely on a different field of law within the totality of a nation's judicial decisions.

Where a particular legal decision, judicial or otherwise, is a matter of central concern, the inquiry may be broadened so as to examine the decision for its ramifications into the whole surrounding body of law and public policy. Our consideration of the *WDA* decision in this connection opened up some quite basic issues of Wisconsin statecraft. It further showed that a legal decision could have powerful impact upon those political-economic issues, at the same time that the legal decision itself was in turn seen to have been probably affected by political-economic forces.

Perhaps there is a special value in the fusion which a legal theorist can make of historical, political, economic, and legal research. It is apparently easier for him to make excursions outside of legal research than it is for those in the outside disciplines to cross over into legal research. Doubtless a study of WDA by an economic or political historian and a separate study of it by a lawyer would not add up to as much as a study which fuses the two approaches. Thus, for instance, in pursuing the latter kind of study we were able to use the historical record to help argue a jurisprudential issue of decisional predictability, and to use legal materials in filling out the historical record.

Meaningful jurisprudential research may indeed extend beyond the lines of inquiry we have chosen. The province of jurisprudence as a whole may be taken to include these areas: (1) *Legal logic or analytics*—and our analyses of judicial techniques falls in this area. (2) *Socio-legal history*—covering "social" (in the broadest sense) origins, in immediate and/or long-range terms, of legal developments and decisions, and "social" operation and consequences of the latter. In this area falls our treatment of the historical background and detailed development of the WDA project, the role of the non-legal in influencing the WDA decision, and the public policy consequences of that decision. (3) *Values, or "justice"*—here the concern being with the "ought" rather than the "is." We have ventured little into this last area, except for the discussion of value-choices involved in the public purpose and internal improvement issues, and the proper role of such policy choices in the process of judicial decision. Faced with so provocative a universe of fact, logical relation, and value as these three areas embody, the legal theorist surely need not confine himself, as he so often does, to abstract verbal manipulations or technical virtuosities.

APPENDICES

DIGESTS OF CASE-AUTHORITIES

APPLICABLE TO MAJOR ISSUES

IN SECOND WDA DECISION

The case-digests below are in two groups: those dealing with the public purpose problem (and its variants, such as municipal purpose and state purpose) and those dealing with the internal improvements problem. Each digest gives the essential facts and the pertinent aspects of the decision. In addition, each indicates under the first sub-head a thumbnail view of what the case stands for in relation to the basic problem being considered, i.e., whether the designated situation was held to meet the public purpose standard, or the requirements for avoiding the internal improvements prohibition, as the case may be.

Thus, one who wishes to skip details and get a quick picture of the cases can simply look at the first of the sub-heads.

In the first seventeen cases (a group dealing with municipal aid to railroads) the first sub-head merely indicates an affirmative or negative answer to the question of whether the public purpose standard was found to have been met, since the basic situation of municipal subscription to railroad stock is the same in all, except where it is noted that the municipal aid was in the form of a donation.

The digests do not cover cases in volumes later than 13 Wis. 2d.

Precedents on Public Purpose

RAILROAD AID CASES

These involve municipal aid, by city, county, town, or village, under authority of the state (which was prevented from direct state aid by the internal improvements restriction of the constitution). These cases usually describe the public purpose involved as municipal purpose.

1 (1859) Clark et al v. City of Janesville, 10 Wis. 136.

Public purpose?: YES (*dictum*).

Facts: Action to recover on city bonds. Were issued for subscription to railroad stock, which subscription was specifically authorized by statute if approved by municipal voters.

Aspects of decision: In addition to holding against plaintiff (reversing the overruling of demurrer) on ground that bond issue invalid because city charter authorizing such bonds hadn't been properly "published," and ruling that cities are not subject to article VIII "internal improvements" and certain other restrictions, expresses opinion that railroad aid is *probably for "municipal purpose"* under article XI, section 1 (declaring that non-banking corporations are not to be created by special act except for *municipal* purpose) even if latter provision be erroneously construed to restrict purposes with which state may invest municipal corporations.

2 (1860) Bushnell v. Beloit, 10 Wis. 195.

Public purpose?: YES.

Facts: Same as above, except were town bonds.

Aspects of decision: Makes same construction of article XI as preceding case, in permitting recovery by bona fide purchaser of bond.

3 (1860) Foster v. City of Kenosha, 12 Wis. 616.

Public purpose?: Not clear (language implies view that subscription to railroad stock is not for municipal purpose. However, court may intend principle stated in #5 below).

Facts: Action to enjoin collection of city realty tax to pay scrip issued upon city's subscription to railroad stock. Statutory charter amendment had authorized special taxes in any amount and for any purpose deemed essential to promote city's common interest and approved by municipal voters.

Aspects of decision: Decision enjoins collection of tax on ground that statutory charter authorization for special taxation, not restricted to taxation for municipal purposes, was unconstitutional, particularly in light of article XI, section 3, hence that part of charter and taxes levied pursuant thereto are void.

4 (1870) Whiting v. Sheboygan & Fond du Lac R.R. Co. et al, 25 Wis. 167.

Public Purpose?: NO (*donation*).

Facts: Action to restrain issuance of county orders for aid to railroads to be paid by county property tax. Specific statutory authorization for such county orders and tax, if approved by county voters, made no mention of county's obtaining stock in railroads; said that railroads were to transport wheat on specified terms.

Aspects of decision: Reverses the dismissal of complaint. While holding such donations to be for an unconstitutional "private purpose," says conclusion is otherwise where city, town, or county takes stock in return for its aid to railroad running through it.

5 (1870) Fisk v. Kenosha, 26 Wis. 23.

Public purpose?: YES *(dictum).*

Facts: Same facts as in #3 above, except is action by bona fide holder of scrip to recover on it (rather than suit to enjoin tax), the scrip showing on its face it was issued by city in aid of railroad.

Aspects of decision: Reverses judgment for plaintiff. Decision that principle of *Foster* case *supra* requires holding the scrip void contains this observation: It is "settled" that municipal corporations may lend their aid to railroads and similar works, but "it is not such an ordinary, general municipal purpose" as to be permitted without "express" statutory provision.

6 (1871) Phillips et al v. Town of Albany et al, 28 Wis. 340.

Public Purpose?: YES *(reluctant).*

Facts: Action to restrain issuance of town bond issue. Bonds were for subscription to railroad stock, specifically authorized by statute if approved by municipal voters.

Aspects of decision: In reversing judgment for plaintiff, court says that as indicated in *Whiting* case (#4 *supra*), court majority would hold otherwise if it were an original question, but "vast pecuniary interests" have grown up on basis of validity of such subscriptions, so strong case for applying *stare decisis.*

7 (1872) Rogan v. City of Watertown, 30 Wis. 259.

Public purpose?: YES.

Facts: Action to recover on city bonds. Some had been issued to subscribe for railroad stock, as specifically authorized by 1856 statute; some been issued as city's "loan of credit" to railroad, as specifically authorized by 1853 statute, which also authorized delivery of bonds "upon such terms as may be agreed upon by the parties."

Aspects of decision: In reversing judgment insofar as unfavorable to plaintiff, says (1) subscription is valid for reasons given in *Phillips* case, *supra;* (2) article XI, section 3, constitution indicates cities can validly loan their credit under legislative authorization. The "upon such terms" clause of statute is to be interpreted as giving discretion on terms for delivery of bonds *as loan of credit;* would be unconstitutional under *Whiting* case (#4 *supra*) if viewed as permitting donation.

8 (1872) Lawson v. Milw. & N. Ry. Co., 30 Wis. 597.

Public purpose?: YES.

Facts: Action to restrain town bond issue and cancel railroad stock subscription, which had been specifically authorized by statute.

Aspects of decision: In affirming judgment for defendant, says that in view of *Clark, Bushnell,* and *Phillips* cases (#1, #2, and #6 *supra*), validity of such subscriptions is no longer an open question.

9 (1872) Olcott v. Supervisors, 16 Wall. (U.S.) 678.

Public purpose?: YES *(donation).*

Facts: Suit to recover on county orders issued for the same railroad aid authorized by Wisconsin statute involved in *Whiting* case (#4 *supra*). *Whiting* decision was prior to trial of this suit in federal court.

Aspects of decision: United States Supreme Court reverses federal circuit court decision that *Whiting* case (#4 *supra*) rendered act invalid. Says issue in *Whiting* case is one of "general law" rather than interpretation of local statute and constitution, hence decision not binding on this court and is declared erroneous Says donation to railroad just as much for public purpose as a stock subscription; that contracts here were made in light of pre-*Whiting* decisional law which indicated their validity, hence can't be invalidated by subsequent legislative or judicial action.

10 (1874) Oleson v. Green Bay and Lake P. Ry. Co. et al, 36 Wis. 383.

Public purpose?: YES.

Facts: Action to restrain delivery of town bonds, issued for railroad stock subscription pursuant to specific statutory authorization. (Same statute as that summarized below in *Perrin* case, #14.)

Aspects of decision: In affirming dismissal of complaint, and ruling that a later law had not repealed the statutory authorization for bond issue, says too late now to question validity of such authorization. *Stare decisis* may be the only justification, but it is sufficient (citing *Phillips* case [#6 *supra*]).

11 (1875) Single v. Supervisors, 38 Wis. 363.

Public purpose?: YES.

Facts: Action to review proceedings by which county subscribed to railroad stock. Statute had purported to ratify previous unauthorized action of county board.

Aspects of decision: Reverses judgment insofar as favorable to plaintiff. In finding a valid ratification, says too late now to question validity of such subscriptions. Says this applies also to argument that conferring power on a specific county violates constitutional provision (article IV, section 23) for "one system of town and county government, which shall be as nearly uniform as practicable." Though this argument would be reasonable as original proposition, precedents on railroad aid have established a "rule of property" which cannot be disturbed.

12   (1878) Bound v. Wis. Cent. RR, 45 Wis. 543.

Public purpose?: YES.

Facts: Action to cancel town bonds issued for railroad stock and to have subscription declared void. Statute authorized municipal tax and bond issue for railroad aid "upon such terms and conditions as shall be agreed upon. . . ."

Aspects of decision: Affirms dismissal of complaint. In declaring that the town's acceptance of the railroad's proposition for a $20,000 stock subscription could not be revoked and was unaffected by later constitutional amendment limiting municipal indebtedness to 5 per cent of taxable property (which was less than the $20,000), court construes the "upon such terms" clause to mean it doesn't permit donation, but only stock subscription. Ryan, J. concurring (on ground taxpayer can't get requested relief without averring refusal of town itself to act) disagrees with latter point. Says statute permitted both, hence invalid, and so stock subscription was too. Thinks majority's view smacks of "policy" against bond repudiation rather than adherence to "legal principle."

13   (1883) Lynch v. Eastern, Lafayette & Miss. R. Co., 57 Wis. 430.

Public purpose?: YES (virtual donation. Decision upholds it without discussing public purpose.)

Facts: Action to restrain delivery to railroad of town bonds issued for railroad stock under specific statutory authority. Stock alleged to be worthless, as being in a defunct railroad which didn't build the road, and to whose property and rights to bonds the present railroad (which built the road) succeeded.

Aspects of decision: Affirms dissolution of temporary injunction. Majority disposes of argument on worthlessness of stock by saying that that has never been a defense to an action on a stock subscription. Says nothing about public purpose doctrine, though dissent contends that upholding this virtual donation to railroad in effect overrules the rule of *Whiting* case (#4 *supra*).

14   (1886) Perrin v. City of New London, 67 Wis. 416.

Public purpose?: Not determined, but shows unfavorable attitude.

Facts: Action to recover on village bonds issued to railroad pursuant to specific 1867 statute (authorizing such issuance by villages, etc., in county through which railroad passed, in exchange for railroad stock or bonds, and *in such amounts and manner as agreed on with railroad*). This statute authorized taxation to pay interest and declared municipalities' liability for principal and interest, but had no provision for taxation to pay principal. Charter of this village restricted incurring of village liabilities to amounts which could validly be raised by taxation in that year; and charter's tax provision didn't mention taxes for such bonds, though it did permit taxes for "extraordinary or special purpose" by vote of people.

Aspects of decision: In affirming the sustaining of demurrer, declares charter's tax authority for "extraordinary or special purpose" refers to a "strictly municipal purpose" and hence not to railroad aid. Since there was no other charter authority for taxation to pay for such bonds and 1867 aid statute had no provision for taxes to pay principal of bonds, bonds were invalidly issued.

Regards as still open, and unnecessary to determine here, whether article XI, section 3, constitution (authorizing legislature to incorporate cities and villages and *limit* their powers) prevents such statutes as 1867 law authorizing local aid to railroads. Says *Oleson* case (#10 *supra*) upholding this same statute, is to be limited to authority of town rather than city or village. *Foster* and *Fisk* cases (#3 and #5 *supra*), "in which the effect of section 3, Article XI upon certain provisions in the charter of the city of Kenosha was determined have never been overruled or shaken." Since 1874 constitutional amendment *limiting* municipal indebtedness so much time has elapsed as to make it unlikely that issue of effect of original section 3 will often arise. "Indeed the general statutes . . . and at least some of the special laws" for railroad aid "contain proper and effectual limitations upon such power." (Though not mentioning it specifically court is evidently concerned over fact that this statute put no limit on local aid.)

15   (1890) Ellis v. Northern Paper Co., 77 Wis. 114.

Public purpose?: NO (*donation*).

Facts: Action to quiet title, one of defendants being a railroad claiming under deed from county which had conveyed the land on agreement that railroad would run between specified points, with depot, etc.

Aspects of decision: Affirms the overruling of demurrer. Says this can't be distinguished from "decision in the *Whiting* case [#4 *supra*]; for, if the county could not donate money or securities to a railroad corporation, it could not give it its lands, which are the property of the county."

Recognizes that United States Supreme Court, contrary to *Whiting* rule, regards donations just as valid as stock subscriptions, and that disparity with federal courts creates "inconvenience," but "we are unwilling to change the rule established in the *Whiting* case." Regrettable that courts have sustained municipal stock subscriptions to railroads, but "we can go no further than we have in sanctioning a bad principle."

[*Note:* For subsequent treatment of this land grant in the United States Supreme Court, see Northern Pacific Railroad Co. v. Ellis, 144 U.S. 458 (1892); Roberts v. Northern Pacific Railroad Co., 158 U.S. 1 (1894).]

16 (1897) State ex rel. Marinette, T. & W. R. Co. v. Tomahawk Common Council, 96 Wis. 73.

Public purpose?: YES (even though the approval of subscription, according to statute, was to be by majority of taxpayers rather than of voters generally or of council.)

Facts: Mandamus to compel city to deliver municipal bonds as stock subscription to railroad, and to levy taxes to pay such bonds. Railroad is seeking to enforce contract allegedly made pursuant to general statute that municipality's acceptance of railroad's proposition for bond issue and stock subscription may be made by signatures of majority of resident taxpayers. Subsequent charter provisions required council approval for city debts; approval by council and by popular vote for bond issues for public improvements up to 5 per cent of assessed valuations; that liabilities contracted are not to exceed taxes authorized by charter for that year, etc.

Aspects of decision: Reverses dismissal of proceedings. Upholds validity of statute authorizing railroad stock subscription to be effective upon approval of majority of resident taxpayers, without submission to people as a whole. Subsequent charter restrictions on indebtedness didn't imply repeal of above statutory authorization. Charter requirements for approval of debts, etc., apply to debts for ordinary municipal purposes. These are not. "It is firmly established in the cases ... that the making of a subscription to the stock of railroad companies, and issuing bonds in payment therefor, are transactions not within the ... purposes for which towns, cities, or counties are created. They have no authority ... to make such contracts, in the absence of some special enabling act authorizing the same."

Perrin v. *New London* (#14 *supra*), is distinguishable on ground that charter's tax limitation was unqualified and applied to village itself, whereas here limitation is on the common council in contracting debts for ordinary municipal purposes, leaving power in city to act other than by common council, i.e., taxpayer method provided in general statute.

17 (1923) Herreid v. Ettrick & Northern R. Co., 179 Wis. 516.

Public purpose?: YES (*dictum*. Statute construed not to authorize aid for already built road.)

Facts: Action to restrain issuance of town bonds in aid of an already completed railroad. Purported statutory authority allowed bond issue for subscription to securities of any company "organized for building any railroad ...."

Aspects of decision: Affirms the injunction. Says that though there is some basis for construing statute otherwise (e.g., refers to railroad "mortgage bonds," which are not usually issued until after railroad completed) it is not to be construed to apply to an already completed railroad. Such statutes authorizing railroad aid confer an "extra-municipal power," one not within scope of usual municipal powers, hence to be strictly construed. "It is well settled that the statute quoted grants to a town the right to vote bonds to aid in the construction of a railroad not yet built." (Citing *Whiting* case, #4 *supra*.)

Note: Some of the foregoing cases involved additional issues that were not deemed material for this analysis. There are also a number of other cases involving procedural points, or the effect of a railroad's deviation from its agreement to build a line all the way between two points (for example, Lawson v. Schnellen, 33 Wis. 288 [1873]) or the validity of an attempted ratification of an originally unauthorized bond issue (Knapp v. Grant, 27 Wis. 147) etc., which do not discuss whether a public purpose exists, but which may assume it in considering other issues.

NON-RAILROAD CASES

18 (1860) Soens et al v. City of Racine, 10 Wis. 271.

Public purpose?: YES (tax assessment for lake shore protection.)

Facts: Action to enjoin collection of special tax assessment levied on plaintiffs' lands in second ward of Milwaukee to help finance building of certain piers and breakwaters, to protect lake shore in second ward from Lake Michigan waters.

Aspects of decision: Reverses injunction against collection of tax. This is not taxation for a private purpose, which is concededly invalid. That private property happens to be protected by a given improvement doesn't make latter private; a public good always involves some private benefit. "To determine whether a matter is of public or merely private concern, we have not to determine whether ... the interests of some individuals will be directly promoted, but whether those of the whole or the greater part of the community will be so. That such was the character of the improvements provided for by the act there can be little doubt."

19 (1860) Hasbrouck v. City of Milwaukee, 13 Wis. 42.

Public purpose?: YES (bond issue for harbor improvements.)

Facts: See same case below, #67.

Aspects of decision: See same case below, #67.

20 (1865) Brodhead v. City of Milwaukee, 19 Wis. 624.

Public purpose?: YES (taxes for bounties to Civil War volunteers and certain others.)

Facts: Suit to restrain municipal property tax levied under authority of statute authorizing such taxes for payment of bounties to Civil War volunteers and to those who procured substitutes for themselves before being drafted, and to give aid to families of volunteers and drafted men, with $200 maximum for any one person or family.

Aspects of decision: Affirms denial of injunction; holds this to be a public purpose. "Counsel on both sides accept as correct the principles laid down in the great leading case of Sharpless v. The Mayor, etc. 21 Pa. St. 147, 168 .... The same principles have frequently been affirmed by this court. The legislature cannot create a public debt, or levy a tax, or authorize a municipal corporation to do so, in order to raise funds for a mere private purpose .... To justify the court in ... declaring the tax void, the absence of all possible public interest in the purposes for which the funds are raised must be clear and palpable—so clear and palpable as to be perceptible by every mind at the first blush. In addition to these, I understand that it is not denied that claims founded in equity and justice ... or in gratitude or charity, will support a tax."

21 (1869) Curtis' Adm'r. v. Whipple, 24 Wis. 350

Public purpose?: NO (aid to private educational institution.)

Facts: Statute specifically authorized town property tax to raise $5,000 for aid in erection of buildings for Jefferson Liberal Institute, a private educational institution. Upon the necessary approval of town voters, tax was levied. Suit by taxpayer alleging wrongful conversion of his property seized for nonpayment of tax.

Aspects of decision: Affirms judgment for plaintiff, and holds act unconstitutional. Stresses that neither the town nor taxpayers thereof as such are stockholders or have voice in management or control of funds, or special privileges. For public purpose there must be "some direct advantage accruing to the public from the outlay, either by its being the owner or part owner of the property or thing to be created or obtained with the money, or the party immediately interested in and benefitted by the work to be performed, the same being matters of public concern; or because the proceeds of the tax were to be expended in defraying the legitimate expenses of government, and in promoting the peace, good order and welfare of society. Any direct public benefit or interest of this nature, no matter how slight, as distinguished from those public benefits or interests incidentally arising from the employment, or business of private individuals or corporations will undoubtedly sustain a tax"—including taxes to meet claims founded in equity and justice and in gratitude. Taxes for charitable purposes supported by separate, peculiar ground.

22 (1872) State ex rel McCurdy v. Tappan, 29 Wis. 664.

Public purpose?: YES; NO (military bounties through town tax compelled by state, regarded as public but not municipal purpose.)

Facts: General statute authorized but did not compel cities, towns, and villages to grant bounties up to $200 to Civil War volunteers. McCurdy, Treasurer of city of Oshkosh, mistakenly thinking a volunteer was credited to quota of city rather than town, paid him $300 under authority of city bounty enactment. Volunteer's claim under *town* of Oshkosh's bounty enactment was assigned to McCurdy, who then failed to recover from town. State private law passed in 1869 requiring town's payment to him of amount (to be judicially determined) paid out to volunteer plus interest plus expenses growing out of town's nonpayment, and *required* town to levy property tax to obtain such amount. McCurdy seeks mandamus to compel town clerk to levy such tax in order to pay the $937 judicially determined to be due.

Aspects of decision: Issuance of mandamus is reversed. Legislature can't *compel* town to pay such bounty and cost of unsuccessful suit to enforce payment, such taxation being not for municipal purpose. Not deciding whether state could *compel* municipality to make or pay for a *municipal* improvement. But where public purpose is *not* strictly of municipal character, state may *authorize* municipal taxes, if there is direct advantage to public; or if tax is for defraying government expenses or "promoting the peace, good order, and welfare of society; or . . . to pay claims founded in natural justice and equity, or in gratitude for public services or expenditure, or to discharge the obligations of charity and humanity from which no person or corporation is exempt." The 1869 private relief violates constitutional provisions for uniform rule of taxation and for single system of town and county government to be as nearly uniform as practicable. Legislative adjudication, in effect, of town's liability and use of court only to ascertain exact amount, was violation of constitutional provision for exercise of judicial power by courts rather than legislature.

23 (1875) Attorney General v. City of Eau Claire, 37 Wis. 400.

Public purpose?: NO (Authorizing city tax for building a dam that *might* have primarily private purpose: leasing water power to factories.)

Facts: Statute authorized city to construct waterworks; to build and maintain dam within city across Chippewa River, with booms, piers, etc., to protect navigability; to lease water power thus created for manufacturing purposes (except what city may reserve to itself for waterworks purpose); to charge rent for boomage and storage of logs, etc., up to specified maximum rates; to issue bonds after approval by popular vote; to apply money from water power rents, etc., to repair of works, bond interest, sinking fund; and to levy annual tax for deficiencies. Attorney General sues in Supreme Court to restrain city from issuing bonds and entering on construction of such works.

Aspects of decision: Holds injunction is to issue upon attorney general's remedying procedural defect in complaint. State can authorize city to erect dam for public purpose—such as its use for waterworks—and to lease surplus power, etc., as incidental to that public purpose. But here such a private purpose as leasing water power to factories is not made dependent on basic public purpose, for city wasn't compelled to build waterworks. Waterworks construction is stated in statute as independent power, so use of dam for public or private purpose is left optional with city. This in effect invalidly gives city power to tax for private purpose.

Dictum that "independently of taxation," would be of "questionable validity" to authorize city to build dam in order to lease power for private use.

[*Note:* After statute was amended to make power to construct dam dependent on power to construct waterworks and limiting the leasing of water power to amount not required for waterworks, was upheld against motion for injunction. State of Wisconsin v. City of Eau Claire, 40 Wis. 533 (1876).]

24 (1879) Jensen v. Bd. of Supervisors of Polk County, 47 Wis. 298.

Public purpose?: YES (statute compelling levy of tax by counties for expenses of laying out road, and by towns for constructing, etc.)

Facts: State's power to appoint commissioners to establish state roads was limited by constitutional amendment of 1871 to roads extending into more than one county. An 1875 law providing for establishing state road in Polk and Burnett counties under direction of state-appointed commissioners is construed in this decision to impose expense of laying it out, including compensation of commissioners and acquisition of land, upon counties, but not expense of constructing it, which under general statutes remains an expense for the towns involved. Plaintiff is contractor suing *county* for work on *construction* of road, done under contract with above state commissioners.

Aspects of decision: Reverses plaintiff's judgment against county, on ground that commissioners' proceedings were defective for want of proper notices, and fact that statute puts cost of construction on towns, rather than county. Denies, however, defendant's contentions on unconstitutionality of statute, including contention as to private purpose. Taxes for providing roads are for a strictly municipal purpose, and municipal taxes for such purpose may be compelled by legislature, though it has been held that taxes not for a strictly municipal purpose can't be so compelled.

[See same case *infra,* #66.]

25 (1892) LeFebre et al v. Bd. of Education of Superior, 81 Wis. 660.

Public purpose?: YES (or perhaps an *exception* to public purpose doctrine, in terms of "equity and justice": circumstances justifying public payment of subcontractor's unpaid claim against contractor for work on school building.)

Facts: School district levied tax to pay amount of plaintiff sub-contractor's claim of $878 against contractor who had abandoned work on school house. School district then refused to pay, and plaintiff sues defendant successor of school district. Excluded evidence would have shown that work done by contractor before abandonment was worth some $5,000 more than he'd been paid for it, that contract could not have been economically completed at the low contract price, that as finally completed building was worth $6,000 more than contract price, and that school district has had the benefit of plaintiff's labor and materials going into the schoolhouse.

Aspects of decision: Reverses judgment for defendant on ground the excluded evidence was pertinent. It would have tended to show consideration for school district's promise to pay subcontractor's claim. Public purpose doctrine obliquely referred to: "In the leading case of Broadhead v. Milwaukee [see #20 *supra*] . . . the tax for paying bounties for volunteers was sought to be enjoined on the ground that there was no sufficient consideration moving to the city to support such a tax. The tax was upheld on the ground of equity and justice. . . . This was a tax also, and more, and the defense in this case is indirectly an attack upon the power of the district to raise this money by taxation. . . . How can it possibly be claimed that the promise and tax in this case are not founded in 'equity and justice'?"

26 (1896) Lund v. Chippewa County, 93 Wis. 640.

Public purpose?: YES (aid by municipality to state institution located therein, pursuant to statutory authorization.)

Facts: Statute established Wisconsin Home for Feeble-Minded, to be under control of State Board of Control, and authorized muncipalities (construed here to include counties) to make donations to it. Ordinance of county in which Home was located donated certain money to Home and provided for issuance of county bonds. Plaintiff taxpayer sues to restrain threatened addition of $3,750 annually in county tax roll for five years, and corresponding levy against county property for paying said bonds.

Aspects of decision: Reverses overruling of demurrer. Quotes general principles as to public and private purpose announced in *Brodhead* (#20 *supra*) and *McCurdy* (#22 *supra*) to show public and municipal pupose exists here. "It must be conceded that the establishment . . . of the 'Wis. Home for Feeble-Minded' was and is a public purpose." And "there are peculiar . . . benefits which will naturally spring from such location . . . . Convenient visitation by friends of . . . inmates is of itself a valuable right."

Says rule in *Whiting* case (#4 *supra*) was overruled by United States Supreme Court in *Olcott* case (#9 *supra*) and "whatever force may be given by this court to the [Whiting] decision ... it is manifest that it ought not to be extended."

Curtis case (#21 *supra*) distinguished since it involved *private* educational institution.

27 (1897) Wis. Keeley Institute Co. v. Milwaukee County, 95 Wis. 153.

Public purpose?: NO (county payments, required by statute, for treatment of "habitual drunkards" without ready means to pay, committed by county court to private profit corporation.)

Facts: Statute provided that "habitual drunkards" who are "pecuniarily unable to procure and pay for treatment for such disease" (statute at another point refers to them as without "means to pay") may by order of county court be sent for treatment to some institution within state for cure of such disease at expense of county in which they reside. Expense not to exceed $130 (for board, medicines, etc., for four weeks). Person not to be sent more than once, and he may reimburse county.

Plaintiff, a private profit corporation sues to recover $130 from county for a four-week treatment of patient turned over to it by county court.

Aspects of decision: Reverses overruling of demurrer. Construing the act as (a) not confined to the helpless and destitute (provision that he be without "means" is construed to mean without "ready means or money" hence doesn't mean he is a pauper) and (b) not concerned with contagious or infectious diseases, compelling a county to make such payments for treatment by a private profit corporation of habitual drunkenness is neither a proper exercise of police power nor within rule requiring taxation to be for public purpose. Cites *Curtis, Whiting, McCurdy, Eau Claire* cases (#21, 4, 22, 23 *supra.*) And act "compels payment without the consent of the county or its taxpayers; and in such cases the purposes for which taxation may be authorized are much more restricted than where such consent is first obtained, as indicated in numerous decisions of this court. Lund v. Chippewa County. [#26 *supra*]."

28 (1899) Wis. Industrial School for Girls v. Clark County, 103 Wis. 651.

Public purpose?: YES (county payments, required by statute for expenses of caring for abandoned, wayward, etc., girls committed by county judge to private, non-profit corporation.)

Facts: R. S. 1878 had imperfectly included provisions of 1875 law on organization of industrial schools but court here construes intent to be to preserve county's liability for children's care as in 1875 law. That law authorized organization of non-profit, non-stock, charitable corporations to conduct at county expense, schools for children who are wayward, vagrant, abandoned, etc., and placed therein by parents or guardian or committed by judge. Plaintiff school organized under such law had for over twenty years prior to this action cared for girls at county expense; seeks recovery for care of girls from 1894 to 1897 in sum of $1,968.64. County contests on ground its liability hadn't been preserved in 1878 revision and, among other grounds, improper use of private corporation.

Aspects of decision: Reverses sustaining of demurrer. *Keeley Institute* case (#27 *supra*) doesn't invalidate this use of private corporation. True, *Keeley* opinion stressed private nature of corporation but that alone wasn't fatal; the "combination of it with the purely private service rendered [treatment of non-contagious disease of persons not necessarily paupers] showed that the entire scheme was private." "The test to be applied in determining whether a particular agency may be employed by the state . . . to perform any particular work, is not whether the agency is public, but whether the purpose is public within the legitimate functions of our constitutional government. If the purpose be public and constitutional, and the agency be an appropriate means to accomplish it, and not expressly or by necessary implication prohibited by state or national constitution, its employment, under reasonable regulations for control and accountability to secure public interests, is legitimate and constitutional."

29 (1902) State ex rel. City of New Richmond v. Davidson, 114 Wis. 563.

Public purpose?: YES (state's discharge of city indebtedness, incurred two years before, to relieve distress from cyclone which had done great damage to life and property in city.)

Facts: City of New Richmond seeks mandamus directly in Supreme Court to compel state treasurer to act in obedience to 1901 statute appropriating $21,400 to discharge city's indebtedness in that amount which it had incurred by borrowing in 1899 from state's trust funds. The borrowing had been to relieve distress from violent cyclone destroying entire business portion of city, killing 115 people and injuring 500 more (total pop.: 1,900), destroying 100 homes, city hall, electric light plant, waterworks tower, tank and pumping station, bridge, 4 churches. Total property destruction: over $750,000.

Aspects of decision: Motion to quash, and demurrer, are overruled.

Cites cases applying public purpose doctrine and says they "seem to be based" upon "implied prohibition" in constitution and that determination of legislature on subject is not conclusive. Quotes from *Brodhead* case (#20 *supra*) that purpose must not only be public but "subserve the common interest and well-being *of the community required to contribute*" in order to show implied constitutional requirement for statewide purpose for state taxation.

Also refers to express constitutional provisions: (1) prohibition against taking person's property for public use without just compensation has the same underlying principle, though involving different theory, as public purpose doctrine in taxation, (2) article VIII, section 5 interpreted to authorize state taxes only to pay "state expenses or such expenditures as are authorized by the constitution."

Concludes that both public purpose and state purpose requirements are met. Quotes *Brodhead* principle that absence of public interest must be clear and palpable, and that equity and justice may support a tax. "This court has held that the administration of the criminal laws is a state affair, and that the officers engaged in such duties represent the sovereign power of the state . . . so . . . the state at large was concerned in the objects of the appropriation in question." If legislature had been in session at time of calamity, it could have appropriated money to bury dead, relieve suffering, prevent disease throughout state. Hence it had power later to reimburse city. "The local authorities were powerless in the presence of such great destruction, suffering and death. The condition of things, so suddenly precipitated, the claims of humanity, and the good of the state called for immediate and extraordinary relief . . . . The people of the commonwealth were bowed in sorrow . . . . "

Concurring opinion: Objects to court's assumption that restrictions on taxation also apply to appropriations. Says state may appropriate money even for local purpose.

30   (1903) State ex rel Garrett v. Froehlich, 118 Wis. 129.

Public purpose?: NO (state paying innocent purchaser of county order issued for treatment of drunkards in private institution under law subsequently held invalid as being for private purpose.)

Facts: After 1895 law for treatment of drunkards in private institutions had been held unconstitutional in *Keeley* case (#27 *supra*), 1901 law appropriated $30,000 for pro rata payment to innocent purchasers of unpaid county orders issued under 1895 law before it was held invalid. Mandamus directly in Supreme Court to compel secretary of state to draw warrant to state treasurer to pay a claim pursuant to 1901 law.

Aspects of decision: Mandamus quashed. Appropriation doesn't meet test stated in *New Richmond* case (#29 *supra*) of "being for a public purpose and such as subserves the common interest and well-being of the people of the state." Other language in that opinion was not intended "to justify a tax for every claim which one private party may have against another private party, though 'founded in equity and justice... or in gratitude or charity.'"

Only difference from *Keeley* case (#27 *supra*) is that the "void claims have been transferred ... to 'innocent purchasers.'" But the latter are no more innocent than those who furnished the treatment. And a transfer didn't change a private purpose to a public purpose or make claim "founded in equity and justice, or in gratitude or charity, against the whole state."

31   (1905) State ex rel Consolidated Stone Co. et al v. Houser, 125 Wis. 256.

Public purpose?: NO (state paying subcontractors on Historical Society building the balance due them from contractor after latter's bankruptcy.)

Facts: Subcontractors furnished stone and brick for building part of Historical Society library. Contractor was paid in full by state, but he didn't pay these subcontractors and went into bankruptcy, resulting in only partial payment to them. Statute appropriated enough to pay them the balance.

Mandamus to compel secretary of state to issue warrants for amounts appropriated.

Aspects of decision: Judgment granting mandamus is reversed. Citing several of the cases *supra* which apply the public purpose doctrine, says this is for a private purpose. Purpose was to "appropriate the public moneys of the state to the payment of private debts."

32   (1908) Lakeside Lumber Co. v. Jacobs, 134 Wis. 188.

Public purpose?: NO (town permitting private party to lay underground steam pipe across town lot, for party's own purposes.)

Facts: Town board permitted lumber company to lay underground steam pipe across town lot, so as to connect its mill with its power plant, provided it was at least three feet underground, and didn't interfere with town property; town could require it to be taken up when necessary to use the ground for any other purpose. Defendant was under contract to furnish power for town's utility plant, and town had already granted him use of the lot and permission to operate factory on it. Lumber company sues to restrain defendant from interfering with laying of the pipe.

Aspects of decision: Affirms dismissal of complaint. Town board's power to hold realty for public uses conferred no power to give to private persons any rights in town property which are "entirely unrelated to any of the governmental functions of the town." This right, in nature of an easement, to lay steam pipe across town lot devotes town property "to a merely private use wholly unrelated to any public town purposes."

33 (1915) State ex rel Owen v. Donald, 160 Wis. 21.

Public purpose?: NO (using state money to purchase lands for primary purpose of creating forestry reserve rather than purpose of helping administer and conserve lands already held by state; or using state money to pay local taxes on certain lands in forest reserve.)

Facts: Statutes made certain state lands a forest reserve, provided for forestry board, and state forester who was authorized to buy more land, sell dead and dying timber, lease some lands for cropping, etc. Appropriation of $50,000 a year for five years for forestry investment fund.

Mandamus to compel secretary of state to audit claim in favor of S Company for balance due on contract by state to buy certain lands pursuant to above authority.

Aspects of decision: Plaintiff's demurrer to defendant's answer (latter raising various issues of unconstitutionality) is overruled.

Lengthy opinion finds numerous constitutional defects (including defective procedure in initiation of 1910 constitutional amendment authorizing forestry program; violation of article VIII provisions on public debt and on internal improvements; and, by including swamp lands in program, violation of article X requirement that proceeds from swamp lands go in part to school fund) and says this on public purpose:

"It is a maxim of the law that the power to appropriate is co-extensive with the power to tax and so has fundamental and inherent limitations. The first of such limitations is implied from the very nature of organized society": must have "public purposes of a governmental character"; tax cannot "be levied to take property from one person and give it to another."

"A state-wide tax could only be levied for state-wide purposes and so on down to ... smallest taxing district. In either case the purpose would need to be public, in the sense of a matter of common or general interest to those upon whom the burden is laid" (citing *New Richmond* case #29 *supra* and non-Wisconsin authorities). "Another limitation on the power of taxation, from the very organic purposes of government is this: at the point where reciprocal benefits end, the power of taxation also ends. The basic idea of exercise of the taxing power and justification for it, is that it involves an exchange of equivalents .... " "There must be some present benefit. It is not sufficient that the forced contribution will be a boon to some future generation." Must remember our government recognizes "inherent rights" of individual. "State tax burdens must rest on a public state-wide constitutional purpose (citing *New Richmond* case, #29 *supra*, *Froelich*, #68, and *Garret*, #30) and ... must fall within the constitutional scope of the term 'expenses of the state' as used in sec. 5, Art. VIII .... The language ... though in form in words of grant, is in fact a limitation."

Viewed as an exercise of police power, would in part meet above constitutional requirement of public purpose and "state expense." With respect to school trust lands, police power could be exercised for reasonable conservation thereof (e.g., realizing on annual forest crops, etc.) and including even "judicious purchasing of adjacent lands to protect the former and increase the proceeds therefrom in the end ... " rather than in a way that would interfere with proper administration of trust lands. "Probably too, under the police power, expense may be incurred to properly care for ... lands granted to state for forestry purposes, and they may be added to at state expense for the primary purpose of utilizing the particular lands and making them valuable in an educational way and for the public purposes of the grants. The primary purpose would not be to create a forest reserve either as a temporary or permanent feature of the state and so violate the inhibition against engaging in 'works of internal improvement'.... " Also, statute authorizing use of state funds to pay local taxes on certain forest reserve lands is invalid; would not be for "state purpose of a governmental nature."

(Concurring opinion disagrees with majority's limits on forestation powers.)

34 (1916) State ex rel Trustees of LaCrosse Public Library v. Bentley,
163 Wis. 632.

Public purpose?: YES (municipal funds for free public library
run by private corporation.)

Facts: LaCrosse Public Library was private corporation maintaining public library for free use of people of city, pursuant to
C. C. Washburn's will which endowed it with $50,000, provided
for seven directors, including mayor of LaCrosse as ex officio member without compensation, and six named citizens, who were to
appoint their successors. Since 1888 city appropriated money
annually for library and since 1903 city levied special library tax
of over $2,000 annually. Charter amendment of 1889 authorized
common council to give this library up to $2,000 annually. *Stats.*
1915, Sec. 931 authorized municipalities to levy taxes for library
funds. Common Council levied tax of $6,000 in 1915 for library
fund, and gave it to this library in 1916.

Library trustees seek mandamus requiring payment of this
$6,000 to the library.

Aspects of decision: Reverses dismissal of mandamus petition.
Stats. 1915 authorizing municipal taxes for libraries doesn't confine power to support of libraries established under those provisions but includes public library like this one. Immaterial that
trustees of this one are not selected by common council, that
mayor is ex officio member, and that "expenditure of the money
raised and the report thereof to the common council is not controlled by the statutory regulations which apply to trustees of
libraries established by cities." These trustees "are in law required
to devote the funds ... for the benefit of all the people of the
city ...." If they are delinquent in their duties, they "would in
equity be responsible ... in the same measure as are the trustees
of libraries established by cities"; and city could always refuse
to grant further support.

Quotes statement in *Wis. Industrial School* case (#28 *supra*)
that a private agency, subject to reasonable controls in public
interest, may be used by government for public purposes.

35 (1916) State ex rel City of Superior v. Donald, 163 Wis. 626.

Public purpose?: YES (distributing to municipalities, portion of
railroad taxes attributable to location of certain terminal facilities
located therein, i.e., not a *local* purpose.)

Facts: Statute provided that after valuing property of railroad as a whole, tax commission was to make separate valuation of "any docks, piers, wharves or grain elevators used in transferring freight or passengers between cars and vessels," and railroad's taxes apportionable to such latter property were to be distributed to towns, villages, and cities in which such property was located.

City brings mandamus action directly in Supreme Court to compell audit of its claims pursuant to above law.

Aspects of decision: Mandamus issued.

In addition to meeting other constitutional objections, court says this law can't be said to appropriate state money "for a local ... and not a state-wide public purpose," for "these funds are not in any true sense state funds, but simply funds belonging to the city of Superior which have been collected by the state as a matter of convenience in the administration of the tax laws and are temporarily held by the state treasurer as custodian only for the city and are to be turned over to the owner upon proper demand."

36 (1919) State ex rel Atwood v. Johnson, 170 Wis. 218.

Public purpose?: YES (taxes for cash bonus to those serving in World War I.)

Facts: 1919 statute provided for levy of income and property taxes (or bond issue if particular county preferred it) to pay bonus to Wisconsin residents who served in armed forces of U.S. during World War I ("Cash Bonus Law").

Plaintiff taxpayer sues directly in Supreme Court to restrain enforcement of statute, claiming unconstitutionality in various respects, including lack of public purpose, undue delegation of legislative power, etc.

Aspects of decision: Demurrer to complain sustained. Against the argument that there was here "no reciprocal benefit such as lies at the foundation of constitutional taxation," says persons carrying on war "are performing services as well for the nation," citing *Brodhead* case (#20 *supra*).

"While there is language in some of the decisions of this court since the *Brodhead* case ... which in the abstract might seem out of harmony with the rule of that case, we feel warranted in saying that the doctrine enunciated there has never been overruled by this court." Further, "assertion of power for a long period ... in adopting legislation similar to that here involved ... is entitled to great weight on the question of public purpose."

37 (1919) State ex rel Atwood v. Johnson, 170 Wis. 251.

Public purpose?: YES (taxes for financial grants for purpose of World War I veterans furthering their education.)

Facts: 1919 statute provided for property and income taxes for purpose of making certain financial grants to enable World War I veterans to further their education ("Educational Bonus Law"). Plaintiff sues directly in Supreme Court to restrain enforcement of statute, making claims similar to those in preceding case (and some in addition, including charge that this lends state credit and makes a state debt contrary to article VIII, sections 3 and 4).

Aspects of decision: Demurrer to complaint sustained.

"If as held in the *Cash Bonus Case* [immediately above] the giving of money to soldiers, which they may spend as they choose, is a public purpose, much more so must be the giving to them of an education. A free government's best guaranty of continuity and security lies in the enlightenment of its people." Purpose here is "to express gratitude and stimulate love of country in those that receive, and in the public at large . . . . "

During Civil War and several years thereafter, eighteen Wisconsin laws were enacted for "war loans and voluntary aid to soldiers and their families" in very substantial amounts; other states as well as federal government have had similar laws. These legislative constructions of constitutional powers, together with prior decisions of this court mentioned in *Cash Bonus Case,* are very persuasive.

38 (1923) State ex rel Dudgeon v. Levitan, 181 Wis. 326.

Public purpose?: YES (teachers' pensions, including certain extra amounts for varying lengths of service *prior* to enactment of law.)

Facts: Mandamus action, directly in Supreme Court to compel payment of death benefit to beneficiary of Professor Dudgeon pursuant to Teachers' Retirement Act of 1921. State treasurer contended that certain amounts computed by annuity board were not proper, and special counsel appointed by governor contended statute unconstitutional insofar as it allows extra amounts to those teachers who were already in service prior to this law.

Aspects of decision: Motion to quash denied.

In addition to upholding statute against various other constitutional objections, court declares provision allowing extra compensation for those teachers who had served prior to enactment of law was not violative of public purpose standard. "If in [the legislature's] judgment the pension system will induce experienced and competent teachers to remain in the service, and that thereby the cause of education will be promoted, the money . . . for the payment of pensions is appropriated for a public purpose unless the court can say that the pension system will have no such result.

This the court cannot do," in view of general opinion on subject, conclusions of learned students, and enactments by twenty-five states of similar legislation.

39 (1924) City of Milwaukee v. Industrial Commission, 185 Wis. 307.

Public purpose?: YES (payment of "death benefit" under workmen's compensation law where, before disability indemnity terminated, death occurred other than as result of the accident.)

Facts: Workmen's compensation law permitted payment of a certain "death benefit" when injured employee's death occurred other than as result of the accident and before disability indemnity terminated. Widow received award pursuant to this law.

Aspects of decision: Circuit court affirmance of award is affirmed. This is not "the taking of public money for a private use." There "is no such independent gift to the dependents. It is no more than a necessary disposition of a balance due to the injured employee himself at the time of his death."

40 (1926) Village of Suring et al v. Suring State Bank, 189 Wis. 400.

Public purpose?: NO (village giving away land to aid a manufacturing company.)

Facts: Village bought certain lands for $2,000. Then, through its president and clerk, and without village board authorization, was transferred to K & W, deed containing these provisos: that K & W would erect mill for manufacturing cheese-boxes and other articles they might decide on; would not remove mill for five years unless was unprofitable, in which case would offer plant to village at price to be fixed by appraisers, and if village didn't buy, K & W could remove mill and deed land back to village.

K & W deeded property to Suring Corporation which they had organized (whose superintendent was village president). Suring Corporation gave mortgage on the property to secure loans from bank which knew conveyance from village to K & W had been unauthorized.

First suit is by bank to foreclose mortgage; second is by village and another to quiet title.

Aspects of decision: Affirms dismissal of complaint in first case, and the quieting of title in the village in second case.

"If it be assumed that the village had power to convey in a proper case, that would not justify a conveyance in this case which was by way of gift of the property to private parties for private benefit. A municipality cannot by statute be authorized to raise funds for such purposes, and bonds issued by a municipality in aid of a manufacturing enterprise are void because the promotion of private manufacturing enterprises is not a public purpose." (Citing *Lakeside* case, #32 *supra,* and *Citizens' Savings and Loan Assoc.* v. *Topeka,* 20 *Wall.* [87 U.S. 655] wherein United States Supreme Court had invalidated statute authorizing municipality to give bonds to company to encourage its establishment of bridge factory in city.)

41 (1928) Loomis v. Callahan, 196 Wis. 518.

Public purpose?: YES (University Regents giving long-term lease on its land to University Building Corporation for $1.00 and for Corporation's constructing and leasing buildings thereon to University at substantial rental, to be paid from operating revenues, with University eventually getting title.)

Facts: [For details, see same case below, #70].

Aspects of decision: [For details see same case below, #70. Closest to public purpose issue is this statement: "It is claimed that the leasing of campus lands to the building corporation is invalid because it gives state property to a private corporation for private purposes without compensation. This contention is based upon a very narrow conception of the transaction and overlooks the general situation and the compensating benefits accruing to the University by virtue of the transaction.... The money with which to construct the buildings is not available, but by leasing the land to a third party, [latter] will finance the erection of building and make it available for the University upon terms which will enable the University in time to pay for the building out of the earnings accruing from its operation.... This certainly furnishes a consideration which supports the lease and renders the transaction immune from the charge that public property is being given to private persons for private use without compensation."]

42 (1928) Curry v. City of Portage, 195 Wis. 35.

Public purpose?: YES (Statute permitting common council to determine whether and to what extent it will reimburse city officials for expenses incurred in successfully defending their official position or conduct before court, board, or commission.)

Facts: City police chief successfully defended himself against proceedings before the city fire and police commission to remove him from office, then sued to recover his expenses from city. Statute authorized city to pay such sum as it saw fit to reimburse officials in such cases; after common council's refusal to reimburse, he sues city.

Aspects of decision: Overruling of demurrer is reversed. Court construes statute as making such payments permissive only, and rejects plaintiff's claim that this would make statute unconstitutional by allowing discriminatory action and permitting use of public funds for private purpose. Without any analogous statute applicable to state officials, state legislature has long followed practice of reimbursing state officials under similar circumstances. "This long-continued legislative practice relieves such appropriations of a private character if, indeed, they are of that character at all" (citing the emphasis on "course and usage of government" in discussion of public purpose issue in Loan Assoc. v. Topeka, 87 U.S. 655, 665). "But more than this, it is now well settled that public moneys may be appropriated for claims founded in equity or justice, in gratitude or charity" (citing *Brodhead, Curtis, McCurdy, LaFebre, Lund, Johnson* cases, #20, 21, 22, 25, 26, 36 *supra*.) "The law simply confers upon common councils the same discretion which the legislature has always exercised" and "does not grant a right to the officer. If such a power be misused it calls for political and not legal remedies. Whether the plaintiff is entitled to mandamus to compel the common council to exercise its discretion need not here be considered."

43   (1930) Will of Heineman, 201 Wis. 484.

Public purpose?: YES (refunds of inheritance tax collected under statute subsequently held unconstitutional by United States Supreme Court.)

Facts: After a state inheritance tax statute had been held unconstitutional by the United States Supreme Court, statute provided for refund of taxes already collected thereunder, including requirement that counties return to state the portion of the tax which had been retained by them.

Petitions for refund were granted; state and county of Marathon appeal.

Aspects of decision: Affirmed.

Court upholds refund statute against objections based on various specific constitutional clauses, and observes: "The statute was passed in recognition of the moral obligation of the state to return moneys collected under a void taxation law. That the appropriation of money by the state for the purpose of discharging its moral obligations constitutes an appropriation for a public purpose, and is within legislative power, is neither challenged nor discussed in the briefs, and this very appropriately, as there is no judicial dissent from that proposition." Can't be said that no moral obligation arose because payment of tax by a taxpayer who could have but didn't challenge validity was voluntary. "The . . . decision of this court in Estate of Ebeling, 169 Wis. 432 ... declared the exaction to be constitutional. Under these circumstances it was within the power of the legislature to recognize a moral obligation on the part of the state to repay the tax."

Collections by counties did "not constitute property held by the counties in their local or proprietary capacities which is subject to constitutional protection. These funds came into their hands as the result of the exertion of [state] governmental power ..., and ... by virtue of the state's control and supervision over its municipalities it may compel [them] to refund these moneys...."

44 (1935) Appeal of Van Dyke: Van Dyke v. Tax Commission, 217 Wis. 528.

Public purpose?: YES (State distributing part of unemployment relief tax funds to municipality on per capita basis, to relieve their financial distress and strengthen their ability to relieve unemployment—is for public *and* state purpose.)

Facts: Statute in 1931-32 special session provided for emergency relief through levy of emergency income tax. About $3,000,000 of funds raised went directly to cities, villages, and towns on per capita basis. Taxpayer petitions for refund of certain income taxes including refund of all the emergency income tax assessed under above law, claiming latter is unconstitutional.

Aspects of decision: Affirms denial of petition for refund. Rejects argument that per capita distribution of funds to municipality meant relief of municipal taxation rather than unemployment relief (which was purpose of special session).

Was for a "public state purpose." Conditions since law was enacted—"continued depression marked by unemployment, distress, and need for extensive public relief—support the conclusion that the legislature wisely sensed the seriousness of the situation. ... In State ex rel New Richmond v. Davidson [see #29 *supra*] ... an appropriation made ... to the city of New Richmond to reimburse it for emergency expenditures by it following a destructive cyclone was considered. That appropriation was held valid ... and to involve a matter in which the state was concerned.... If that appropriation was for a public purpose concerning the state as a whole, how much more certainly may it be said here that the appropriation was for a public purpose in which the state as a whole was concerned."

[On "internal improvements" issue, see same case below, #72].

45 (1936) Wendlandt v. Hartford Accident and Indemnity Co., 222 Wis. 204.

Public purpose?: NO (city subsidy, through money and services, for erection and operation of shoe factory, under specified conditions.)

Facts: New London city officials contracted with shoe manufacturing company as follows: (a) company would erect factory with at least 20,000 square feet floor space, not of wood, and preferably of brick or concrete; to begin operation within six months; to pay $1,000,000 wages within first ten years, with annual minimum after first year of $50,000 (and if annual amount falls below $50,000, difference to be made up following year), and $400,000 minimum during first five years; to furnish $100,000 penal bond, to be reduced year by year in proportion that wages paid in year bears to $1,000,000; (b) city would furnish free water for five years and city official representing citizens would pay company $100,000.

Prior to contract, practically all taxpayers had signed petition urging payment of the $100,000 from public funds and stating willingness to pay special tax for it during next five years.

City paid the $100,000 (some of it raised by borrowing); factory began operating January, 1927; by 1932 city had recovered the $100,000 by special taxes (though interest on its bank loans and amount of special tax not paid by a large taxpayer was absorbed by city out of own funds). Shoe company breached contract in 1930. City officials sue surety on remaining amount of penal bond, approximately $86,600.

Aspects of decision: Dismissal of complaint affirmed. Contract is invalid and bond was so closely a part of the whole illegal transaction as to be "permeated with illegality."

"However well-intentioned the citizens of New London were in attempting to promote the well-being of the city by inducing a new industry to locate there, ... the ... plan and scheme was to induce the officers ... including the members of the council, to act officially but clearly contrary to the prohibition of the statutory law of this state, and against public policy as universally declared. To permit a recovery on the bond here would, to say the least, tend to encourage the citizens of other municipalities ..., under the stress of excitement and dominated by so-called public-spirited motives, to induce their officers to act contrary to law and to public policy.... 'To refuse to grant either party to an illegal contract judicial aid for the enforcement of his alleged rights under it tends strongly toward reducing the number of such transactions to a minimum.' "

[*Note:* Public purpose doctrine is apparently intended in court's above reference to such contracts being contrary to statutory law "and against public policy as universally declared." Statutory law referred to was argued in defendant's brief as follows: (1) Sec. 67.12 (1) allows city to borrow funds "to pay its ordinary and current expenses"—which doesn't fit this case; (2) Sec. 62.12 (6)(b) prohibits council from appropriating funds for any purpose not authorized by statute—and this purpose was not; (3) Sec. 348.28 makes it a crime for a public official to make contract not authorized or required by law, and Sec. 343.20 punishes officer who converts funds to use of self or other person not the owner. Brief also argued that every city resident has interest in preservation of city funds, so even if true that owners of 95 per cent of taxable property signed petition, that is immaterial.]

46 (1938) State ex rel WDA v. Damman, 228 Wis. 147.

Public purpose?: YES; NO (State funds to private non-profit corporation for promoting municipal and co-operative utilities through generalized activity is for public and state purpose; but promoting formation, acquisition, etc., of *particular* enterprise violates *state* purpose requirement though it is possibly for a public purpose.)

Facts: 1937 statute designated WDA (an existing, private, non-stock, non-profit corporation organized under general corporation law for promoting municipal and co-operative operation of utilities) as instrumentality for executing following functions with appropriation of $10,000 and $60,000 annually thereafter beginning July 1, 1937: (1) to promote municipal power districts under chapter 198 of Statutes, and co-operative or non-profit corporations to engage in enumerated types of utility service; (2) to promote acquisition, construction, operation, etc., of any plant, equipment or facilities for such service by co-op, non-profit corporation, municipality, municipal power district or other government unit; (3) to make studies of state's utility resources, studies looking to cheap and abundant supply of utility services, and studies for coordination of water power and fuel power development with regulation of rivers for water supply, flood control, etc.; (4) to collect and disseminate information related to execution of foregoing functions; and to cooperate with federal government and its agencies in execution thereof.

WDA not to use state funds for activities repugnant to state constitution if carried on by state; but this law doesn't prevent WDA use of non-state funds for internal improvements or other lawful purposes. State not responsible for obligations of WDA.

WDA authority to use state funds ends if articles are amended to provide profits for members, directors, or officers, or amended to change manner of distribution of property on dissolution or to authorize activities (which are actually engaged in) which are specified neither in Act nor articles. WDA records to distinguish between uses of state and non-state funds, and to submit annual report to governor on activities performed with state funds; and state fund disbursements to be audited by secretary of state. WDA to have access to information in hands of state departments and can ask Public Service Commission to get further information; and governor may require any state department employee to assist WDA.

Mandamus to compel secretary of state to audit three obligations incurred by WDA: (1) Murray claim for services in conducting survey of state resources; (2) Maloney claim for promoting creation of co-op in Crawford County; (3) Tuttle claim for mimeographing form letters addressed to 508 municipal officers concerning WDA's services.

Aspects of decision: First decision (Jan. 11, 1938): Reverses the issuance of mandamus; declares law invalid as unconstitutional delegation of sovereign power to private corporation.

Decision on rehearing (June 21, 1938): In addition to holding that previous ruling as to delegation was erroneous and rejecting the "internal improvements" objection and miscellaneous other constitutional objections, holds that WDA's activities of *generalized* nature are for *public and state purpose,* but promoting formation, acquisition, etc., of any particular enterprise violates *state* purpose requirement, though it is possibly for a public purpose. Hence Maloney claim for promoting particular co-op should not be audited; Murray claim for survey of state resources should be; and so should Tuttle claim for mimeographing form letters (even though letters called attention not only to services which WDA could, under majority opinion, legally perform, but also offered particularized services for community in question; would be harsh to kill whole expenditure for this overstatement).

Appropriation for a private purpose, of money raised or to be raised by taxation "would be to take the property of one citizen or group ... without compensation and to pay it to others, which would constitute a violation of the equality clause as well as a taking of property without due process of law." Reviews Wisconsin and other cases on each side of line, and says no "rule of thumb" exists to distinguish between public and private purposes. In general: legislature has wide discretion to determine what is public purpose; there is some guidance in past course and usage of government; numerous statutes since 1853 have given state aid to private societies like agricultural societies, historical societies, veterans' associations; an expenditure is not deprived of public character by mere fact that it benefits some more immediately than others, or that it is "paid to or through a private corporation or agency" (explaining *Curtis* and *Whiting* cases, #21, 4 *supra,* on ground of absence of state control there to see funds were actually used for public purpose by private corporations). Refers to *Froehlich, New Richmond,* and *Owen* cases (#30, 29, 33 *supra*) as establishing a "state purpose" requirement.

Applying foregoing paragraph to this statute: (1) survey and research provisions are "state-wide expenditures for a clearly public purpose." And fair inference that information was intended not for sole benefit of company but to be state property and available to all citizens—in view of persumption of constitutionality. (2) Provisions for promoting "generally the organization of municipal power districts and co-ops" are for "public and state purpose" and "are to be construed to authorize encouragement of co-operatives and power districts by general educational activities of the sort permitted in the case of agricultural co-operatives, but not to authorize ... activities directed to the creation of any particular power district or co-operative ...." (3) Provisions which authorize promoting acquisition, construction, operation of plant by co-op, city, power district, etc., are invalid as not for *state* purpose though possibly a public purpose. "We pass the question whether it is a public purpose ... [but] to urge and assist a particular group or municipality to construct or acquire a particular plant ... is a private, local and proprietary matter with which the state has no concern. The appropriation is not for a state purpose within the rule of the *Froehlich* and *New Richmond* cases ...." This is particularly true with reference to municipal ownership because that question is determined universally by local referendum uninfluenced by expenditure of state funds, and policy of home-rule amendment would also be contradicted.

Concurring opinion by Fritz, J; separate dissenting opinions by Fowler, J. and Fairchild, J.

47 (1939) State ex rel Voelkel v. Thiessen, 232 Wis. 126.

Public purpose?: YES (use of public funds to reimburse property owners who paid water main assessments, to put them on same basis as owners who in prior and later years were not required to pay.)

Facts: From 1913 to 1928 City of Oshkosh itself bore cost of laying water mains; from 1928 to 1934 cost was partly paid through assessments against abutting property owners; from 1935 on city returned to policy of bearing cost itself. 1937 law declared that where, in any municipality, cost of water main installation or extension had been in some instances assessed against abutting property owners and in other instances not, such municipality could reimburse those owners who had paid. City accordingly passed resolution authorizing repayment to such owners over three-year period.

One such owner brings mandamus to compel city officials to make reimbursement.

Aspects of decision: Circuit Court's issuance of mandamus is affirmed.

"The assertion that there can be no moral obligation on the part of the city to reimburse the water consumers of the city of Oshkosh who have paid assessments, and thereby place them upon a basis of equality with other consumers who have contributed nothing" is erroneous. The moral obligation existed, and many cases have held that appropriations for discharge of moral obligations are for public purpose.

48 (1940) State ex rel American Legion 1941 Convention Corp. v. Smith, 235 Wis. 443.

Public purpose?: YES (State funds, to be spent through private, non-profit corporation, for financing actual holding of American Legion convention in Wisconsin: serves both public and state purpose. Not so for use of state funds to bring convention to Wisconsin.)

Facts: 1939 Statute appropriated $50,000 for expenses of (a) bringing 1941 American Legion convention to Milwaukee and (b) holding and operating it there. American Legion 1941 Convention Corporation of Milwaukee, an existing non-stock, non-profit corporation, was designated as instrumentality for execution of above functions. Corporation not to use state funds for activities repugnant to state constitution if carried on by state, but this not to prevent corporation's use of non-state funds for above statutory purpose or other lawful purpose. State not to be liable for any corporation obligations. Corporation records to distinguish between state funds and others. Disbursement of state funds to be audited by secretary of state. If to obtain convention corporation must make deposit with national organization, secretary of state shall draw his warrant upon certification by corporation officers of amount so required. At the end of fiscal year following convention, corporation to submit report to governor of activities performed with state funds.

Mandamus against state treasurer to compel honoring of warrant issued by secretary of state for $27,050 (deposit required by national organization) as part of above appropriation; and request for declaratory judgment that law is valid.

Aspects of decision: Mandamus denied, since provision for deposit is unconstitutional (as undue delegation, as loan of state credit, etc.) but part of law is declared valid, i.e., all except provisions for deposit and for use of state funds to *obtain* convention for Milwaukee; use of state funds for *holding* of convention in Wisconsin does serve both a *state-wide* and *public* purpose.

Quotes general principles on public and state purposes from *WDA* case (#46 *supra*). In view of statutory preamble on nature of American Legion and facts about it in petition, legislature could reasonably conclude that appropriation would promote patriotic sentiment and preserve American ideals. "These are clearly public purposes of state-wide importance and particularly so in this critical period ... [of] reversion in other countries to systems of despotism . . . . " Cites *Johnson* case upholding soldier's bonus (#36 *supra*). Many instances of similar appropriations for conventions of patriotic organizations.

Fact that purposes have nation-wide significance doesn't alter their state-wide character. Fact that convention is in one city doesn't render purpose local rather than state-wide. Participants are from all parts of state and benefits derived are not merely local.

Using state funds for *bringing* convention to Milwaukee would not be for public purpose. "The attempt to bring the convention here may not be successful. That is at best a gamble and lies so largely in the field of conjecture and speculation that the possibility of serving a public purpose" or deriving direct public benefit "is so uncertain and remote that it cannot be considered a public purpose."

Separability clause should be applied, just as in WDA case.

49 (1942) Kiel v. Frank Shoe Mfg. Co., 240 Wis. 594.

Public purpose?: NO (city's payment of money and exempting of premises from rent and taxes for five years and conveyance of realty thereafter, in return for company's moving plant to city and meeting certain payroll requirements.)

Facts: City of Kiel sues to recover $12,000 which it had paid to shoe manufacturing company under agreement that company would move its plant from Milwaukee to Kiel; that plant would be rent and tax free for five years (at end of which, if company had performed its part, city was to convey certain realty to company free of encumbrances); that city would pay $2,000 to company for repairing building to be occupied by it, and $10,000 when company had completed removal to Kiel; that company was to maintain average annual payroll, exclusive of corporation officers, of $40,000 or more for five years. Complaint alleged fraudulent misrepresentations by company that company was prosperous and that it had decided to leave Milwaukee because of labor trouble.

Aspects of decision: Affirms overruling of demurrer.

Arrangement was "beyond the power of the city, and for that reason, illegal and void, therefore not in any legal sense a contract," citing *Wendlandt* case, #45 *supra.*

(Also rejects arguments that taxpayer rather than city should sue; that statutory sixty-day period for bringing suit to test validity of municipal contract had expired; and that complaint hadn't stated a cause of action.)

50 (1942) State ex rel Smith v. Annuity and Pension Bd. of Milwaukee, 241 Wis. 625.

Public purpose?: NO (granting pension funds to public employee already retired, in amount greater than that to which he was entitled at time of retirement.)

Facts: 1941 amendment to Milwaukee employees' retirement system law provided that all who were formerly active members of retirement system established in 1937 and who were compulsorily retired on or after Jan. 1, 1941, were to get additional retirement allowance (if prior allowance was less than $60 per month, were to get allowance of $3 per month for each creditable year of service, with maximum of $60 monthly). This amendment was passed June 28, 1941, and became operative for Milwaukee city employees when adopted by Milwaukee common council in October 1941.

Petitioner had been retired from city employ on Jan. 1, 1941, and brings mandamus to require Annuity and Pension Board of Milwaukee retirement system to certify, pursuant to above 1941 amendment, additional monthly retirement allowances for period from Jan. 1, 1941.

Aspects of decision: Reverses overruling of motion to quash mandamus.

Petitioner being no longer a municipal employee or member of retirement system at time of 1941 amendment, latter amendment could not lawfully attempt, as it did, to grant further public funds beyond the pension he was contractually entitled to at time of retirement. This was using public funds for private purpose. Refers to classification of cases cited in *WDA* case (#46 *supra*) as illustrating difference between public and private purposes.

Amendment couldn't be justified in terms of purpose of the Teachers' Retirement Law sustained in *Levitan* case, #38 *supra,* of retaining seasoned teachers in service and promoting efficiency by setting up pensions based on prior as well as future service. As for *Fritzke* case, 201 Wis. 179, claimant there was on leave of absence without pay at time the law was extended to truant officers; wasn't separated from service like claimant here.

51 (1948) State ex rel Martin v. Giessel, 252 Wis. 363.

Public Purpose?: NO (alloting state funds to local housing authority to defray part of cost of veterans' housing project constructed by such authority.)

Facts: 1947 laws created Wisconsin Veterans' Authority and appropriated to it from general fund, an amount equal to one-half of net proceeds of intoxicating liquor occupational tax, and authorized such authority to make allotments to local housing authority on basis of 10 per cent of cost of any veterans' housing project constructed by such local housing authority. W.V.A. allocated $15,600 to city housing authority of Port Washington and directed that $1,000 be paid forthwith. Director of Department of Budget and Accounts refused to audit and approve. Attorney General sought mandamus directly in Supreme Court to compel such auditing and approval.

Aspects of decision: Petition for mandamus is denied.

This cannot be said to be a *public* purpose on basis of previous cases upholding state benefits to veterans (see cases, *supra,* of *Brodhead,* #20, *Atwood,* #36, *American Legion,* #48) for "if it is a grant to the veteran it does not treat all equally." Also agrees with 1946 attorney general opinion that when state funds are used to assist a particular local housing authority for veterans, they are being used for other than a *state-wide* purpose.

[*Note:* These seem to be incidental observations. Court states at one point that sole issue is whether internal improvements prohibition of constitution has been violated, and concludes it has. Same case below, #74].

52 (1949) Heimerl v. Ozaukee County, 256 Wis. 151.

Public purpose?: NO (law authorizing municipality to contract for building private roads and driveways.)

Facts: 1947 law authorized town, city, or village to enter into contracts to build, grade, drain, surface, and gravel private roads and driveways; and authorized county to enter into agreements with municipality to perform any such work for it.

Action for declaratory judgment to have law declared invalid, and for injunction to restrain Ozaukee County from doing private road work for its municipalities in accordance with county board resolution.

Aspects of Decision: Affirms judgment holding the law unconstitutional.

Building of private roads is not "allied with a public purpose." Public "receives no direct or indirect benefit," and municipalities are being improperly authorized to engage in private business.

To be distinguished from other statutes involving clearly "governmental" functions, for example, soil conservation law; or law authorizing counties (a) to manufacture, sell, distribute agricultural lime to be sold at cost to farmers, and to acquire lands for such purpose, (b) to buy or receive tractors, bulldozers, etc., to clear lands for weed-control, and operate or lease them for work on private lands, charging fees for the service and rental of equipment on cost basis. Even if county were ultimately to be reimbursed, it would have had public funds *invested* in this *private* work. "Taxation for a private purpose is prohibited by the clause of the federal Constitution that guarantees to every State a republican form of government (Sec. 4, Art. IV) as such a form of government forbids the raising of taxes for anything but a public purpose." Quotes approvingly Ohio case against municipal operation of garage in competition with private garages, and Massachusetts case against public operation of business of selling wood and coal. "In order for a municipality to employ taxes to carry on a competitive business ... must involve a public function or be concerned with some element of public utility."

Powers granted are too broad: (1) not limited to cases of necessary ingress and egress, that is, of getting to and from public road; private road could be built or repaired "solely for the pleasure and convenience of the owner and to beautify his property"; (2) though county board has set up price structure for work to be done on contract, *statute itself omits* any price structure that would protect all taxpayers equally; (3) no exception made for those instances where *private* road-builders are equipped to operate, as in present case. "Thus it competes with private persons.... The right to engage in work is a property right. This property right cannot be infringed upon."

Distinguishes case of connecting a municipal utility with individual user's premises: costs are covered by charges to customer rather than by taxes; as to sewers supported by taxes, customer normally pays for sewer from his property line to the buildings and not only owns but maintains it; utilities other than such sewers retain control over such facilities, which are subject to governmental regulation—not so the private road. (Broadfoot, J. writes dissenting opinion.)

53   (1952) State ex rel Thomson v. Giessel, 262 Wis. 51.

Public purpose?: NO (increased monetary benefits to those teachers who had retired prior to, and wouldn't benefit from, the more liberal 1951 retirement law, and could meet certain requirements, including payment of a $100 contribution to general fund.)

Facts: 1951 law provided that teachers who retired before June 30, 1951, and would not benefit from the more liberal retirement law of 1951 were to be paid an additional $1 monthly benefit for each year of teaching experience, provided they met certain requirements, including making a $100 contribution to general fund.

Attorney General seeks mandamus directly in Supreme Court to compel budget director to audit certain vouchers for additional benefits as above described. Director's return to writ alleges unconstitutionality of statute, and attorney general demurs.

Aspects of decision: Attorney General's demurrer overruled; mandamus denied.

"When the applicants rest their claims on their former service they are entangled with Sec. 26, Art. IV, Constitution [prohibiting extra compensation to public officer, contractor, etc., after services rendered or contract entered into]. When they free themselves from that by relying only upon the new consideration [i.e., payment of the $100] to support a new contract they put themselves into the class of other private citizens, with former teaching status as an identifying mark only, and the special benefit granted them is a use of public funds for a private interest and hence unconstitutional . . . ."

Soldiers' bonus cases are distinguishable because statutes there contained declaration of legislative purpose to show gratitude for patriotic service; and even if this statute contained analogous declaration would be insufficient, since "noble and useful as the profession of teaching . . . may be, as much may be said for most other forms of service to the public." [Dissenting opinion filed by Currie, J.; joined in by Fairchild, J.]

54   (1953) State ex rel Thomson v. Giessel, 265 Wis. 185.

Public purpose?: YES (statutory authorization for construction and operation of toll highway—which when paid for would become state property—by non-profit, private corporation, which was to receive no state funds and could not, through its revenue bonds or otherwise, create a state obligation.)

Facts: See case #75 below.

Aspects of decision: See case #75 below. *Note:* Court's brief reference to public purpose idea seems to be mainly for purpose of argument that use of private corporation for public purpose need not be invalid *delegation* of legislative power, rather than argument that public funds should not go for private purpose. Closest thing to idea of public funds being used was tax-exemption (for corporation property and income, and for bonds, including transfer, income therefrom, profits from sale thereof) and fact that a Commission created to *study* feasibility of project was given $250,000.

55 (1953) State ex rel Thomson v. Giessel, 265 Wis. 207.

Public purpose?: YES (state payments to towns from general fund, on basis of forest land acreage therein.)

Facts: Constitutional prohibition re internal improvements was amended in 1924 to permit state appropriation for acquiring, preserving, and developing forests—annual amount not to exceed two-tenths of one mill of state's taxable property.

From tax funds above authorized, statutes authorize payments to *counties* on basis of acreage of county-owned forest lands for development of county forest reserve under supervision of Conservation Commission.

Statutes also authorize appropriation from *general* fund, to *towns,* on basis of acreage of forest lands therein, but with no requirement that funds be used for forestry purposes.

Action by attorney general directly in Supreme Court for mandamus to compel auditing of above payments to *towns.*

Aspects of decision: Mandamus granted.

(1) The two-tenths of one mill limit specified in constitution has no reference to these payments to *towns* but only to appropriations for acquiring, preserving, and developing state's forests. There is no requirement, as in case of counties, that funds be used for forestry purposes. And though these appropriations "are related to the forest crop law, they are not an integral part thereof. The landowner is induced to enter his lands under the Forest Crop Law because of the limitation upon the taxation thereof.... Acreage payments to the towns in which his lands are located cannot in any way affect his taxes on his forest crop lands."

(2) These expenditures are for *public purpose*. Cites *Brodhead* and *New Richmond* cases (#20 and #29 *supra*) and approvingly makes this quotation from Carmichael opinion quoted in *WDA* case (#46 *supra*): "The existence of local conditions which, because of their nature and extent, are of concern to the public as a whole, the modes of advancing the public interest by correcting them or avoiding their consequences are peculiarly within the knowledge of the legislature ... and it would require a plain case of departure from every public purpose which could reasonably be conceived to justify the intervention of a court."

56 (1953) Tonn et al v. Strehlau et al, 265 Wis. 250.

Public purpose?: YES (town funds appropriated pursuant to statute, to non-stock, non-profit fire department.)

Facts: Pursuant to Wisconsin Statutes a volunteer, non-profit, non-stock fire department was organized, and town board appropriated funds to it. On plaintiffs' refusal to pay consequent tax, their lands were sold at tax sale.

They seek to have the funds returned to town, and tax sale certificates declared void.

Aspects of decision: Dismissal of complaint is affirmed.

Regarding contention that "because the appropriation was made directly to a privately organized corporation ... the purpose of the appropriation and tax was private and not public," court cites *WDA* case (#46 *supra*) to contrary and quotes statement therein that when appropriation for public purpose is under proper government supervision, "it is not invalid merely because it is paid to or through a private corporation or agency."

57 (1953) State ex rel Thomson v. Giessel, 265 Wis. 558.

Public purpose?: YES (increased monetary benefits to teachers who had already retired prior to more liberal retirement law of 1951, if they registered as available for substitute teaching or other educational service.)

Facts: 1953 law made available to school teachers who had retired prior to the more liberal retirement law of 1951, added compensation of $25 monthly (not to exceed $100 when added to normal retirement benefit) if they registered as available for substitute teaching or for other educational service.

Mandamus action brought directly in Supreme Court by attorney general to compel budget director to audit a requisition for certain materials necessary for administration of statute. His return to writ alleged unconstitutionality of statute.

Aspects of decision: State's demurrer to budget director's allegation of unconstitutionality is upheld; writ is issued.

One of budget director's arguments was that "the act makes an invalid appropriation of public moneys for a private purpose." But this "is based upon the erroneous assumption that the payments prescribed are for services previously rendered." Legislature's stated purpose of inducing this class of retired teacher to register and thereby improving efficiency of school system is a public purpose. We can't question legislature's motives by regarding this law as subterfuge to evade previous decision on 1951 law (which hadn't required the teachers involved to hold themselves available for future service). (See case #53 *supra*.)

58 (1954) State ex rel Larson v. Giessel, 266 Wis. 547.

Public purpose?: YES (legislative provision for administrative refund of license tax which had been inadvertently imposed by the same legislature.)

Facts: Under laws relating to registration and licensing of motor vehicles, there was an exemption for small trailers (not more than $1\frac{1}{2}$ tons gross weight) if not used for hire. By a revision of these laws on June 12, 1953, the day on which legislature recessed until October 1953, such trailers became subject to an $8 annual registration fee. At the adjourned session, legislature enacted law stating that because it had "inadvertently" removed the previous exemption, it "hereby finds that it is a matter of public policy that this error be rectified by returning the fees collected," and it appropriated funds to motor vehicle commissioner to make refunds.

Mandamus is brought directly in Supreme Court to compel director of department of budget and accounts to audit voucher for payment of a refund.

Aspects of decision: Writ of mandamus is ordered issued.

After recognizing the public purpose doctrine, and the general exception in terms of principle that "a legislative act providing for a refund of taxes or license fees is valid if there exists a *moral obligation* to support the same," and after saying a declaration by a *subsequent* legislature of inadvertence or mistake by prior legislature would seem to be ineffective to establish the necessary moral obligation, court says: "However, we believe that a declaration by the same legislature that enacted the statutes imposing the tax or license fee, set forth in a subsequent chapter adopted at the same session, which declares that the prior taxing or licensing act was passed as a result of inadvertance or mistake, is entitled to be accepted as a verity by this court" and establishes the necessary moral obligation. [Fairchild, C. J., dissents without opinion.]

59 (1955) State ex rel Holmes v. Krueger, 271 Wis. 129.

Public purpose?: YES (increased monetary benefits to Milwaukee public school teachers who had retired before June 11, 1947, and elected to come under the new provisions before Jan. 1, 1952, with payment of $100 into retirement fund.)

Facts: 1951 law provided (*Stats.,* Sec. 38.25) that Milwaukee public school teacher annuitants who had retired before June 11, 1947, were to be paid an additional $1.00 per month, for each year of accredited teaching service, up to thirty-five years (and sum of annuity and increase not to exceed $1650 per year), provided they elected by Jan. 1, 1952, to come under these provisions and paid in $100.

Trustees of the fund plus one of annuitants seek mandamus in Circuit Court to compel city treasurer to honor pension payroll reflecting increased payments pursuant to above law.

Aspects of decision: Overruling of defendant's motion to quash is affirmed.

Refers to, and distinguishes, the language of earlier case [see quoted paragraph, #53 *supra*] and says it "was addressed to an argument ... that the statute provided for a new contract between the state and the retired teachers. That case was decided upon the ground that the effect of Sec. 42.535 *Stats.* was to grant compensation to public servants after the services were rendered and to public contractors after the contracts were entered into, in violation of Sec. 26 of Art. IV. ... In that case we were dealing with retired teachers who had rendered services in this state outside of ... Milwaukee [,] with a different section of the statute, with teachers who were to be paid directly from the state treasury, and upon a petition that raised different issues and which alleged different facts than those presented here. After Sec. 42.535, *Stats.* had been found to be unconstitutional, the legislature enacted a new statute that accomplished the same result and that statute was held to be constitutional [#57 *supra*]. Now retiring teachers who served within Wisconsin but outside of Milwaukee receive additional retirement benefits.

"Each case must be decided upon the facts and issues presented. This court has held several times that the expenditure of public funds for a moral obligation is an expenditure for a public purpose. ... The question of moral obligation was not before us in the first state teachers retirement case [#53 *supra*], although it was contended that the payment could be made out of gratitude for the services performed. ... There is a distinction between gratitude and a moral obligation.... We hold that the expenditures authorized under Sec. 38.25, *Stats.* are in satisfaction of a moral obligation and the expenditures are for a public purpose."

(Also rejects contentions that statute violates article IV, section 26 and "equal protection" clauses of both constitutions, and that it creates contracts void for lack of consideration.)

(Dissent by Gehl, J., joined by Brown, J., stresses that the "only difference between Sec. 42.535, the statute which we struck down [in #53 *supra*] and Sec. 38.25 ... is that the former was intended to provide additional benefits to retired teachers throughout the state, and the latter would provide additional benefits only to the retired teachers of the City of Milwaukee.")

60 (1957) Hermann v. City of Lake Mills, 275 Wis. 537.

Public purpose?: NO (transfer of municipal property for less than fair market value, to promote industrial expansion.)

Facts: Complaint of plaintiff taxpayers alleged that City of Lake Mills adopted resolution to sell certain park real estate for $4500 to Creamery Package Manufacturing Company; that the parcel had cost the city $7579; that common council had received from one Seward an estimate of $8000 as the parcel's value; that plaintiffs had offered to purchase it for $7500 and had protested to common council that $4500 was far below the true market value. Answer of defendant city officials denied that value was higher than $4500; alleged that plaintiffs' offer was not bona fide, good faith, responsible offer; and that it was in city's best interest that the sale be made to the corporation, which intended to erect office and engineering building that would employ fifty persons in addition to the four hundred and fifty the corporation already employed in its Lake Mills plant. Defendants moved for summary judgment, with affidavits stressing above emploment benefit to city and fact that corporation intended to use part of parcel for employee parking (since 1945, city had devoted two acres of parcel to public parking lot, in which employees of this corporation whose plant adjoined, customarily parked).

Taxpayers seek to avoid the sale and enjoin further steps effectuating it.

Aspects of decision: Circuit Court's dismissal of complaint and granting of summary judgment for defendants is reversed, and case remanded for further proceedings.

Taxpayers attacking a sale of municipal property must show illegality, fraud, or clear abuse of discretion. Would be clear abuse of discretion if proved that city was in effect making gift of part of value of property. A "transfer of municipal property to a manufacturing corporation in return for a payment representing only part of the fair market value of the property, which is knowingly made for the purpose of promoting industrial expansion, is . . . beyond the power of the municipality" (citing *Kiel* and *Suring,* #49 and #40 *supra*). True, consideration necessary to support the sale need not be money, so judgment below would be affirmed if corporation had been bound to devote part of parcel to municipal parking lot, but there was no such commitment, and corporation intended to afford parking only to its own employees.

Question of value of parcel was a material issue of fact to be litigated, hence was error to enter summary judgment.

61 (1960) Glendale Development, Inc. v. Bd. of Regents, 12 Wis. 2d. 120.

Public purpose?: YES (University Regents' sale (as part of plan for profit-making development of shopping center to be leased to private enterprises) of lands at $6,000 per acre to non-profit corporation and donation of purchase price to said corporation out of anonymous gift funds earmarked for discretionary use by Regents and whose use for present purpose was approved by anonymous donors; and where affidavits as to value of lands were conflicting but showed probability of large future profits to University, and Regents' exercise of discretion was concurred in by Building Commission.)

Facts: (See digest of same case under #80 below.)

Aspects of decision: Supreme Court affirms sustaining of demurrer to taxpayer's action and granting of summary judgment in defendants' favor.

Plaintiff's contention "that public property was given for a private purpose . . . goes to the sufficiency of the consideration received by the regents for the land sold to Kelab, Inc. and also the gift from the anonymous donation. . . ." But these cannot be challenged here since there was no fraud, illegality, or abuse of discretion. Affidavits on value of lands were conflicting but price received per acre "was comparable with that received for other tracts out of the Hill Farms and much higher than for some tracts"; per acre price of such a large tract is naturally smaller than for a small tract; and consideration must also be "given to the many advantages, financial and otherwise, accruing to the university by virtue of the creation and operating of the shopping center."

(For Fairchild, J. dissent see digest under #80 below.)

62 (1961) Fulton Foundation v. Wis. Dep't of Taxation, 13 Wis. 2d. 1.

Public purpose?: YES (retroactive exemption from gift tax due but not yet paid.)

Facts: In December 1948, Fulton Foundation was incorporated as non-stock, non-profit corporation and two of the three organizers made substantial gifts of stock to it in that month. A 1949 law, broadening the scope of gift-tax exemptions, applied in terms to all transfers in 1949 and subsequent years "and to all transfers of property prior to 1949 on which the gift tax has not been paid prior to the enactment hereof." No gift taxes had been paid on the Fulton transfers prior to enactment of this law. Department of Taxation assessed a gift tax on the transfers, claiming the retroactive exemption was an unconstitutional expenditure of public funds for a private purpose and a denial of equal protection of the laws. Wisconsin Board of Tax Appeals modified and affirmed Department's denial of petition for abatement of assessment.

Aspects of decision: Circuit Court reversal of Department and Board position is affirmed.

Exceptional situations in which Department is permitted to question constitutionality of tax statutes it administers should be limited to situations "involving issues of great public concern," and only the public purpose issue here qualifies. A "general law retroactively granting exemptions from taxes recently accrued or paid is not an expenditure of public funds for a private purpose." A legislative determination of public purpose "is implict in all statutes which grant tax exemptions general in scope. Ordinarily such a legislative determination is conclusive upon this court." There is a time limitation applicable to attempted retroactive exemptions compelling refund of already paid taxes. But was clearly not exceeded here "with respect to the application of the retroactive exemption to the unpaid gift taxes due on the 1948 transfers. . . . "

Hence there was here no expenditure of public funds for private purpose; and "anything stated by way of dictum in State ex rel Larson v. Giessel [#57 *supra*] which would conflict with such determination is withdrawn."

Fairchild, J. dissents.

In denying motion for rehearing: We should also have treated the "equal protection of the laws" issue as being one of great public concern which Department should be permitted to raise.

Legislative classification must be sustained "if there is any conceivable basis in reason therefor." "Our opinion in State ex rel Larson v. Giessel [#58 *supra*] is open to the interpretation that a refund of taxes already legally collected, by way of a granting of a retroactive exemption from tax would constitute an expenditure of public funds for a private purpose. We see no reason to now either repudiate or affirm such interpretation. It is sufficient to sustain the classification made by the legislature to point out that a conceivable basis for the same is the reasonable doubt as to whether the exemption would have been constitutional if it had required the refund of taxes already paid."

Plaintiff's statutory deposit with treasurer "in effect is one in escrow and the amount of the same in no sense constitutes public funds. Therefore the making of the refund in no sense can be considered an expenditure of public funds for a private purpose."

(Dissent by Brown, Fairchild, Hallows, JJ., from "the conclusion that the retroactive feature of the statute is valid.")

Precedents on Internal Improvements Prohibition

63 (1859) Clark v. City of Janesville, 10 Wis. 136.

Whether avoids internal improvements ban: YES (City is not within the constitutional prohibition.)

Facts: Action to recover on city bonds. Were issued for subscription to railroad stock, specifically authorized by statute if approved by municipal voters.

Aspects of decision: Reverses overruling of demurrer. Although deciding that bond issue invalid because city charter authorizing such bonds hadn't been properly published, rules that city is not within constitutional prohibition on internal improvements [article VIII, section 10]. Says all of article VIII applies to state only, with possible exception of section 1 provision that rule of taxation to be uniform.

History of other states had shown that financial distress resulted from state itself engaging in internal improvements and that such works were better done by private enterprise, assisted by interested municipalities. "Hence the constitution prohibits the state to become a party to such works, or to loan its credit, but contains no prohibition of a similar character [for] these local corporations; and, on the contrary, expressly recognizes their power to loan their credit [by authorizing state in article XI, section 3 to restrict their power to tax, loan credit, etc.] which must have contemplated their becoming parties in carrying on internal improvements, for it was for this purpose that this power in such corps. had been commonly exercised."

Hence not subject to objection of doing indirectly what can't be done directly: "The thing that can't be done directly is to contract a *state* debt for works of internal improvement .... Nor is it liable to the logical objection of deriving power from a source where it does not exist. The state may have power to grant a power, and at the same time not have power to execute it. This is clearly shown by reference to this very prohibition against its being a party [to] internal improvements. No one doubts that it may authorize a railroad company to build a railroad. But it could not build one itself."

[Dixon, C. J. concurs; Cole, J., files dissenting opinion.]

64 (1860) Bushnell v. Beloit, 10 Wis. 195.

Whether avoids internal improvements ban: YES (town is not within the constitutional prohibition.)

Facts: Same as above, except were town bonds.

Railroad had violated the agreement made with town at time of subscription (that town would get one director on railroad board, etc.). There were also certain irregularities with respect to following statutory procedure for such subscription.

Plaintiff is suing as bona fide assignee of railroad; and bonds were payable to bearer.

Aspects of decision: Affirms judgment for plaintiff. Uses same arguments as in *Clark* case, directly above.

Says framers of article VIII thought it "best to leave ... construction [of internal improvements] to private enterprise and associated capital rather than that the state should have anything to do with them. It was not supposed that towns and counties, whose inhabitants were mostly farmers, or that even cities would involve themselves in debt for these works. Probably if the country had then had the experience of the last 10 years and had seen the ... financial ruin which [has come] to towns, counties, and cities ... by subscribing to the capital stock of railroad companies and issuing their bonds therefor," a constitutional provision would have covered them too. "But this was not done; and we cannot construe the constitution as though such a prohibition was there."

True that some cases (for example, famous Sharpless v. Mayor, 21 Penn St. 147) go on ground that the particular state involved can carry on these works itself, hence could authorize localities to. "But ... the true reason is that when the legislature is authorized to create municipal corporations and no limit is imposed by constitution as to power which shall be conferred upon them, ... extent of such powers rests in the discretion of the legislature."

65 (1860) Hasbrouck v. Milwaukee, 13 Wis. 42.

Whether avoids internal improvements ban: YES (municipal construction of harbor, but only to extent authorized by statute.)

Facts: 1853 law authorized city of Milwaukee to issue bonds up to $50,000 "to raise money to be expended in the construction of a harbor" in Milwaukee; and 1856 law raised the maximum to $100,000. City's contract for construction of harbor exceeded latter maximum. 1857 law authorized "such an amount of ... bonds ... as may be necessary to complete the harbor."

Action by contractor to recover $73,000 allegedly due him for labor and materials in construction of harbor.

Aspects of decision: Affirms sustaining of demurrer.

"The power of municipal corporations, when authorized by the legislature, to engage in works of internal improvement ... and to defray the expenses [thereof] by ... taxing ... has always been sustained on the ground that such works, although ... in general operated and controlled by private corporations, are ... indispensable to the public interests and public functions."

But this power cannot be exercised without legislative authority. Since first two statutes authorized expenditures only up to $100,000, contract providing for greater expenditure was void as to the excess, and 1857 law was insufficient legislative ratification (wasn't procured by assent of city or acted upon or confirmed by it).

66 (1879) Jensen v. Bd. of Supervisors of Polk County, 47 Wis. 298.

Whether avoids internal improvements ban: YES (state roads—where state put cost of laying them out on counties, and cost of constructing on towns.)

Facts: See Facts stated in #24 *supra.*

Aspects of decision: See #24 *supra.* On internal improvements issue, observes that there is no violation of constitution since state is not standing the cost but putting it on counties and towns. Nor is it material that state-appointed commissioners direct the work: "It is no more a work of internal improvement carried on by the state because it directs the work to be done by officers specially appointed ... than it would be were the same work directed to be done by the proper officers of some ... towns ... or counties."

"This question ... was finally disposed of by this court in Bushnell v. Beloit ... [see #64 *supra*] and has not been questioned since."

67 (1881) Sloan, Stevens and Morris v. State, 51 Wis. 623.

Whether avoids internal improvements ban: NO (allowing recovery against state of judgment for legal services rendered to state in defending replevin suits by trespassers on lands granted to state for construction of railroad.)

Facts: State agents, acting pursuant to statute, had seized logs cut by trespassers upon lands granted to state in aid of construction of railroad. Plaintiffs, who were employed by governor for legal services in defending replevin suits against these agents, are suing for value of their legal services after secretary of state refused to audit their claim and legislature refused to appropriate money for it. Statutes provided for a trepass fund, to which proceeds of sale of such seized logs were allocated.

Aspects of decision: Complaint dismissed.

Reviews constitutional provisions on state debt and on internal improvements; and notes that state had duty as trustee of lands granted to it, to protect lands from spoliation and compel trespassers to reimburse trust fund to extent of damages done. Concludes that "if this action is sustained and the plaintiffs recover, the judgment will be an indebtedness of the state, and must be paid out of the state treasury like any other judgment whether any of the trespass funds remain in the treasury or not." This would violate constitution; but statutes do provide for payment of expenses of this kind out of trespass funds and plaintiffs should make their claim pursuant thereto. [Cole, C. J., with Taylor, J. concurring, *dissents:* "It is said that any judgment which this court may render in favor of the plaintiffs must be paid out of the general fund in the treasury, and thus the state will become liable for a debt in carrying on an internal improvement. But the state is in no danger of incurring any such liability, because it has an ample trust fund out of which it may indemnify itself on paying the judgment. It will doubtless charge the amount paid on the judgment to that fund."]

68 (1902) State ex rel Jones v. Froehlich, Secy. of State, 115 Wis. 32.

Whether avoids internal improvements ban: NO (appropriation for a state commission to strengthen levee system in vicinity of Portage on Wisconsin River.)

Facts: 1901 law appropriated up to $20,000 for "constructing and strengthening the levee system already existing in the vicinity of Portage on the Wisconsin River . . . ." Commission appointed by governor to conduct work. For a surveying bill incurred by commission and approved by governor, secretary of state refused to issue warrant, on ground law was invalid.

Commissioners bring mandamus to compel issuance of warrant.

Aspects of decision: Reverses the granting of mandamus.

Gives historical background of Wisconsin constitutional prohibition on internal improvements and says concept of internal improvement "included those things which ordinarily might in human experience be expected to be undertaken for profit or benefit to the property interests of private promoters, as distinguished from those other things which primarily and preponderantly merely facilitate the essential functions of government. Of course, this line of classification does not exclude possibility that the dominant characteristics of one class may be present in illustrations of the other. A toll-earning canal which gathers spreading waters within its banks may promote public health, as also may a drainage system undertaken for improvement of the lands of those who construct it. Improvement of the grounds of a state institution may improve access to, and enhance the value of private property. But in each case, the dominant purpose is obvious, and therefore the classification along the line of distinction above stated."

Gives list of what have been considered internal improvements in various states, including roads, wharves, levees, etc. Levee is internal improvement even if main purpose be promoting navigability, water power, or reclamation. "In any of these, there is enough of pecuniary benefit to warrant belief in the possibility at least, that they may be undertaken by private enterprise or local association. Indeed, a part at least of the system which the act of 1901 proposes to construct and strengthen was the result of the private enterprise of Green Bay and Mississippi Canal Company subsequently taken over by the United States." Any "general governmental purpose likely to be accomplished" is so "indirect" and "slight" as not to change this classification.

69 (1915) State ex rel Owen v. Donald, 160 Wis. 21.

Whether avoids internal improvements ban: NO (state contract to purchase land, as part of comprehensive forestry program involving creation of forest reserve, development of water power and lumbering operations thereon, etc.)

Facts: See case #33 *supra.*

Aspects of decision: See case #33 *supra.*

On internal improvements issue, concludes that state's contract for purchase of land pursuant to forestation program was invalid, since such program violated internal improvements prohibition. Says that forestation program has been treated by legislature itself as internal improvement, in view of its attempts in 1907, 1909, 1911, and 1913 to amend constitution to permit it; that *Froehlich* case (#68 *supra*) took broad view of meaning of "internal improvement," so that it didn't necessarily exclude projects with a public purpose, and wasn't restricted to some channel of trade or commerce; that similar views were indicated in Journal of Constitutional Convention and been held by most other courts. Indicates, however, that many aspects of forestry program might *not* be invalid.

[Concurring opinion by Winslow, J. says court should state clearly that forestation is not internal improvement, except for lumber manufacturing aspect of program.]

70 (1928) Loomis v. Callahan, 196 Wis. 518.

Whether avoids internal improvements ban: YES, but not specifically discussed by majority (construction of campus buildings by non-profit building corporation composed of University of Wisconsin officials which got loan from State Annuity Board, such buildings being built on University land and leased to Board of Regents at rental to be paid from operating revenue, with University eventually getting title.)

Facts: Statute authorized plan by which certain campus buildings were to be erected by a University Building Corporation on land leased from Regents for which it paid $1 rental and leased buildings to Regents at annual rental, with Regents eventually paying for buildings out of operating revenues. University Building Corporation was non-profit corporation whose members were current and future Secretary of Board of Regents, business manager and comptroller of University of Wisconsin. It got fifteen-year loan from Annuity Board of State Retirement System of $400,000 at 4½ per cent and thirty-year loan of $326,000 at 4½ per cent, on security of the Corporation leasehold interest in the realty involved.

Suit by taxpayer to enjoin members of Annuity Board from loaning funds of Retirement System to University Building Corporation.

Aspects of decision: See #41 *supra*.

Majority opinion rejects various constitutional objections, for example, says state is not contracting "debt," since for the property it acquired state is not committed to pay from any source other than revenues arising from operation of the property. But says nothing on whether state is being *party* to an *"internal improvement"*; evidently assumes it is not.

[*Dissent* by Eschweiler, J. says this violates constitution, including provision against state contracting debt for, or being party to internal improvements, "the use of these funds so being trans-

ferred from a trust fund under the control of one set of state officials to be spent by another set . . . is for a work of internal improvement," citing *Owen* case, #69 *supra*. "Though these two sets
of state officials, the borrower and the lender do not appear to be
dealing . . . much at arms' length, nevertheless they carry on all
their doings as agents of the State. Not a dollar of this money is
to be used, except as directed and controlled by the board of
regents, and therefore the state itself . . . is . . . a party . . . in carrying on such works of internal improvement."]

71   (1929) State ex rel Hamman v. Levitan, 200 Wis. 271.

Whether avoids improvements ban: YES (law authorizing establishment by Conversation Commission of a wild-life refuge,
game preserve, fur farm, and fish hatchery on Horicon Marsh,
and construction of dams in connection therewith. Avoids ban
on internal improvements because comes within specific constitutional authorization for "parks.")

Facts: 1927 laws authorized: (1) that a wild-life refuge, game preserve, and fur farm be established on Horicon March in Dodge
County, under supervision of Conservation Commission; (2) that
commission may establish fish hatchery in connection therewith;
(3) that commission shall buy or acquire by condemnation, all or
part of Horicon Marsh and construct such buildings and provide
such equipment as needed for authorized purposes; (4) that commission may build and maintain dams near city of Horicon to
regulate Rock River flood waters and restore public waters of
Rock River on Horicon Marsh to natural levels existing prior to
private drainage thereof; (5) that proceeds from fur farm and all
other income from state property be paid, within one week from
receipt, to conservation fund; (6) that $25,000 be appropriated
annually for ten years, for purchase of land, construction of buildings and equipment, and operation of the wild-life refuge, game
preserve, and fur farm.

Title of act described it as creating specified subsections and
"relating to a state wild life refuge, fur farm and dam on the
Horicon Marsh, and making an appropriation."

Action brought directly in Supreme Court to restrain expenditure of above moneys on ground of violation of constitution.

Aspects of decision: Injunction is denied. (1) No violation of
article IV, section 18 requirement that "no . . . local bill . . . shall
embrace more than one subject, and that shall be expressed in the
title." Purpose of act is to authorize a wild life refuge on Horicon

Marsh, and the other things mentioned are simply "incident" to this purpose. "There must be a dam to raise the water level. When the wild life refuge is instituted, certain incidental steps in the judgment of the legislature should be taken, such as the establishment of a fish hatchery... the control of the flood waters of Rock River. If any one of these subsidiary steps were to be entered upon by the state as a sole and distinct enterprise, other and serious questions would be presented. It is very doubtful whether the legislature could authorize the state to enter into the business of raising fur. It is equally doubtful whether it could authorize the agricultural college to enter into the business of raising wheat, tobacco, or other agricultural products. However the state does all of these things as a necessary and proper incident to the carrying on of a school of agriculture. If the authorities charged with execution of the law should depart from the fundamental purpose and make the incidental the dominant purpose, it is quite probable they could be brought within their proper sphere by court action. The erection of a dam for the purpose of controlling flood waters would undoubtedly be a work of internal improvement. Here the dominant purpose is the creation of a wild life refuge, and as an incident to it the establishment of a fur farm, dam, and a fish hatchery. We see nothing in the title of the bill which... makes it unconstitutional as violation of sec. 18 of art. IV."

(2) It is *"unnecessary ... to consider"* whether this is an internal improvement within meaning of article VIII, section 10, since it is specifically authorized by article XI, section 3a, added in 1912, which authorizes state or city establishment of parks. "[A]lthough this project does not conform to the popular idea or notion of a park," the term is often used (as in case of some national parks) in a wider sense. We shouldn't narrowly construe this constitutional amendment intended to promote general welfare. Proper employment of leisure through recreation is important social problem, and legislature has broad discretion as to best use of public funds to provide such recreation.

[Concurring opinion by Crownhart, J., "would prefer to have the judgment based on the police power of the state." Viewed as exercise of such power, there is no violation of internal improvements ban.]

72 (1935) Appeal of Van Dyke: Van Dyke v. Tax Commission, 217 Wis. 528.

Whether avoids internal improvements ban: YES (state reimbursing counties and cities to extent of 25 per cent of labor cost on public works undertaken for unemployment relief—where state's "primary purpose" was to assist in unemployment relief rather than be party to works of internal improvement.)

Facts: See #44 *supra.*

Aspects of decision: See #44 *supra.*

In rejecting internal improvements objection, says: "It is true that some of the moneys which were paid out by the industrial commission, pursuant to . . . sec. 2 (2) . . . which permitted reimbursement to the county or city of 25 per cent of the labor cost of public works undertaken to provide for the unemployed, went into such public works, but the primary purpose of the state was not to become a party to carrying on works of internal improvement but to reimburse the counties and cities which had made work simply for the purpose of providing employment to the unemployed."

73 (1938) State ex rel WDA et al v. Damman, 228 Wis. 147.

Whether avoids internal improvements ban: YES (state funds to private, non-profit corporation which was to promote carrying on of public utility enterprises by co-operatives, municipalities, and power districts.)

Facts: See #46 *supra.*

Aspects of decision: See #46 *supra.*

In rejecting internal improvements objection, says that state's encouraging others to form these types of utility enterprises does not make state a party to such works. Says constitution drafted by first convention (and "rejected by the electorate largely because of objections to other provisions") had coupled with the prohibition on state's carrying on internal improvements, a provision that state shall encourage internal improvements by individuals, associations, corporations. This "demonstrates convincingly that there was deemed to be and is such a material distinction between those two activities that the mere encouragement of others to engage in such works was not considered to constitute the carrying on, or being a party in the carrying on, of such work . . . . [T]here is likewise no occasion now to hold that it was intended by Sec. 10, Art. VIII . . . to prohibit encouragement by the state of the making of such improvements by others," citing *Jensen* #24 *supra, New Richmond* #29 *supra, Van Dyke* #44 *supra,* and *Raub,* 106 Kan. 196.

74 (1948) State ex rel Martin v. Giessel, 252 Wis. 363.

Whether avoids internal improvements ban: NO (allotting state funds to local housing authority to defray part of cost of veterans' housing project constructed by such authority.)

Facts: See #51 *supra.*

Aspects of decision: See #51 *supra.*

On internal improvements issue, says: "It would appear almost axiomatic that if housing is a public venture, it constitutes an internal improvement. If it is not a public improvement, then certainly the government could have no basis for entering into the field, for it must then be private business." Constitutional restriction is not diminished by existence of alleged emergency in housing. Even if housing program comes within police power, latter power is subject to restriction of internal improvement prohibition. Providing "structures for the housing of private individuals" is to be distinguished from "providing structures necessary for the discharge of the state's functions." Agrees with 1946 attorney general's opinion that when state uses funds to give specific assistance to local housing authority for veterans, it is a party in carrying on works of internal improvement; language of court opinion suggests hostility to general assistance as well. Cites *Froehlich* and *WDA* cases (#68 and #73 *supra*) as stating applicable legal principles.

75 (1953) State ex rel Thomson v. Giessel, 265 Wis. 185.

Whether avoids internal improvements ban: YES (statutory authorization for construction and operation of toll highway, which when paid for would become state property, by non-profit private corporation, which received no state funds and could not through its revenue bonds or otherwise create a state obligation.)

Facts: 1953 laws: (1) created a turnpike commission of five members to be appointed by governor, with appropriation of $250,000, to ascertain feasibility of turnpike or toll highway to run roughly between St. Croix or Pierce counties near Minnesota border, and Rock, Walworth, or Kenosha counties near Illinois border; (2) authorized formation of non-profit, non-stock turnpike corporation with powers to construct and maintain turnpike projects, including power to acquire land through specified condemnation procedure, to fix and collect tolls, to lease land to private persons for gas stations, motels, etc., to issue bonds to be paid out of revenues and not to be secured by mortgage or property and not to be a debt of state or political subdivisions. Members of commission mentioned above may, after determining that toll highway over above route is in public interest, incorporate as a turnpike corporation under this law, with governor's consent. Tax exemption for corporation property and income, and for bonds (including transfer, income therefrom, profits on sale thereof). When bonds have been paid or sufficient amount set aside in trust for payment, project belongs to state as toll-free public highway.

Attorney General requests Supreme Court to mandamus the auditing of commission's allottment request for $155 and requisition of typewriter, and to declare above statutory provisions valid.

Aspects of decision: Mandamus granted; declaratory judgment that statutory provisions are valid.

Rejects various constitutional objections, and on internal improvements issue says: "Even if we should concede that the construction of toll roads is a work of internal improvement and not exempted by the 1908 amendment to Art. VIII, sec. 10 concerning 'public highways,' the prohibition of that section of the constitution is not violated, since it applies only to such works as may be engaged in by the state." State is neither engaging in the work, nor contributing funds to it, nor incurring debt on account of it. Stresses that a turnpike corporation is not a state agency.

76 (1954) State ex rel Thomson v. Giessel, 267 Wis. 331.

Whether avoids internal improvements ban: YES (construction of addition to state office building.)

Facts: Statutes authorized a State Building Commission to construct new buildings or additions for state offices, and to incorporate a non-profit Wisconsin State Public Building Corporation, which could become lessee of state-owned land and construct thereon buildings and necessary equipment. Corporation could (1) *lease* these buildings to State Building Commission on appropriate terms for rental, maintenance, and ultimate purchase by state, and the buildings, until acquired by state, would be operated by State Building Commission so as to pay costs, interest, and yield surplus sufficient to pay principal amount in not more than fifty years and (2) *mortgage* its interest in land and buildings to secure loan from State Investment Board. Under authorization of 1953 law, in order to finance a state office building addition and pay off almost $1,000,000 balance due on existing building to State Insurance Fund, the existing office building and land as well as land for new addition was leased to Building Corporation, which mortgaged this leasehold interest to secure $4,200,000 loan from State Investment Board.

Mandamus by attorney general directly in Supreme Court to compel approval of voucher for the almost $1,000,000 balance due on existing building, as first step in above financing plan; also, asked declaratory judgment that relevant statutes (Secs. 14.86, 14.88) and proposed financing plan are valid.

Aspects of decision: Demurrer to declaratory judgment request upheld; complaint dismissed. In addition to other constitutional holdings [that is, that the Statutes don't violate article IV, par. 7, section 31 on special or private laws; that the "Building Corporation is not an agency or instrumentality of the State but a private corporation organized for a public purpose"; that the State Building Commission's obligation to pay rentals to Building Corporation, under a lease entered into for state's benefit and advantage, is not a "debt," and is not a case of state's credit being given or loaned in aid of private parties; but that the Building Corporation's mortgaging of its leasehold interest as above stated violated article VIII, section 4 against state's incurring a debt, for state would feel "coercion . . . to pay an indebtedness for the payment of which existing state property or an interest therein had been pledged as security"], court rules *these buildings are not internal improvements,* quoting a statement from *Donald* case, #69 *supra* on government buildings.

[*Note:* Court declares, in ruling that state debt provision had been violated, that insofar as *Loomis v. Callahan* (#70 *supra*) may be interpreted as permitting "encumbering of an interest in existing state property as security for a loan," it is overruled. Gehl, J. dissents on this point as to which *Loomis* case is overruled.]

77 (1955) State ex rel Thomson v. Giessel, 271 Wis. 15.

Whether avoids internal improvements ban: YES (construction of University off-campus dormitories; also, though not specifically discussed on internal improvements issue, construction of indoor athletic practice building and addition to state office building.)

Facts: (1) University of Wisconsin Regents leased to Wisconsin University Building Corporation, a non-profit corporation, for fifty years at $400 monthly rental, the land on which Camp Randall Memorial, an indoor athletic practice building was to be constructed by the Corporation. Said Corporation, on same date, subleased to Regents the identical land and any improvements thereon for fifty years at $400 monthly rental plus additional rentals calculated to enable Corporation to retire indebtedness to be created in construction, that is, $600,000 to be borrowed by Corporation from banks (remaining $900,000 to come from Regents under statutory revolving fund). Pursuant to sublease, Corporation assigns rentals so that Regents pay directly to banks, for application to indebtedness. (2) Regents proposed to lease to said Corporation two off-campus land parcels for fifty years and rental of $1.00 plus Corporation agreement to construct dormitories thereon; with Corporation subleasing same land and any improvements thereon to Regents for fifty years at rental enabling Corporation to retire construction indebtedness. Corporation proposed to borrow from Allstate Insurance Company up to $125,000, to be secured by promissory note and pledge of rental agreement; remaining $184,000 to come from funds made available by State Building Commission. (3) Building Commission proposed to sell to Wisconsin State Public Building Corporation (a non-profit Corporation whose organization was authorized by Building Commission pursuant to *Stats.* 1953, sec. 14.86) for $125,000, land adjoining state office building, on which Corporation would erect office building and lease it to Commission. Corporation would obtain funds for land and building by borrowing from Allstate Insurance Company up to $4,600,000, secured by mortgage on premises. Lease is expressly made subject to the mortgage, and rents to be paid by Commission are pledged to Allstate.

Statute provided that state's obligation to pay rent to a building corporation is subject to available appropriations.

Attorney General seeks declaratory judgment directly in Supreme Court, adjudging that proposed constructing, and financing, and statutory authorization in *Laws* 1955, c. 144 are valid, and that director of budget and accounts should approve vouchers, etc., issued to him by Regents or Building Commission concerning above programs.

Aspects of decision: Demurrer overruled; judgment for plaintiff. In addition to other constitutional holdings [that is, that the above-summarized arrangements do not create state "debt" or loan the credit of the state in violation of article VIII, sections 3, 4, 6, 7, of constitution, or violate article XI, section 3a authorizing states and cities to acquire realty for certain purposes and erect improvements thereon and convey any such realty not necessary for such improvements] holds that the *off-campus dormitories were not internal improvements,* since they not only provided a place to eat and sleep but would afford "educational opportunity," they were an integral part of the University. "Any structure which is used by the state university for the purpose of education is excluded from being a work of internal improvement." Cites *Donald* case, #69 *supra,* and 1954 office-building case, #76 *supra.* On this ground, court distinguished *Veterans' Housing Case,* #74 *supra.*

78 (1957) Cutts v. Department of Public Welfare, 1 Wis. 2d 408.

Whether avoids internal improvements ban: YES (construction of state school for delinquent boys.)

Facts: Laws 1955, c. 404 authorized the erection of a state school for delinquent boys within the Kettle Morain State Forest, on a site to be determined by state building commission. Pursuant to this law the commission purchased a site within the forest from the conservation commission. Taxpayers seek declaratory judgment that the statute is unconstitutional.

Aspects of decision: Reverses the overruling of demurrer to complaint. In the course of various constitutional holdings [that is, that the law was not an invalid delegation of legislative power; that it did not violate article VIII, section 10 as a non-forestry use of state forest land; that it did not violate article XI, section 3a standards for conveyance of certain state lands] court observes that the boys' school is not a work of internal improvement, citing Donald case, #69 *supra.*

79 (1959) Redevelopment Authority of City of Madison v. Canepa, 7 Wis. 2d 643.

Whether avoids internal improvement ban: YES (carrying on a blight-elimination, slum clearance, and urban-renewal project through land condemnation and other activities, by Redevelopment Authority of City of Madison, created by and in some respects controlled by the city, pursuant to provisions of state law which described any Authority created thereunder as an "independent, separate and distinct public body and a body corporate and politic.")

Facts: A 1958 state law provided for carrying on of blight-elimination, slum clearance, and urban-renewal projects by Redevelopment Authorities which were to be appointed by and in some respects controlled by the city (e.g., through approval of the Authority's plan, financial aid, and control of its budget). The law described such an Authority as an "independent, separate and distinct public body and a body corporate and politic," and authorized it to acquire private property by condemnation proceedings without submitting to a jury the issue of necessity therefor. Plaintiff Redevelopment Authority seeks a declaratory judgment in Supreme Court, against certain property owners, that latter provision doesn't violate article XI, section 2 of Wisconsin constitution: "No municipal corporation shall take private property for public use, against the consent of the owner, without the necessity thereof being first established by the verdict of a jury."

Aspects of decision: Court declares the no-jury provision of statute unconstitutional, and separable so as not to invalidate remainder of law.

Defendants, in course of arguing that the Authority was an agency of the city and hence subject to the constitutional provision, contended that if Authority was not such agency the law would be invalid, because it authorized Authority to contract debts and carry on internal improvements which state itself could not do. Court replied there would be no such invalidity, *regardless of whether Authority be regarded as city agency.* "It has been held from almost the beginning of the state that while the state is subject to the provisions [on debt and internal improvements], governmental units created by the state and carrying on their public functions in particular localities or geographical subdivisions of the State are not so subject [citing Bushnell, #64 *supra,* Clark, #63 *supra,* and Jensen, #66 *supra*]. Defendants' argument in this regard is founded upon [the statutory reference to Authorities as] 'state-created agencies' and 'state agencies,' and upon plaintiff's stress upon the same language in order to demonstrate that the Authority is not an agency of the city; we do not attach great significance to this particular language because in a sense all governmental bodies created under the constitution of the state, including cities and villages, could be termed 'state agencies.' We have no doubt that this statute would not violate the state-debt and internal-improvement provisions of the constitution even if construed so as to classify the Redevelopment Authorities as independent from the cities in which they operate."

(Court goes on to analyze the relations between city and Authority and concludes the city exercised sufficient control so that the jury provision of constitution was applicable and invalidated the no-jury portion of the statute.)

80 (1960) Glendale Development, Inc. v. Bd. of Regents, 12 Wis. 2d 120.

Whether avoids internal improvement ban: YES (development of shopping center by Hilldale, Inc., a business corporation whose stock was owned by non-profit University of Wisconsin Foundation, Hilldale paying rental for lands which had been acquired by a non-profit corporation (organized by friends of University) as a gift from the Regents. The purchase price of $6,000 per acre, which was deemed by the Court a fair price, was paid by the non-profit corporation through funds donated to it by Regents from their anonymous gift funds.)

Facts: University of Wisconsin Board of Regents sold at $6,000 per acre, 33.83 acres of its Hill Farms agricultural land in vicinity of city of Madison, to Kelab, Inc., a non-stock, non-profit corporation organized by friends of University. Regents made gift of purchase price to Kelab out of anonymous gift fund, over which Regents had unrestricted control. Under non-amendable provisions of Kelab's articles, its net income was to go to University, as well as its assets on dissolution. Kelab in turn leased the land, for thirty to fifty years to Hilldale, Inc., a business corporation formed to develop a shopping center there, all of its stock being owned by University of Wisconsin Foundation, a non-stock, non-profit corporation formed to aid University. All dividends received by Foundation on Hilldale stock, as well as rentals received by Kelab for land, would be turned over to Regents. On dissolution of Hilldale, all its assets, as well as the land, would revert to Regents.

Taxpayer's action in Circuit Court to set aside Regents' sale of the lands.

Aspects of decision: Supreme Court affirms sustaining of demurrer and granting of summary judgment in defendants' favor.

"This court has repeatedly held that nonstock, nonprofit corporations organized by friends of the university for its benefit, could do things which neither the state nor the university could do directly, that such corporation is not an arm or agency of the state and does not engage the state in work of internal improvement or create a state debt." Though affidavits on value of lands involved were conflicting, they showed that $6,000 per acre sales price "was comparable with that received for other tracts out of the Hill Farms and much higher than for some tracts." In addition to initial cash price for land, consideration must be given to probability of great future profits, shown in affidavits of defendants' experts.

(Dissent by Fairchild, J.: "Assuming the correctness of the Regents' conclusion that because of the special character of their possession of the 'anonymous' funds, such funds, unlike the state land, could be dedicated to make possible the construction of a shopping center, it has not been established that the amount of money collected from Kelab is equal to the value of the land . . . .

Assuming as we must [in this request for summary judgment] that if that issue were tried, plaintiff might prevail," then would follow that state property, to extent of difference in value, had been dedicated to creation of shopping center, and internal improvement ban been violated. "It has never been decided that state property may be conveyed to one of these friendly entities at less than a fair price so that it can build a commercial establishment.")

RELEVANT CONSTITUTIONAL ARTICLES AND TEXT OF THE WDA LAW

Below are the articles of the Wisconsin Constitution to which specific reference is made in the text and Appendix A, and the text of the WDA law. The portions of the constitution are taken from the *Wisconsin Blue Book, 1962;* provisions of the WDA law are from *Laws,* 1937, c. 334.

Wisconsin Constitution

Article I, section 1: All men are born equally free and independent, and have certain inherent rights; among these are life, liberty and the pursuit of happiness; to secure these rights, governments are instituted among men, deriving their just powers from the consent of the governed.

Article I, section 13: The property of no person shall be taken for public use without just compensation therefor.

Article IV, section 4: The members of the assembly shall be chosen biennially, by single districts, on the Tuesday succeeding the first Monday of November, by the qualified electors of the several districts, such districts to be bounded by county, precinct, town or ward lines, to consist of contiguous territory and be in as compact form as practicable.

Article IV, section 18: No private or local bill which may be passed by the legislature shall embrace more than one subject, and that shall be expressed in the title.

Article IV, section 23: The legislature shall establish but one system of town and county government, which shall be as nearly uniform as practicable.

Article IV, section 26: The legislature shall never grant any extra compensation to any public officer, agent, servant or contractor, after the services shall have been rendered or the contract entered into; nor shall the compensation of any public officer be increased or diminished during his term of office. . . .

Article IV, section 28: Members of the legislature, and all officers, executive and judicial, except such inferior officers as may be by law exempted, shall before they enter upon the duties of the respective offices, take and subscribe an oath or affirmation to support the constitution of the United States and the constitution of the state of Wisconsin, and faithfully to discharge the duties of their respective offices to the best of their ability.

Article IV, section 31: The legislature is prohibited from enacting any special or private laws in the following cases. . . . 7th. For granting corporate powers or privileges, except to cities. . . .

Article VI, section 2: The secretary of state shall keep a fair record of the official acts of the legislature and executive department of the state, and shall, when required, lay the same and all matters relative thereto before either branch of the legislature. He shall perform such other duties as shall be assigned him by law. . . .

Article VIII, section 3: The credit of the state shall never be given, or loaned, in aid of any individual, association or corporation.

Article VIII, section 4: The state shall never contract any public debt except in cases and manner herein provided.

Article VIII, section 5: The legislature shall provide for an annual tax sufficient to defray the estimated expenses of the state for each year, and whenever the expenses of any year shall exceed the income, the legislature shall provide for levying a tax for the ensuing year, sufficient, with other sources of income, to pay the deficiency as well as the estimated expenses of such ensuing year.

Article VIII, section 6: For the purpose of defraying extraordinary expenditures the state may contract public debts (but such debts shall never in the aggregate exceed one hundred thousand dollars). . . .

Article VIII, section 7: The legislature may also borrow money to repel invasion, suppress insurrection, or defend the state in time of war; but the money thus raised shall be applied exclusively to the object for which the loan was authorized, or to the repayment of the debt thereby created.

Article VIII, section 10: The state shall never contract any debt for works of internal improvement, or be a party in carrying on such works; but whenever grants of land or other property shall have been made to the state, especially dedicated by the grant to particular works of internal improvement, the state may carry on such particular works and shall devote thereto the avails of such grants, and may pledge or appropriate the revenue derived from such works in aid of their completion. [1908—Provided, that the state may appropriate money in the treasury or to be thereafter raised by taxation for the construction or improvement of public highways] [1945—or the development, improvement and construction of airports or other aeronautical projects] [1949—or the acquisition, improvement or construction of veterans' housing] [1960—or the improvement of port facilities.] [1924—Provided, that the state may appropriate moneys for the purpose of acquiring, preserving and developing the forests of the state; but there shall not be appropriated under the authority of this section in any one year an amount to exceed two-tenths of one mill of the taxable property of the state as determined by the last preceding state assessment.]

Article IX, section 3: The people of the state, in their right of sovereignty, are declared to possess the ultimate property, in and to all lands within the jurisdiction of the state; and all lands the title to which shall fail from a defect of heirs shall revert or escheat to the people.

Article X, section 1: The supervision of public instruction shall be vested in a state superintendent and such other officers as the legislature shall direct; and their qualifications, powers, duties and compensation shall be prescribed by law. . . .

Article XI, section 1: Corporations without banking powers or privileges may be formed under general laws, but shall not be created by special act, except for municipal purposes, and in cases where, in the judgment of the legislature, the objects of the corporation cannot be attained under general laws. All general laws or special acts enacted under the provisions of this section may be altered or repealed by the legislature at any time after their passage.

Article XI, section 2: No municipal corporation shall take private property for public use, against the consent of the owner, without the necessity thereof being first established by the verdict of a jury.

Article XI, section 3: Cities and villages organized pursuant to state law are hereby empowered, to determine their local affairs and government, subject only to this constitution and to such enactments of the legislature of state-wide concern as shall with uniformity affect every city or every village. The method of such determination shall be prescribed by the legislature. . . . [Note: miscellaneous earlier provisions of article XI, section 3 are referred to in summary form in various App. A case-digests].

Article XI, section 3a: The state or any of its [1956—counties,] cities, [1956—towns or villages,] may acquire by gift, [1956—dedication,] purchase, or condemnation lands for establishing, laying out, widening, enlarging, extending, and maintaining memorial grounds, streets, [1956

—highways,] squares, parkways, boulevards, parks, playgrounds, sites for public buildings, and reservations in and about and along and leading to any or all of the same; and after the establishment, layout, and completion of such improvements, may convey any such real estate, so as to protect such public works and improvements, and their environs, and to preserve the view, appearance, light, air, and usefulness of such public works. . . .

Article XIII, section 3: No member of congress, nor any person holding any office of profit or trust under the United States (postmasters excepted) or under any foreign power; no person convicted of any infamous crime in any court within the United States; and no person being a defaulter to the United States or to this state, or to any county or town therein, or to any state or territory within the United States, shall be eligible for office of trust, profit or honor in this state.

Wisconsin Development Authority Law

Section 1. A new chapter is added to the statutes to read:

Chapter 199
Wisconsin Development Authority

199.01 DESIGNATION OF INSTRUMENTALITY. Wisconsin development authority, a nonstock, nonprofit corporation now in existence, is hereby designated and selected as an instrumentality for the execution of certain duties and functions provided in section 199.03; provided, that such designation and the authority conferred upon said corporation by this chapter shall terminate forthwith if the articles of organization of said corporation shall at any time be amended so as to provide profits for its members, directors or officers in any form, directly or indirectly, or so as to change the mode or manner of distribution of property upon dissolution; provided, also, that such designation and the authority conferred upon said corporation by this chapter shall terminate forthwith if the articles of organization of said corporation shall at any time authorize the corporation to engage in any activities and pursuant thereto said corporation actually does engage in any activities except those provided by section 199.03 and except also those which are part of or in connection with the acquisition, ownership, construction, operation or management of any plant, equipment or facilities, or any part thereof, for the production, transmission, distribution or furnishing of light, heat, water or power, the transmission of telephone messages, or the rendering of street or interurban railway or bus services, and the furnishing of technical, supervisory or management services therefor. The acceptance by Wisconsin development authority of any funds appropriated to it by section 20.514 shall be conclusively deemed to be its complete acceptance of the provisions of this chapter.

199.02 USE OF STATE FUNDS. Wisconsin development authority shall not use or expend any of the funds appropriated to it by the state for any activities or functions which would be repugnant to the constitution of the state if carried on by the state, but nothing in this chapter shall be construed to prevent said corporation from using or expending funds which it may derive from other sources than the state to works of internal improvement or such other lawful purposes as it may deem proper. The state shall never be liable or responsible for any debt or obligation of Wisconsin development authority.

199.03 DUTIES AND FUNCTIONS OF WISCONSIN DEVELOPMENT AUTHORITY. Subject to the provisions of section 199.02 Wisconsin development authority shall use and expend the funds appropriated to it by section 20.514 solely for the execution of the following duties and functions:

(1) To promote or encourage the organization or creation of municipal power districts in the state under chapter 198;

(2) To promote or encourage the organization or creation of cooperative associations and nonprofit corporations to engage in the production, transmission, distribution or furnishing of light, heat, water or power, or the rendering of street or interurban railway or bus services;

(3) To promote or encourage the acquisition, ownership, construction, operation or management of any plant, equipment or facilities, or any part thereof, for the production, transmission, distribution or furnishing of light, heat, water or power, or the rendering of street or interurban railway or bus services, by any cooperative association or nonprofit corporation, or any group or combination of cooperative associations or nonprofit corporations;

(4) To promote or encourage the acquisition, ownership, construction, operation or management of any plant, equipment or facilities, or any part thereof, for the production, transmission, distribution or furnishing of light, heat, water or power, or the rendering of street or interurban railway or bus services, by any of the cities, villages, towns, municipalities, municipal power districts, or other political or governmental units of the state, or any group or combination thereof;

(5) To survey the resources and facilities, existing and potentially available, for the production, transmission, distribution and furnishing of light, heat, water and power in the state; to make studies and surveys for the economical development, use and conservation of such resources and facilities as will best provide an abundant and cheap

supply of these essential services for industrial, agricultural, commercial, governmental, transportation and domestic purposes; and to make studies and surveys for the coordination of water power and fuel power developments with the regulation of rivers by storage or otherwise for water supply, navigation, flood control, soil conservation, public health, recreational and other uses;

(6) To collect and disseminate information and engage in research, planning and educational activities necessary or useful for the execution of its duties and functions under this section;

(7) To cooperate with the federal government and its agencies in the execution of its duties and functions under this section.

199.04 INFORMATION, ASSISTANCE, ADVICE AVAILABLE TO WISCONSIN DEVELOPMENT AUTHORITY. In the performance of its duties and functions under section 199.03 Wisconsin development authority shall have access to all available information collected by any department of the state and may call upon the public service commission to obtain further information. The public service commission is hereby authorized to gather such information under section 196.02. The governor may direct that assistance and advice be given said corporation in the performance of its duties and functions under section 199.03 by any officer, agent or employe of any department of the state.

199.05 ACCOUNTS AND RECORDS. The accounts and records of Wisconsin development authority shall be so kept as to distinguish clearly between the uses made of funds appropriated by the state and the uses made of funds derived from other sources, and all disbursements of funds appropriated by the state shall be audited by the secretary of state in the manner provided by law.

199.06 ANNUAL REPORT. Wisconsin development authority shall prepare and submit to the governor at the end of each fiscal year a report of its activities during that year performed with funds appropriated by the state.

199.07 SEVERABILITY OF PROVISIONS. If any provision, sentence, clause or word of this chapter or the application thereof to any person or circumstance shall be held invalid, the remainder of this chapter and the application of such provision, sentence, clause or word to other persons or circumstances shall not be affected thereby.

Section 2. A new section is added to the statutes to read: 20.514 WISCONSIN DEVELOPMENT AUTHORITY. There is appropriated from the general fund to Wisconsin development authority, a Wisconsin corporation, on the effective date of this section ten thousand dollars and annually thereafter, beginning July 1, 1937, sixty thousand dollars for the execution of its duties and functions under section 199.03.

Section 3. This act shall take effect upon passage and publication.

Approved July 1, 1937.

NOTES AND INDEX

KEY TO

ABBREVIATED REFERENCES

IN THE NOTES

A	Assembly bill
AG	Opinions of the Wisconsin Attorney General
AJ	Assembly Journal
App. A	Appendix A to this volume, containing digests of numbered cases. The number following "App. A" is the case number in the Appendix; page references are to original publication of case, not to this volume.
Cardozo	Benjamin N. Cardozo, *Nature of the Judicial Process* (New Haven, 1921); *Growth of the Law* (New Haven, 1924).
Carley	David Carley, "Legal and Extra-legal Powers of Wisconsin Governors in Legislative Relations," 1962 *Wisconsin Law Review* 3–64; 280–341.
CB	*Cases and Briefs*, Wisconsin Supreme Court, August Term, 1937, State ex rel WDA v Damman.
CDT	Chicago Daily Tribune
Childs	Marquis Childs, *The Farmer Takes A Hand* (New York, 1952).
Clemens	Eli W. Clemens, *Public Utility Regulation in Wisconsin Since Reorganization of the Commission in 1931* (Ph.D. thesis, Univ. of Wis., 1940).
Const.	Wisconsin Constitution

Crow   William L. Crow, "Legislative Control of Public Utilities In Wisconsin," 18 *Marquette Law Review* 80 (1934)

CT   *Capital Times* (Madison, Wis.)

Frank   Jerome Frank, *Law and the Modern Mind* (New York, 1930); *Courts On Trial* (Princeton, 1949).

HJ   House Journal

ILC [M]   Majority Report of Interim Legislative Committee on Water and Electric Power, SJ 1950–1977 (1929).

ILC [UO]   Report of Interim Legislative Committee on Water and Electric Power [Unanimous Observations], SJ 2006–2042 (1929).

JH   Joint Hearings Before Committee on Finance and Assembly Committee on State Affairs On Bills 608A and 266S. Creating WDA (Commonly Known As the Little TVA), April 22, 1937 (Mimeo., Legislative Reference Library).

JR   Joint Resolution

Laws   *General Laws* (session laws)

Laws (P. & L.)   *Private and Local Laws* (session laws)

Llewellyn   Karl N. Llewellyn, *The Bramble Bush* (1930; Oceana ed., N.Y., 1951); *The Common Law Tradition* (Boston, 1960).

MB   WDA Corporate Minute Book

MJ   *Milwaukee Journal*

ML   *Milwaukee Leader*

MS   *Milwaukee Sentinel*

Muller   Frederick W. Muller, *Public Rural Electrification* (Washington, 1944).

Patterson   Edwin W. Patterson, Jurisprudence (Brooklyn, 1953).

PSCR   Public Service Commission of Wisconsin, *Reports*

REC   Rural Electrification Coordination

RGH   WDA, Report to Governor Heil, June 27, 1939 (typewritten).

Richardson   Lemont Kingsford Richardson, *Wisconsin REA: The Struggle to Extend Electricity to Rural Wisconsin, 1935–1955* (Madison, 1961, University of Wisconsin Experiment Station, College of Agriculture).

RREC   A Report of Rural Electrification Coordination, Oct. 1935 to Jan. 15, 1938, by John A. Becker, Director.

RS	Wisconsin Revised Statutes
S	Senate bill
SJ	Senate Journal
SL	U.S. Statutes At Large
SP	*Sheboygan Press* (Sheboygan, Wisconsin)
SS	Special session
Stats.	Wisconsin Statutes
WBB	*Wisconsin Blue Book*
WGPP	WDA, *Wisconsin Gets A Power Program* (1938 pamphlet).
WSJ	*Wisconsin State Journal* (Madison)

NOTES

In consulting these Notes, the reader should refer to the preceding Key to Abbreviated References in the Notes.

The text paragraphs usually contain not more than one or two note numbers, though a greater number of ideas in the paragraph are being footnoted. To help correlate the material in each note with the material in the text, a system of slashes and key words has been employed in the notes. The slashes correspond with the separate ideas being footnoted, and often correspond with separate sentences in the text. Where the Key lists more than one work by an author, the note refers to the author's last name and the year of publication of the cited work.

Page references to cases in Appendix A refer to the original publication of the cases, not to this volume.

Chapter I

1. *First authorization: Laws* 1895, c. 294. / *Davidson:* AJ 44 (1907). / Clemens 1. This pioneering honor was stated as being shared with New York, which enacted its law in the same year. / *Legislation: Laws* 1907. c. 499, Sec. 1797m–74, Sec. 1797m–76, and Secs. 1797m–78 through 1797m–86. / Crow 87.

2. *Laws* 1915, c. 380, Sec. 1596–9m. See WBB 79–85 (1929).

3. JR 5A. / The unanimous recommendations were for "a survey to determine advisability of state constructing and operating storage reservoirs"; for "an investigation by the Railroad Commission of Wisconsin with respect to reasonableness of spread of rates to different classes of consumers"; for "activity looking toward more uniform rate structure, calling on Railroad Commission of Wisconsin and utilities to cooperate by appointment of committee if necessary," and for "legislation enabling the Railroad Commission of Wisconsin to consider two or more municipalities in a uniform rate-making district." ILC [UO] 2041–42. / On its first recommendation the Majority Report stated: "We recommend the adoption of a Joint Resolution to create Section II of Article VIII of the Constitution to enable the state to take over and recapture its water powers and to generate, buy, distribute and sell electric power. This recommendation is made to enable the state to take advantage of the recapture provision in our present water law. This was enacted by the legislature of 1915, was

signed by Governor Philipp and was not in any sense a radical or factional measure. It has, moreover, stood the test of the courts, having been sustained as constitutional by the United States Supreme Court in the case of Fox River Paper Co. v. Railroad Commission of Wisconsin, 274 U.S. 631 (1927)." ILC [M] 1971.

4. ILC [M] 1971–72; 1963–64; 1977.

5. *1929 recommendations:* JR 32A and JR 38S; 593A and 361S. / *Right to compete:* 596A; see also 13S and 359S. / *Municipal indebtedness:* JR 74. This resolution covered indebtedness in extending, improving, and operating of utilities as well as in acquiring and constructing them. A 1919 provision (*Laws,* c. 595) had already permitted acquisition, or other development of utilities through use of revenue bonds (to be paid from the revenue of the utility itself rather than municipal funds in general); and the obligations thus incurred had been held by the Wisconsin Supreme Court to be not subject to the constitutional limitation on municipal indebtedness. But the court had also declared that indebtedness for utility improvements and extensions after the acquisition or construction were subject to the constitutional limitation. State ex rel Morgan v. Portage, 174 Wis. 588 (1921). This difficulty was in addition to the fact that revenue bonds could not be so readily and favorably sold as municipal bonds not so restricted. The public power situation as of 1929 and the hopeful prospects for the 1931 legislature are described by Assemblyman Reis in "Wisconsin's Power Fight," 129 *Nation* 298 (1929).

6. *Platform:* WBB 447–48 (1931). / *Message:* SJ 31–32 (1931).

7. JR 71 (*Laws* 1931, 948); *Laws* 1931–33, 1297–98.

8. SJ 32 (1931); *Laws* 1931, c. 50.

9. *Governor's request:* SJ 32 (1931). / *Resolutions:* JR 31 (*Laws* 1931, 923); JR 111 (*Laws* 1931–33, 1281); in 1935, JR 166A passed the Assembly, but it and JR 100S were unsuccessful in the Senate. / *Corporation: Laws* 1931, c. 314. The corporation, which was also referred to in the law as a "state department," was to be run by five Governor-appointed directors, and was to help municipalities in working out plans for power districts; help municipalities, power districts, and state departments with information and advice concerning purchase, construction, improvement, and operation of any utility facilities; represent the state's interest before the Federal Power Commission and Interstate Commerce Commission; contract with utilities, subject to certain limitations; and make a survey of the state's utility resources and establish a state-wide integrated plan for their most efficient development—this plan to be subject to Public Service Commission approval and possible amendment.

10. *Laws* 1939, c. 236. See Reis, "Power Legislation in the State of Wisconsin," in 16 *Minnesota Municipalities,* September 1931, p. 347, quoted in Crow, 100. Reis was the Assemblyman in the 1929 legislature who was active in support of public-power bills, was secretary of the Interim Legislative Committee on Water and Electric Power, and a signer of that Committee's majority report already referred to. / *Laws* 1939, c. 236. For at least two years the State Utilities Corporation did not function at all. WBB 382 (1933). It spent $331.19 in the fiscal year 1933–34. WBB 370 (1935).

11. *1931 bills:* 10A; 10S. / *1933 bills:* 559A, 68S, 110S; *1935 bills:* 153A, 138S; *1937 bills:* 2A; see also 17S. Some light is thrown on the problem by newspaper comment. An Open Letter to Editor Evjue of the Madison *Capital Times* from the Wisconsin Dairymen's News criticized him for having attacked three Pro-

gressive Senators (Panzer, McDermid, Kannenberg) for voting against the "municipal competition bills" in the Senate. The letter stated that these bills were not Progressive-sponsored but rather sponsored by the Wisconsin League of Municipalities; that municipal ownership is not always a logical plan for a utility; and that municipal utilities have been reluctant to serve farmers outside the area of the municipality, for tax reasons. CT April 13, 1937.

12. In 1934 the Progressive wing of the Republican party presented itself successfully to the voters as an independent party. The platform stressed that "our economic system has failed" and that drastic measures were necessary. As for public utilities, they "should be publicly owned. Especially is this necessary in the case of electricity, where private ownership has robbed the investor and deprived the people of the full use of electricity on the farm and in the home." WBB 476–78 (1935). In the 1936 platform the same note was sounded, as well as support for public corporations: "Progressives favor the establishment of public corporations similar to the TVA to perform such functions of government as the welfare of the people makes necessary. These corporations shall pay taxes as private corporations.... Especially are these corporations necessary to furnish electric power to industry, home and farm.... Reactionary Republicans and reactionary Democrats in the legislature have voted to prohibit public ownership of power in Wisconsin. For example, a Wisconsin TVA is now impossible.... Progressives favor granting municipalities the right to compete with privately owned plants...." WBB 274, 278–79 (1937).

13. JH 9-10.

14. At the hearings on the bill, it was stated by John Becker, who was in charge of the state agency known as Rural Electrification Coordination, that the "municipal power district law has been on the statute books since 1931; and, as yet, in spite of the fact that in several localities the people of this state voted to organize municipal power districts ... not one of them has even started building its lines. The first one, in Polk and Burnett counties, is still in the courts of Wisconsin. Several others ... have not even gotten that far. Also, we have an agency on the law books of the state [evidently the State Utilities Corporation] but that agency has not been active; it failed to give direction and assistance to interested parties." JH 24. That the Polk-Burnett district referred to was invalidated by the Supreme Court in June 1937, and that the power-district law was full of legal problems requiring court interpretation, see Clam River Electric Co. v. Pub. Serv. Comm., 225 Wis. 198 (1937).

15. On December 31, 1919, the total number of municipally owned electric utilities in Wisconsin reached a high of 105; during 1919–1930, there was a decrease to 85; and no increases had occurred by 1937. In 1935 these 85 plants, located mainly in smaller cities and villages, were serving 70,200 or 10.6 per cent of the state's electric customers, whereas the 8 largest private companies were serving 85 per cent. Wisconsin Public Service Commission, *Extent and Results of Municipal Ownership of Electrical Utilities in Wisconsin* 1, 3 (1937). The cited study also revealed that 25 of the existing municipal utilities were originally purchased from private utilities, and 60 were started as municipal utilities; that municipal rates were lower than private rates; that while most municipalities used to generate their whole supply, the trend of the preceding 15 years had been the other way, so that in 1936, 22 per cent of them were generating their whole supply, 10 per cent were generating and purchasing, and 68 per cent were purchasing their whole supply.

16. Emergency Relief Appropriation Act of 1935, 49 SL 115. For an in-

sider's account of other steps along the way, see Morris L. Cooke, "The Early Days of the Rural Electrification Idea 1914–1936," in 42 *American Political Science Review* 431 (1948). See also Childs 35–69. The original order, Exec. Order 7037, is reprinted in Geffs and Hepburn, "Public Authorities and Co-operatives to Promote the Use of Electricity," 25 *Georgetown Law Journal* 827–28 (1937). The 1936 law is found at 49 SL 1363.

17. Richardson 42; Speech by Governor La Follette on Oct. 13, 1938 at Barron, Wis., in La Follette papers, State Historical Society of Wisconsin.

18. Richardson 42–46.

19. Richardson 48–51; 117–18; 123–36; 141–44; Clemens 286.

20. RREC 1, 3.

21. Muller 24.

22. *Stats.*, c. 185; Secs. 93.07(17), 94.15; Sec. 40.22(11)(a) starting 1936, and 40.46(8) since 1953.

23. Richardson 43–44, 63–80; Clemens 310; Childs 62–63, 74–77.

24. Opinion accompanying modification of Order 2-U-965, 13 PSCR 541–42 (1936).

25. Opinion accompanying Order 2-U-965, 11 PSCR 596, 601 (1936); Richardson 65. / Modification of Order 2-U-965, 13 PSCR 539 (1936).

26. 13 PSCR 554 (1936); 132, 135–36.

27. *Laws* 1937, c. 17 (Rush Act, sponsored by Progressive Senator Rush). Other 1937 enactments included provisions facilitating the filing of right-of-way easements (c. 44; c. 405) and the executions of mortgages by the cooperative (c. 143), and miscellaneous enactments, either beneficial or clarifying, dealing with approvals of franchises or permits, right to get through cities and villages, etc., including a specific declaration that no cooperative organized under the cooperative corporation law to furnish heat, light, power, or water to its members only was a public utility under chaps. 196 and 197 regulating public utilities (c. 365). / Richardson 77–80.

28. Testimony of Thomas M. Duncan, JH 24; see also 16.

29. Wisconsin Department of Agriculture (REC Division), *A Comparison of Rural Electric Rates in Wisconsin* 30 (1941), shows the *increase* in number of *rural* electric customers, 1928–1940:

	Privates		Municipals	Co-ops
1928	6,349		93	——
1929	4,645		210	——
1930	5,606		362	——
1931	3,374		48	——
1932	345	(decrease)	75	——
1933	85		4	——
1934	1,726		224	——
1935	1,425		221	——
1936	5,829		243	——
1937	11,215		569	3,754 (first co-op energized June 1937)
1938	6,284		824	6,629
1939	3,200		100	6,150
1940	3,700		100	6,527

The same publication indicates (35–36) that at the end of 1940 the *total number* of rural electricity customers was 69,938 for private utilities; 5,382 for municipals; 23,219 for electric co-ops. Total miles of line were 21,816; 1,168; and 10,921 respectively. Total revenues from rural customers were $4,579,496; $268,693; and $1,034,645 respectively. For detailed status of the various co-op projects as of August 1936, see 13 PSCR 539, 544 (1936).

30. Carley 20–42; 280–308.

31. The organizers were Herbert W. Parisius, of Rice Lake; John A. Becker, of Hartford; Ferris M. White, of River Falls; John A. Anderson, of Barron; Harry H. Jack, of Hortonville; Kenneth W. Hones, of Colfax; Herbert L. Mount, of Milwaukee; Thomas F. Davlin, of Berlin; Charles B. Perry, of Wauwatosa; and Edward W. Morehouse, Glenn D. Roberts, and Edwin E. Witte, all of Madison. "Most of the incorporators," said the *Milwaukee Journal* of March 31, 1937, "are actively identified with the Progressive Party." The articles of incorporation are reprinted in the Wisconsin Supreme Court Record of the litigation. CB 163–175.

32. There were also provisions dealing with election and duties of corporate officers and directors, provisions governing admission and expulsion of members by majority vote and limiting membership to fifteen; and a requirement that amendments to the articles must be made at a special meeting by vote of four-fifths of the members. The non-profit character of the corporation was indicated by Article Third ("No dividend or pecuniary profits shall be declared or paid to the members thereof. No member shall be deemed to have any property interest in this corporation."), and Article Tenth (declaring that while corporate dissolution was generally to be in the manner provided by chap. 181 of the Statutes, any property remaining after payment of all obligations and expenses was to become the property of the state).

33. A minor deviation was that under the bill, the informational, educational, research, and planning functions mentioned in parenthetical clause (3), were to be only those necessary or useful for executing the duties and functions mentioned in the bill (rather than for executing all the corporate purposes).

34. The articles, as indicated in the text *supra* in parenthetical clause (7), contained a broader provision, for cooperation with federal, state, local governmental units, and non-governmental persons or groups.

35. ML March 29, 1937. So, too, Assemblyman Biemiller was reported as saying in a radio speech that state operation is a "reserve power which would become an integral part of the program only if scientific studies revealed the need of it in future years." CT April 7, 1937.

Chapter II

1. MJ April 11, 1937. The same news story observes: "The two committees that heard the bill . . . are manned by administration men. Sen. Walter Rush [P., 24th District] of the senate committee did his rush job well. His committee handed the senate bill right over to the finance committee. Chairman J. D. Millar [P., Dunn] of state affairs bungled the job. His committee voted for another hearing. Then the chairman tried to right the error by rounding up his committeemen in the assembly lobby and persuading them to sign a new report to send the assembly bill to the finance committee. The maneuvering created a big stir. The assembly slapped its state affairs committee for its unusual method of disposing of an important bill." See also CT April 9, 1937.

2. CT April 9, 1937, and April 16, 1937; MJ April 9, 1937.

3. J. D. Semrad, Boscobel, member of Joint Farmers' Legislative Committee; J. J. Handley, Milwaukee, Secretary of Wisconsin State Federation of Labor; Adam Poltl, mayor of Hartford; Charles Madsen, Luck, of the Inter-County Municipal Power District; Harry Jack, Hortonville, President of Wisconsin Cooperative Milk Pool. CT April 9, 1937.

4. Those reported as so arguing were: Roy Brecke, Milwaukee, Wisconsin Petroleum Association; A. J. Fiore, Madison fuel dealer; Jacob Uhrmann, Wisconsin Association of Retail Meat Dealers; W. E. Brown, Milwaukee, Allis-Chalmers Mfg. Co.; Richard Lehmann, Milwaukee; William Ryan, Madison, Wisconsin Power & Light Co.; Walter Sanders, manager of Plymouth municipal electric system; C. E. Kohlhepp, Milwaukee, Wisconsin Public Service Corp.; Glenn Rork, Eau Claire, Northern States Power Co. It was further reported that William Ryan, for Wisconsin Power & Light Co., argued the bill was making a "delegation of public authority to a private corporation"; that A. J. Fiore, Madison fuel dealer, argued generally against co-ops and government enterprise in business; and that C. E. Kohlhepp, Wisconsin Public Service Corporation, disputed the statement that Wisconsin power rates were not low enough to attract industry here. CT and MS April 9, 1937.

5. JH 3, 4, 6.

6. Concerning his reference to the federal corporations, completeness of the analogy may be questioned on the ground that these corporations were more closely tied to the government, by government stock ownership or government personnel among the directors, than was WDA.

7. JH 7, 10, 11. He noted that the State Historical Society had an existing appropriation of over $60,000; the State Horticultural Society, $6,000; the Potato Grower's Association, $2,000; the State Dairymen's Association, $6,000; Foreign-type Cheesemakers' Association, $1,000; Cheesemakers Association, $600; Central Wisconsin Cheesemakers, Buttermakers, and Dairymen's Advancement Association, $500; Livestock Breeders Association, $2,000; various county agricultural societies, over $125,000.

8. JH 11–15.

9. The reason, he said, for the articles' general clause allowing the exercise of all powers conferred by law was to overcome unintended implications from the specification of particular powers. The specification was not intended to be "inconsistent with" WDA's use of general corporate powers (to sue and be sued, etc.) under Section 182.01 of the Statutes giving such powers "when no inconsistent provision is made by law or its articles of organization." He referred also to the use of the general clause in articles of federal government corporations. His conclusion, like Sinykin's, was that WDA was restricted to the utility field, and was prevented by Section 180.07 of the Statutes from substantially changing its purposes through amendment of the articles. JH 20–23.

10. JH 24–25. On the State Utilities Corporation, see Chap. I, note 9.

11. JH 26–27, 44–50.

12. *WDA in coal & oil business:* This fear was voiced by Ernest Miller, Sheboygan County Gasoline Retailers and Dealers Association; Sam Trainor, Marathon County Oil Co., Wausau; Al Mosher, Milwaukee Badger Oil Co., purporting to represent twenty-one small merchants in twenty-one Wisconsin cities; Robert A. Lee, Wisconsin Retailers Association, representing gasoline retailers; Charles J. Grabbe, Milwaukee Western Fuel Co., also representing

coal dock companies at Superior and Ashland. And it was an oil industry representative who made the introductory statement preceding the testimony of the opposition—Roy Brecke, Wisconsin Petroleum Association, described as comprising nearly four hundred independent oil jobbers. They generally did not come to grips with the legal argument of Sinykin and Roe. The only attempt was by Al Mosher, who pointed to the uncertainty of the idea of a "substantial" change in the articles of incorporation. JH 28, 32, 58. / *Government in business:* A. J. Fiore, Fiore Coal and Oil Co., Madison; A. E. Wallace, Fuel Merchants Association of Milwaukee and Milwaukee County; Louis Faber, Milwaukee retailers. JH 29, 34, 62.

13. JH 34–41. Dr. Miller, who said he represented twenty-three hundred taxpayers in Racine, declared that under the bill there would eventually be hundreds of thousands of new employees who would be harnessed into political activity; and that taxes were already taking away people's homes and leading to Communism. JH 41.

14. JH 51–62. Sibold's point on taxes was also made by W. H. Kuh, Marinette, who said that while he was on the Marinette Industrial Board trying to attract industry to Wisconsin, the difficulty he experienced was not with power rates but with the tax situation. He felt that industrialists would be further repelled from entering the state by the feeling that WDA was an entering wedge for the state's entry into private enterprise. JH 63.

15. CT April 23, 1937 (quotation). Other press summaries on the same day are in WSJ, MS, MJ, SP.

16. CT April 17, and May 4, 1937. The vote was 45–40, with fifteen members absent or not voting, and seven Progressives jumping party ranks to vote for the resolution.

17. 26 AG 170(1937). The opinion quoted the statement in the *Froehlich* case (App. A #30) that "internal improvement" includes "those things which ordinarily might, in human experience, be expected to be undertaken for profit or benefit to the property interests of private promoters, as distinguished from those other things which primarily and preponderantly merely facilitate the essential function of government." It referred also to the statement in the *Donald* case (App. A #33) that internal improvements include "not merely the construction or improvement of channels of trade or commerce, but any kind of public works, except those used by and for the state in performance of its governmental function, such as a state capitol, state university, penitentiaries, reformatories, asylum, quarantine buildings, and the like, for the purposes of education, the prevention of crime, charity, the preservation of public health, furnishing accommodations for the transaction of public business by state officers, and other like recognized functions of state government." The attorney general's opinion further noted such Wisconsin court holdings as that the improvement of the Fox River (App. A #67) and levees (App. A #68) were internal improvements; and the holdings of courts in other states with a similar constitutional restriction that the following were internal improvements: lighting plants, water works, gas works and the like; bridges; ditches; grain elevators; grist mills; river channel improvements, levees, wharves, irrigation, reservoirs, and canals; railroads, highways, ferries, street railways; oil refineries; petroleum pipelines; streets and sidewalks. / Regarding charter restrictions, he said WDA was "authorized to engage in 'works of internal improvement' within the public utility field . . . ." It is "limited to activities in

the public utility field by the articles of incorporation, which under sec. 180.07, subsec, (1), Stats., cannot be substantially changed . . . ." / Under the bill, "the corporation is prohibited from using state funds for any purpose that the state itself could not use them for. Inasmuch as the state by the constitution is prohibited from engaging in 'works of internal improvement,' . . . the corporation could not use any state funds for such purposes." However, the state could carry on educational or promotional activities in relation to such internal improvements (citing State v. Raub 106 Kan. 196 [1920]). He referred to the unchallenged Wisconsin practice of appropriating state money to private corporations for carrying on work in which the public has an interest, as in the case of the "State Historical Society, Wisconsin agricultural experimental association, Wisconsin horticultural society, Wisconsin potato growers' association, Wisconsin livestock breeders' association, Wisconsin cheesemakers' association, and county agricultural societies."

18. The Budlong [R., Marinette] amendment on property taxation was Am. 1A, rejected 59 to 38 on May 12. AJ 1501 (1937). Assemblymen Biemiller and Sigman [P., Manitowoc, 2nd.] were quoted as saying the property was not exempted from taxes, and no amendment was necessary. SP May 12, 1937. / The Daugs amendment restricting WDA functions was Sub. Am. 1A, rejected 91 to 4 on May 12. AJ 1503 (1937). / The "steam" quotation is from MS May 7, 1937. The amendment, proposed by Vernon Thomson (later to be Attorney General, Governor, and member of Congress) was Sub. Am. 2A, held not germane by vote of 53 to 43, sustaining the Speaker's ruling. AJ 1503. The amendment would also have cut down the appropriations to $1,000 on passage and $10,000 annually thereafter.

19. The Cavanaugh [D., Langlade] amendment, Sub. Am. 3A, declared that notwithstanding any provisions in the corporate articles, WDA's powers were those granted by the bill. And these powers were to cover light, heat, and power only, and only for purposes of rural electrification. Am. 1A to this (again by Cavanaugh) would have expanded the bill's prohibition against using state funds for activities the state itself couldn't constitutionally engage in, by similarly restricting the use of funds from federal or other agencies, and by covering activities violating the bill or the state's corporate laws; but it was rejected 53 to 38 on May 13. AJ 1522 (1937). Am. 2A [Halvorsen, P., Vernon] to this same substitute amendment was adopted, adding "water" to light, heat, and power and including the regulation of rivers in the studies of coordination of power resources; but then the substitute amendment as thus amended was rejected 52 to 43 on May 13. AJ 1522. / The Catlin [R., Outagamie, 1st.] amendment was Am. 5A, rejected 54 to 39 on May 13. AJ 1523. The bill's provision that the bill didn't prevent WDA's use of non-state funds for "works of internal improvement or such other lawful purposes as it may deem proper" would have been amended by inserting after "improvement" the words "within the public utility field." / On May 12, Assemblyman Theisen said the transcript had just been received by some members and that all of them, as well as the public, should have a chance to read it by means of publication in the official state paper. His motion to defer action to permit preparation of the necessary appropriation measure was defeated 63 to 32. SP May 12, 1937; AJ 1500.

20. In order: the Hoesly [P., Green] amendment was Am. 2A adopted 93 to 4 on May 12. AJ 1501 (1937). The Fuhrman [P., Shawano] amendment was Am. 3A adopted 67 to 30 on May 12. AJ 1502. (Assemblyman Biemiller was quoted

on the "interstate" point in SP May 12, 1937.) The Nehs [P., Clark] amendment was Am. 4A, adopted 92 to 4 on May 12. AJ 1502 (1937). / CT May 12, 1937 (Biemiller and Thomson).

21. AJ 1646 (1937). / The amendment as to state responsibility for WDA obligations was Am. 4S by Nelson [R., 11th District] adopted June 3 (no vote recorded). SJ 1252 (1937). The amendment to exclude telephone companies was Am. 2S, by Rowlands, adopted 20 to 11 on June 3. SJ 1251. And the amendment conditioning the powers granted by the bill upon WDA's confining itself to activities specified in the bill and existing articles was Am. 1S, by McDermid [P., 12th District] adopted 21 to 11 on June 3. SJ 1251. Am. 1S, to the latter amendment, by Callan [D., 9th District] which would have tightened this conditioning by recognizing only the activities specified in the bill, was rejected 17 to 15 on June 3. SJ 1250.

22. The first amendment, by Roethe, was Sub. Am. 1S, rejected 17 to 15 on June 3. SJ 1097 (1937). WDA would have been created as a state department as well as a corporation. The amendment contemplated funds "from other sources" too, apparently federal; and appropriated $5,000 currently and $20,000 annually thereafter. / Sub. Am. 2S by Sauld [D., 20th District] was rejected 17 to 15 on June 8. SJ 1294. It appropriated $1,000 currently and $30,000 annually thereafter. / The "request" amendment, by Clancy [D., 21st District] was Am. 1S, to the above Sub. Am. 2S, rejected 17 to 16 right before the latter was rejected. SJ 1294. A rather similar independent amendment offered by Clancy was Am. 6S, under which the promotion of the acquisition, construction, or operation was to be only on request from the cooperative, non-profit corporation or governmental unit. It was rejected 17 to 15 on June 8. SJ 1295. / Am. 7S by Coakley [R., 15th District] was rejected 19 to 13 on June 8. SJ 1295. / The election, etc., amendment, by Clancy, was Am. 5S, rejected 17 to 15 on June 8. SJ 1294. If WDA used state funds for election purposes or in connection with a referendum or election held in a city or village, it was to be subject to the provisions of the Corrupt Practices Act. / The news story, SP June 7, 1937, erroneously refers to the author as Sen. Roethe instead of Sen. Clancy. It was Am. 3S, rejected 17 to 15 on June 3. SJ 1251. Two related amendments should be noted here. Am. 8S, by Bolens [D., 20th District] was like Am. 3S, with the addition of an authorization for WDA's investigation of the rates of broadcasting stations; it was ruled not in order, on June 8, as having been rejected previously by the rejection of Am. 3S. SJ 1296. Am. 9S by Bolens, added to WDA's functions the investigation of "the rates and profits of all existing broadcasting stations so that the legislature shall have a suitable yardstick to measure the necessity of public ownership of broadcasting stations or regulation of charges imposed on the public." It was ruled not germane on June 2. SJ 1297.

23. The radio station amendment was Am. 3A by Tehan [D., Milwaukee, 4th.] rejected 50 to 40 on June 23, AJ 2184. It was like Sen. Clancy's Am. 3S. / Cavanaugh's Sub. Am. 2A was rejected 52 to 42 on June 23. AJ 2185. / Sub. Am. 3A by Krueger [D., Dodge, 2nd.] was rejected 56 to 40 on June 23. AJ 2186. It would have appropriated $10,000 currently, and $100,000 annually thereafter. / Am. 1A by Shimek [D., Kewaunee] (on polls) was rejected 52 to 39 on June 23. AJ 2184. / Sub. Am. 1A by Genzmer [D., Dodge, 1st.] was rejected 54 to 37 on June 23. AJ 2185. Powers conferred on WDA by the bill were to terminate unless its articles provided that membership in the corporation be subject to the governor's approval, and that the power to borrow and to issue

obligations not go beyond $100,000,000. Appropriations under the proposal were to be $10,000 currently and $500,000 annually thereafter. / Am. 2A by Shimek was rejected 51 to 37 on June 23. AJ 2183. From the original bill's provision that it did not prevent WDA's use of non-state funds for internal improvements "or such other lawful purposes as it may deem proper," the amendment would have eliminated the latter clause. / AJ 2245, 2282 (final votes).

24. WSJ June 17, 1937. The writer was Morris H. Rubin, later editor of *The Progressive* magazine.

25. The two opposition Republicans were Duel and Shearer. Six senators were paired. The ten recorded as absent or not voting were Bolens, Callan, Clancy, Coakley, Dempsey [D., 33rd District], Galasinski [D., 7th District], Morrissey [D., 19th District], Roethe, Saul, White [R., 10th District] (a group which included the most active opponents of the bill). SJ 1382.

26. SJ 1387, 1389. Newspapers took the view that Sen. Coakley had outsmarted himself in appealing the chair's ruling. "Had Coakley not appealed, when the bill was taken to court, judges might have ruled the presiding officer was correct in his ruling. However, since the Senate is the judge of its own actions and the Senate voted to uphold Rush's ruling, the courts can no longer decide that the ruling was invalid." CT June 17, 1937; to same effect, WSJ June 17, 1937. The Wisconsin Supreme Court was subsequently to deal with the problem by upholding the correctness of the original ruling. See note 14, Chapter III, for text.

27. WSJ June 17, 1937. The "arrest" had been on Sen. Kannenberg's successful motion that the chief clerk subpoena all senators absent without leave. SJ 1392.

28. WSJ June 17, 1937; CT June 17, 1937.

29. WSJ June 17, 1937. By one report, Sen. Rowlands "purposely left the chamber so that a call could be put on the Senate and the coalition bloc prevented from leaving the chamber a third time." CT June 17, 1937.

30. The Assembly's concurrence in the Senate bill was by 56 to 19; the Assembly bill had been passed 55 to 36; and the Senate passed its own bill by 16 to 14 (with one Progressive supporter of the bill paired, and another Progressive supporter absent). The Senate had 16 Progressives as against 9 Democrats and 8 Republicans. The Assembly had 48 Progressives as against 31 Democrats and 21 Republicans. WBB 428-34 (1937). The Progressives were solidly for the bill in both houses, and it is clear that several Democrats and Republicans supported the bill in the Assembly, while only two supported it in the Senate.

31. CT May 9, 27, 1937. / SP June 3, 1937.

32. CT June 10, 1937.

33. MS April 14, 1937. / SP May 12, 1937.

34. CDT May 14, 1937; MJ May 1, 1937; SP June 3, 1937.

35. WSJ May 15, 1937; SP May 20, 1937; SP June 7, 1937.

36. SP May 20, 1937; CT June 18, 1937. Similar statements on unconstitutionality were made by Assemblyman Fitzsimons [D., Fond du Lac, 1st.] and by Senator White. SP May 12 and June 17, 1937.

Chapter III

1. MJ July 8, 1937. / CT July 16, 1937.

2. WDA employed: (1) V. M. Murray for three days (August 2–4) on the task of surveying the state's resources and facilities for production, transmission,

distribution, and furnishing of light, heat, power, and water in the state; (2) Norris Maloney for two days (August 3–4) on the task of promoting and encouraging the creation of a cooperative association in Crawford County, to engage in furnishing light, heat, power, and water, and dissemination of information relating thereto; (3) H. I. Tuttle, Inc., for mimeographing five-hundred and eight copies of a form letter addressed to executive officers of municipalities, informing them of the services WDA stood ready to perform, and of the availability of certain Public Service Commission chart comparisons of private and municipal rates. / Judge Reis issued the alternative writs, and after a hearing denied motions to quash the writs and ordered issuance of peremptory writs on September 14. The facts in this note and the text paragraph appear in the printed record of the appellate litigation. CB 2–157.

3. "The constitutional convention of 1847 had before it (prior to amendment) a mandatory provision that the state 'shall' encourage works of internal improvement. In a process of sundry amendments, this was omitted and the present language substituted that the state shall *not be a party*. No inference can be drawn from this that the state *may* not encourage. No inference can be drawn that encouraging means being a party. Indeed, the fact that prior drafts of the section provided *both* that the state *shall* encourage and shall *not* be a party proves logically that, in the minds of the draftsmen, these two things were the opposite of each other." CB 52. (Emphasis in original.)

4. The position on the *Van Dyke* case (App. A #72) seems based on a questionable reading of it. The court there said (at 544): "It is true that some of the moneys which were paid out by the industrial commission pursuant to sec. 2 (2) . . . which permitted reimbursement to the county or city of twenty-five per cent of the labor cost of public works undertaken to provide for the unemployed, went into such public works, but the *primary purpose* of the state was not to become a party to carrying on works of internal improvement, but to *reimburse the counties and cities* which had made work simply *for the purpose of providing employment* to the unemployed." (Emphasis supplied.) Was the court upholding state financial support for works of internal improvement "because someone else made the work" as Judge Reis suggests, or because the financial aid was given with an eye primarily towards unemployment relief and relief of local governments in connection therewith?

5. The other authority referred to is the *Jensen* case (App. A #66). The court there said that no violation of the constitutional restriction had occurred where the state did not stand the expense of the state roads, but had put the cost of laying them out on the counties, and the cost of constructing them on the towns.

6. CB 56. For the "first blush" point, he referred to language in prior cases including the *Brodhead* case (App. A #20).

7. CB 57.

8. The soldiers' bonus case is Johnson (App. A #37); the New Richmond case is App. A #29.

9. Cited were the Johnson case (App. A #37) (state "credit") and the Loomis case (App. A #70) (special act charters).

10. CB 64.

11. *Reis's background:* It will be recalled that as an assemblyman, he sponsored the 1927 resolution for investigation of the power problem and signed the majority report. / *Past Association:* "Defendant points to two defeated

constitutional amendments in the 1931 and 1933 legislatures which would have permitted the state to enter the electric power business. (We might add Jt. Res. 81,A in the 1927 session and Jt. Res. 32,A in the 1929 session, the original 'water power' resolutions, with which we are not wholly unfamiliar.") CB 53–54. / *Briefs:* "Exactly 250 typewritten pages of briefs were submitted, mostly legal size. We . . . desire to thank counsel of all litigants for a clear-thinking and thorough presentation (and at all times on a high plane) which has enabled us to sift the issues and condense the result." CB 51.

12. *Favorable:* CT Sept. 12, 1937. It had a front-page, bold-face headlined story, together with full reprint of the opinion. There was a similarly featured story the same day in WSJ. / *Unfavorable:* Editorial, MJ Sept. 13, 1937.

13. One *amicus curiae* brief arguing this issue was submitted by William Ryan, in behalf of himself; the other was by R. M. Rieser, J. W. Rector, and Roy G. Tulane (with Olin and Butler, "of counsel"), in behalf of Wisconsin Municipal Utilities Association, Wisconsin Petroleum Association, Fuel Merchants Association, Frank H. Meyers, Frank Zelhoefer, and Richard F. Lehmann (President of United Taxpayers Cooperative Association of Wisconsin). / For the defendant-appellant, secretary of state, special counsel was Harold E. Stafford, Chippewa Falls. John Ernest Roe, as special counsel, and attorney for WDA, signed respondents' brief, together with Attorney General Orland S. Loomis, Norris E. Maloney as attorney for intervening relators (Murray, Maloney, H. I. Tuttle, Inc.), and Charles B. Perry, "of counsel."

14. The attempted passage on June 16 without the necessary quorum "was a nullity. . . . Therefore the status of the bill in the senate continued as it was before the votes were taken on June 16, 1937, until that house subsequently acted effectively by voting the passage of the bill when the required quorum was in attendance. By that passage and the subsequent valid action by the assembly and the governor, ch. 334, Laws of 1937 was fully enacted." App. A #46, at 155.

15. App. A #46 at 163–65.

16. App. A #46 at 161–62. The two named cases are App. A #28 and #41.

17. For approving comment on the court decision see WSJ, Editorial Jan. 12, and Jan. 13, 1938; for disapproval: CT, Editorials Jan. 12, and Jan. 17, ML Jan. 14, 1938. For general press coverage on Jan. 11, see CT, WSJ and SP. / *First quotation:* CT Jan. 12, 1938. / *Second quotation:* SP Jan. 17, 1938.

18. SP Jan. 11, 1938. / "Some of those who have studied the opinion do not agree with Governor La Follette that it goes as far as he intimated to capitol newspapermen. There is general agreement that it knocks out the Wisconsin Agricultural Authority which was authorized to be created along lines similar to WDA. . . . But whether the WDA decision will endanger other funds is extremely problematical." The State Historical Society is distinguishable because it is "generally regarded as an unofficial arm of the state government," public officials being *ex officio* members of the board. And agricultural and other societies depend only slightly on state aid. "In many circles the belief is that this 'scare' was put out only as a 'smoke-screen' on behalf of the progressives to win support for their power program. Progressives regarded the decision as a body blow to them, while members of other political parties hailed it as a protection to the people . . . ." SP Jan. 17, 1938. / It was observed that Governor La Follette had not appointed any directors of the state utility corporation, that Governor Schmedeman did in 1933, and that while the "board is not

Progressive ... Gov. La Follette could make two appointments now, and he could get a majority next year. Its appropriation is only $1,000 a year but with his emergency board powers, Gov. La Follette could endow it with whatever funds he thought it needed. It could handle federal utility grants and do other things not banned by the constitution. Its directors get $25 per diem—not bad plums if the board meets often enough." MJ Jan. 16, 1938.

19. *Printed Arguments In Support of Motion for Rehearing*, at 2, 3, 5 (in CB). Detailing the prior neglect of the delegation issue, the argument stated the issue had not been "raised by counsel for the Secretary of State in either the Circuit or Supreme Courts until the oral argument in the Supreme Court. Such oral argument was then supplemented by a short reply brief filed several days after argument. The treatment of these considerations by respondents' counsel was also limited to a short reply brief and summarization on oral augment ...."

20. "The decision, from a constitutional view point, and in its possible effect not only upon numerous existing appropriations but upon the future course of government, ranks in importance with *Borgnis v. Falk Co.* (1911) 147 Wis. 327, upholding the Workmen's Compensation Act, and *State ex rel. Wis. Inspection Bureau v. Whitman* (1928) 196 Wis. 472, upholding broad delegations of power to administrative tribunals."

21. *Brief On Motion for Rehearing* 5 (in CB).

22. For the business interests involved see note 13 *supra*. / The argument on scanty presentation was that one who moves for rehearing must include at that time the substance of his authorities supporting the motion, rather than merely promise to reveal them if the rehearing is granted; and if he needs more time to present authorities, can ask the court for more time. / The Ryan *amicus* brief, cited in note 13 *supra*, had also discussed the issue at length.

23. See statement of this invitation in *Brief of Plaintiff and Respondent In Support of Argument On Rehearing*, 2 (in CB).

24. In addition to the brief of the three law professors (129 pp.), was one by county fair associations (44 pp.; counsel were James F. Malone, Beaver Dam; Herb J. Smith, DePere; Frank W. Lucas, Madison); one by veterans' associations (56 pp.; counsel were Attorney General O. S. Loomis and William H. Dietrich, Jr., Special Counsel); one by seventeen corporations receiving state aid (100 pp.; counsel were Attorney General O. S. Loomis and Ralph M. Hoyt, Special Counsel); and one by the Wisconsin Agricultural Authority (149 pp.; counsel were Attorney General O. S. Loomis and N. S. Boardman, Assistant Attorney General). WDA's brief on rehearing was 172 pp.; that of *amici curiae* representing utility and business interests was 45 pp.; that of the secretary of state was 67 pp.; and that of *amicus* William Ryan was 35 pp.

25. The WDA brief did not treat so intensively the governmental use of private corporations on the *federal* level, or the importance for the general problem of public administration, of the hybrid legal technique represented by the WDA act.

26. McCulloch v. Maryland, 4 Wheat. (U.S.) 316, 436 (1819).

27. App. A #28 (school) and 34 (library). The library decision approvingly quoted this statement from the school opinion: "The test to be applied in determining whether a particular agency may be employed by the state or some particular subdivision thereof by legislative authorization to perform any particular work, is not whether the agency is public but whether the purpose is

public within the legitimate functions of our constitutional government." / On the last point citation was made to Alabama Power Co. v. Ickes, 302 U.S. 464 (1938) denying the right of Alabama Power Co. to enjoin federal loans to municipalities for engaging in the power business; and Milwaukee Horse and Cow Commission Co. v. Hill, 207 Wis. 420, 430-32 (1932) denying an injunction to restrain the state fair board from leasing to certain individuals some stock barns on the state fair grounds for a horse and cattle market.

28. The statute involved had provided for certain types of instruction to be given by private industrial schools organized under the statute and for discretionary power in the school's officers "to bind out any child committed to it, as apprentices or servants during their minority, to such persons and to learn such proper trades and employments as in their judgment will be most for the future advantage of such child. Such officers may also in their discretion give away to any suitable person for adoption any such child during its minority." RS 1878, sec. 1786.

29. *Appointment:* It was pointed out that confining the governor's power of appointing the regulatory Dentistry Board and Board of Pharmacy to a selection from those nominees suggested by the dental and pharmaceutical societies respectively had been upheld in State ex rel. Milwaukee Medical College v. Chittenden, 127 Wis. 468 (1906) and State v. Heinemann, 80 Wis. 253 (1891). [Note: The issue was not specifically discussed in the last mentioned case.] / *Eminent Domain:* In Pratt v. Brown, 3 Wis. 603, 610 (1854) the Court had said, with reference to a milldam statute, "The time has gone by when it is proper to discuss or question, judicially, the power of the legislature to exercise the right of eminent domain resting in the sovereignty of the state by delegation to incorporated companies." See also Newcomb v. Smith, 2 Pinney 131, 137 (1849); Bohlman v. Green Bay & Minn. Ry. Co., 40 Wis. 157, 168 (1876); Blair v. Milwaukee E.R.&L.Co., 187 Wis. 552 (1925). A federal case cited, sustaining congressional delegation of the eminent domain power to a private bridge company, was Luxton v. North River Bridge Co., 153 U.S. 525 (1894). / *Children:* For example, People ex rel. Board of Charities v. N.Y.S.P.C.C., 161 N.Y. 233 (1900); Corbett v. St. Vincent's Industrial School, 177 N.Y. 16 (1903); Hager v. Kentucky Children's Home, 119 Ky. 235 (1904). / *Animals:* For example, A.S.P.C.A. v. City of N.Y., 205 App. Div. 335, 199 N.Y.S. 728 (1923), upholding statutory authority for a private humane society's recovery of fines imposed by New York courts for cruelty to animals. The money was regarded as compensation for public services performed by the society, acting in an administrative capacity for the state. The brief pointed out (p. 82) that the earlier New York case, which had been relied on in the first WDA decision (Fox v. M.&H.R. Humane Society, 165 N.Y. 517), was not based on a delegation ground. / *Education:* For example, People v. Brooklyn Cooperage, 187 N.Y. 142 (1907); Furlong v. South Park Commissioners, 340 Ill. 363 (1930). / *Public improvements:* For example, Clendaniel v. Conrad, 3 Boyce (Del.) 549 (1912); Commonwealth ex rel. Kelly v. City of Pittsburgh, 183 Pa. 202 (1897). / *Police powers:* For example, Slaughter House Case, 16 Wall. (U.S.) 36, 64 (1872); Scholle v. State, 90 Md. 729 (1900); Parke v. Bradley, 204 Ala. 455 (1920). / State ex rel. Wisconsin Inspection Bureau v. Whitman, 196 Wis. 472 (1928) (insurance). See also Wis. Tel. Co. v. Pub. Serv. Comm., 206 Wis. 589, 597 (1932).

30. In Re Appointment of a Revisor of Statutes, 141 Wis. 592, 598, 615, 617 (1910); State v. Hogue, 71 Wis. 384 (1888).

31. *Investigation and recommendation:* Legislators appointed to discharge functions of investigation and recommendation were held not covered by a law which, roughly, prohibited legislators from holding "public office" during their legislative term. Mulnix v. Elliott, 62 Colo. 46 (1916); Curtin v. State of Calif., 61 Cal. App. 377 (1923). Although Hall v. State, 39 Wis. 79 (1875), held that a state geologist employed under legislative authority by the governor to make a geological survey of the state was a public officer so that he could not claim rights under the contracts clause of the federal Constitution for continuance of his employment, this conclusion was reversed by the Supreme Court, 103 U.S. 5 (1880). / *Executive functions:* U.S. ex rel. Noyes v. Hatch, 1 Pinney (Wis.) 182 (1842), declared certain legislatively appointed commissioners for the sale of territorial lands to be not "civil officers," who, under the Territory's organic act, would have to be appointed by the governor. Also cited were County Bd. of Supervisors v. Parker, 3 Wall. (U.S.) 93 (1866) (where commissioners appointed by the Wisconsin legislature to act for the county in subscribing for railroad stock and issuing bonds in payment were not county officers within a constitutional provision that such officers be appointed by the county board or elected); Sieb v. Racine, 176 Wis. 617 (1922) (where a superintendent of city schools, with comprehensive statutory duties of administration, was held an employee rather than an officer, within the meaning of a statutory prohibition against salary increases to city officers during their appointed or elected terms); State ex rel Baraboo v. Page, 201 Wis. 262 (1930) (where mandamus was an improper remedy to compel the official city printer to publish city council proceedings, since he was not a public officer). / *Tax:* State ex rel Carey v. Ballard 158 Wis. 251 (1914). / *Directly affecting rights:* Wagner v. City of Milwaukee, 177 Wis. 410 (1922); Gibson Auto Co. v. Finnegan, 217 Wis. 401 (1935).

32. *Public officer:* In addition to the requirements cited by the court, of taking an oath and being an elector, the brief pointed to these other constitutional provisions as signifying that WDA might not be a public officer: article XIII, section 11, prohibiting the giving to, or receipt by, the incumbent of an office, of any free pass or frank for traveling, transport, transmission of message or communication; article XIII, section 3, disqualifying from office in this state, anyone holding office under U. S. or a foreign power, and anyone convicted of infamous crime or a defaulter to state or nation; article XII, section 9, providing that all officers whose office may be created by law shall be elected by the people, or appointed. / *Implied powers:* giving exhibitions, fairs and picnics; erecting libraries; establishing wages and regulations for municipal utilities; buying and selling electrical equipment; establishing codes of maximum prices of materials and maximum hours of labor; inaugurating a civil service or merit system; employing lawyers and others, including doctors specializing in treatment of electric burns; instituting suits against monopolies tending to hamper municipal ownership; issuing notes and letters of credit; electing, in WDA elections, their children and children's children so as to establish a "dynasty or divine right of kings at public expense"; and creating another corporation to carry out its powers. (Brief, pp. 61–63.) Moreover, there was said to be broad freedom in the exercise of these powers: it could choose to employ speakers; to loan funds; to publish pamphlets, newspapers, and periodicals; to maintain educational institutions; to grant franchises, licenses, or permits; to center its activity in one locality, or on one or a few of its possible functions. / *Appointment:* Citing Dowling v. Lancashire Ins. Co., 92 Wis.

63 (1896), the brief declared that one department may not appoint to a public office which is exclusively within the function of another department.

33. *Eminent domain:* It is "not similar or comparable to the sovereign power exercised by a public official or commission. It is not the power by which a state, in its sovereign capacity, thinks, acts, determines, or administers its affairs in the execution of its laws." Brief 56. / *Sovereign power, etc.* Brief 12–50, 53. / *Re school opinion:* Brief 11, 49–50.

34. For more information on these briefs see notes 13 and 24 *supra.*

35. App. A #46 at 166, 174–75.

36. App. A #46 at 175, 176. The *Whiting* and *Curtis* cases are App. A #4 and 21.

37. App. A #46 at 176, 178, 180.

38. App. A #46 at 180: An enactment may properly "make provision for the care and education of children as wards of the state [citing App. A #28]; pay bounties to volunteers in the military service of the country [citing App. A #20]; pay cash bonuses to those who served in the World War [citing App. A #36]; give educational assistance to veterans of the World War [citing App. A #37]; provide old-age and unemployment aids, Steward Machine Co. v. Davis, 301 U.S. 548 . . . ; Carmichael v. Southern Coal & Coke Co., *supra;* Helvering v. Davis, 301 U.S. 619, 672 . . . ; provide special aid to farmers . . . where [they] might otherwise suffer in health or die from want of food, Cobb v. Parnell, 183 Ark. 429 . . . ; give aid to the sufferers of a tornado where necessary to avoid a public calamity affecting the whole state" [citing App. A #29]; create "a state reclamation board with authority to purchase farm lands for resale upon convenient terms to soldiers, sailors, and industrial workers who desired to settle on farms," State ex rel. Bd. of Reclam. v. Clawson, 110 Wash. 525; establish "a municipal wood, coal and fuel yard for sale to the inhabitants of a city at cost," Laughlin v. City of Portland, 111 Me. 486.

39. App. A. #46 at 181: "Statutes offering bounties for the manufacture of sugar were held to be private in purpose. Oxnard Beet Sugar Co. v. State, 73 Neb. 57 . . . ; Michigan Sugar Co. v. Auditor-General, 124 Mich. 674 . . . ; Minn. Sugar Co. v. Iverson, 91 Minn. 30 . . . ; Dodge v. Mission Tp. (8th Cir.) 107 Fed. 827. The same conclusion was reached with reference to laws and ordinances conferring special benefits upon shoe factories and other manufacturing corporations. Wendlandt [App. A #45]; Cole v. LaGrange, 113 U.S. 1 . . . ; Parkersburg v. Brown, 106 U.S. 487 . . . ; Citizen's Savings and Loan Assoc. v. Topeka, *supra; Suring* [App. A #40]. . . . The same ruling was made with respect to federal loans to livestock raisers in In re Opinion of the Judges, 59 S.D. 469 . . ." and a "statute authorizing taxation to administer the Keeley cure to habitual drunkards who are unable to pay for treatment [App. A # 27 and 30]" and "a statute authorizing a town to levy a tax to aid in the erection of a private educational institution [App. A #21]."

40. App A #46 at 182. This was "doubtless in recognition of the fact, as was stated in Laughlin v. City of Portland, *supra,* that: 'Times change. The wants and necessities of the people change. The opportunity to satisfy those wants and necessities by individual efforts may vary . . . . On the one hand, what could not be deemed a public use a century ago, may, because of changed economic and industrial conditions, be such today. . . . Its two tests are: First, the subject matter, or commodity, must be one "of public necessity, convenience or welfare". . . . The second test is the difficulty which individuals have in providing it for themselves.' "

41. App. A #46 at 183. The opinion based the "state purpose" doctrine on constitutional language. "Sec. 5, Art. VIII ... requires the legislature to provide an annual tax sufficient to defray the estimated expenses of the state for each year, and it has been held in [App. A #29, 30, and 33] that an appropriation by the legislature must not merely be public in purpose but a proper expenditure by the state."

42. App. A #46 at 184, 185, 194. The court referred, at 189, to the past "course and usage of government" in Wisconsin's encouragement of agricultural cooperatives and its authorization to municipalities to acquire and operate their own utilities, in concluding that it could not "condemn as private in purpose the encouragement of cooperatives and power districts generally." The *Froehlich* and *New Richmond* cases are App. A #30 and 29.

43. App. A #46 at 186–87.

44. App. A #46 at 192–93. The cases are App. A #24, 29 and 44. In connection with the *Van Dyke* case, the court also referred to a Kansas case (Kansas having a similar constitutional prohibition) holding that a state's encouragement of local governments' construction of highways through appropriations for educational, advisory, regulatory, and coordinating activities did not violate the prohibition. State ex rel. Hopkins v. Raub, 106 Kan. 196 (1920).

45. *Corporate power:* App. A #46 at 194–98. It has been held, the court pointed out, that the corporate power or privilege referred to by the constitution is one occurring in the act creating the corporation and is thus part of the corporate charter—which is not the case here. / *Delegation of judicial power:* The auditing provision in Sec. 199.05 is merely a "restatement of the duty imposed upon him by the constitution itself" to act as "ex officio auditor" (article VI, section 2) for all state disbursements. / *State's credit:* A violation occurs only when the giving or loaning of credit "results in the creation by the state of a legally enforceable obligation on its part to pay to one party an obligation incurred or to be incurred in favor of that party by another party." Not so here, where "all that is done by the state is to incur liability directly or only to such other party, as for example where the state lawfully employs someone to perform an authorized service for the state." / *Compensation:* The fact that two members of the legislature that passed the act were members of WDA was legally irrelevant. The act did not provide compensation to members or officers of WDA. There was no showing that either of them received compensation from WDA, or that compensation would be out of state funds or by virtue of the act. If either one received compensation for services to the corporation in his private capacity, it would not constitute an increase in compensation for public service. Texts of these articles are in Appendix B.

46. App. A #46 at 198, 199. The text (Sec. 199.07) is in Appendix B. The clause is entitled, said the court, to "great weight," but "if so little of the act remains as not to leave a 'living, complete law capable of being carried into effect consistent with the intention of the legislature which enacted it in connection with the void part it is the duty of the court to decline to sustain the act in part in spite of a separability clause."

47. App. A #46 at 200–01. The court's reference to 585 copies is apparently an error; the number referred to earlier in the opinion, and in the court record, is 508.

48. App. A #46 at 200.

49. App. A #46 at 202–03.

50. App. A #46 at 205, 209–10. Power districts, he observed, had under chap.

198, certain powers to condemn property, or take over other utilities which other utility corporations did not have. "We are here not directly concerned with the favoritism involved in giving to power districts powers which other utility corporations do not possess, but to exercise favoritism in granting aid in organizing a class of corporations already highly favored, accentuates and increases the degree of constitutional violation involved in extending the aid." He regarded as similarly invalid the favoritism to cooperatives and non-profit corporations.

51. App. A #46 at 210–15. On the issue of favoritism to co-ops, he thought it significant that the case of Weco Products Co. v. Reed Drug Co., 225 Wis 474 (1937) held unconstitutional the provisions of the Fair Trade Act exempting cooperatives and non-profit associations from the act.

52. App. A #46 at 217–220. If the legislature had wanted to establish "another educational institution," he said, it "doubtless would have given some consideration to sec. 1, art. X of the constitution" [see Appendix B] for supervision of public instruction; and he also referred to existing statutory requirements concerning public instruction and powers of cooperatives [Secs. 185.08 and 40.22 (12)].

53. WSJ June 22, 1938. / CT June 22, 1938.

54. MJ June 24, 1938. / WSJ June 21, 1938.

Chapter IV

1. WGPP 11. / Laws 1939, c. 15 repealed Stats., c. 199 which had been created by the 1937 law and had authorized WDA's public operations.

2. RGH. This report, covering the period July 1, 1938–March 21, 1939, consists of four typed pages, and was consulted in the Wisconsin Legislative Reference Library. / The pamphlet [WGPP] also showed the extent of rural electrification through REA funds, to October 1, 1938: twenty-four Wisconsin projects (twenty-three cooperatives and one municipally-owned plant) had been loaned $8,566,800—of which $7,527,100 was for 6,831 miles of distribution line, to bring electricity to about 21,300 previously unserved Wisconsin farm families; $775,000 was for construction of a cooperatively-owned generating plant and transmission lines; $184,000 was for wiring and plumbing loans; and $28,700 was for operating loans and purchase of a small private plant.

3. WGPP 14, 19, 21. It stated that if a community wished to form an electric cooperative and approached WDA, the latter "can inform that community how electric cooperatives may be organized, and it can point out the advantages and benefits to be derived from electric co-ops. It can supply any other related information that is purely educational in character and state-wide in scope," including advice on requirements for federal REA loans.

4. The tax study findings were declared to be "instrumental as factual data prompting the drafting of chap. 132 of the Laws of 1939." The latter law declared that electric cooperatives were to pay an annual license fee of 3 per cent of total gross receipts, in lieu of all other general property and income taxes. / A mimeographed bulletin was distributed on residential electric rates of all incorporated Wisconsin communities of more than five hundred population; and rural retail electric rates were compiled, but curtailment of state funds prevented general distribution. / The miscellaneous uncompleted studies were of: (1) existing and potential power facilities in the state; (2) possible integration and coordination of state power resources; (3) rural electric line standards

considered in the light of modern engineering practice; (4) Wisconsin water resources from the standpoint of formulating a statewide plan on hydro-electric power, soil conservation, and flood control; (5) the power factor in the production costs of industry; (6) effective load-building methods.

5. *Laws* 1939, c. 321. The new agency was to "gather, digest, and disseminate all available information on rural electrification, to cooperate with the federal government and its agencies and any private or municipal company in carrying out its program of rural electrification, to coordinate the efforts of rural electric cooperative associations and private and municipal companies in this state all to the end that electric service shall be made available to all Wisconsin farmers desiring such services and presently without it." The appropriation as of August 10, 1939, was $5,000 and annually beginning July 1, 1939, it was to be $15,000. While the session-law states it was creating Sec. 94.81 of the Statutes, this was re-numbered by the Revisor and appeared in the Statutes as Sec. 94.90.

6. The transfer was by *Laws* 1945, c. 283 which repealed Sec. 94.90 and pertinent appropriation (Sec. 20.60 (26)), and enacted Sec. 36.195 together with 20.41 (21) (the latter appropriating $2,000 for the balance of the fiscal year ending June 30, 1945, and, annually beginning July 1, 1945, $5,000 for execution of functions under Sec. 36.195). All records and equipment of the division in the Department of Agriculture were to be transferred to the new division in the College of Agriculture; and personnel for the new division might come either from the old one, or from civil service lists, or from existing staff of the College. The 1949 Statutes, Sec. 20.41 (21), record a slight change in appropriations: $5,400 on July 1, 1949, and $5,500 annually beginning July 1, 1950. / The repealing act is *Laws* 1951, c. 319, Sec. 128. The College of Agriculture functions continue to be stated in Stats. Sec. 36.195.

7. The pamphlet was found in the corporate records of WDA. The records indicate that the pamphlet was used by John Becker, WDA's General Manager (who was then on leave from fully active duty for reasons of health), in a trip to Washington, D.C. for the above-mentioned purpose. / Payroll data was as of Nov. 30, 1940. The largest number employed in the preceding two years had been seventy-two. Currently, in addition to the general manager on leave, there was an acting manager and chief engineer; field personnel, consisting of six resident engineers supervising field construction, and twenty-six assistant engineers, staking foremen, and stakers; office employees consisting of two draftsmen, two stenographers, one with inventory duties, and two with accounting duties. In addition, as "consultants" were three civil engineers, one turbo-generating engineer and one diesel engineer. / The officers listed were *President,* W. E. Rabe, farmer, officer of various cooperatives; *Vice President,* F. E. Brewer, lawyer; *General Counsel,* J. E. Roe, lawyer; *Secretary,* T. F. Davlin, contractor and lawyer, member and formerly chairman of the Wisconsin Highway Commission; *Treasurer,* Carl Fries, retired merchant, holder of various civic posts. The directors (who during the fiscal year 1939–40 received $10 per diem and mileage for attendance at four meetings held) were, in addition to the president and secretary above, W. E. Owen, farmer, active in cooperatives; K. W. Hones, farmer, President of Farmers' Equity Union; H. W. Parisius, Assistant Regional Director and former State Director of Farm Security Administration.

8. MB #2 and 3.

9. MB #3. An "immediate policy of retrenchment" was called for at the

board meeting of March 27, 1942. An audit of July 22, 1942 showed cash in bank of $11,297, estimated income receivable of $15,201, and the following comparative table:

Excess of earnings over cost

To June 30, 1939 .... $21,299
Year ended June 30, 1940 13,332
Year ended June 30, 1941 5,877
Year ended June 30, 1942 .... −7,848 (loss)

10. MB #3 and 4. As discussed in Chapter I, WEC was formerly WREC or "Statewide." It had been given a $5,000 loan by WDA at a Board meeting of Sept. 23, 1942. In the 1944 transaction, $500 was in cash and $1500 was a note. The auditing data in the table on WDA financial data are compiled from MB #3 and 4.

WDA Financial Data, 1943–52

		Assets				
Fiscal year	Cash	Estimated Income Receivable	U.S. bonds	Note receivable (WEC)	Liabilities	Surplus
1943	5,332	6,639	5,000		2,942	14,063
1944	4,392	4,147		1,500	1,106	9,163
1945	1,837	1,546	8,500		293.90	11,661
1946	1,116	1,310	8,500			11,251
1947	1,765		8,500			10,251
1948	1,227		8,500			9,811
1949	761		8,500			9,353
1950	333		8,500			8,820
1952	425		7,500			8,002

11. MB #4. On Jan. 10, 1953, the University Regents accepted the funds for the project.

12. MB #4. / Richardson 51–56.

Chapter V

1. 228 Wis. 147, 175: "The validity of an appropriation must be judged by the validity of any tax which might be levied to support it, and . . . for the state to appropriate for a private purpose money raised or to be raised by taxation would be to take the property of one citizen or group of citizens without compensation and to pay it to others, which would constitute a violation of the equality clause as well as a taking of property without due process of law."

2. The "benefit" idea is found, for example, in the *Donald* case, App. A #33 at 126 and in the *Curtis* case, App. A #21 at 354–55. / Article I, sec. 13 was specifically invoked by the *New Richmond* court, App. A #29 at 577. It is the typical public-use or "eminent domain" clause which acted in some other states as an analogue, if not the source, of the public purpose restriction on taxation and spending. See Ellis Waldron, *The Public Purpose Doctrine of*

Taxation, 418–421 (Ph.D. thesis, University of Wisconsin, 1952). / The *Heimerl* reference is App. A #52 at 158.

3. The *Heimerl* reference is App. A #52 at 160. / The point on executive vetoes applies to Gov. Philipp's veto of a 1917 bill authorizing cities to sell the common necessities of life to their inhabitants, and of a 1919 bill authorizing municipal depots and plants for purchase, manufacture, and distribution of dairy products; and the 1921 attorney general's opinion holding unconstitutional a bill that would have authorized municipal food markets in second-class cities. See AJ 1077–1080 (1917); 1338–39 (1919); 1537–39 (1921). There was a similar basis for Gov. Philipp's misgivings when he signed a 1917 bill increasing the number of cities which could engage in the ice and fuel business. AJ 1211–12 (1917). The 1917 emergency year was a busy one for vetoes on public purpose grounds. Philipp had also vetoed in that year a bill authorizing and ratifying county payments, up to $500, to those who construct and operate ferries. AJ 661–62 (1917). / The *Curtis* reference is App. A #21 at 354 / *Cooley:* People v. Salem, 20 Mich. 452, 484–85: "By common consent also, a large portion of the most urgent needs of society are relegated exclusively to the law of demand and supply. It is this in its natural operation, and without the interference of government, that gives us the proper proportion of tillers of the soil, artisans, manufacturers, merchants, and professional men, and that determines when and where they shall give to society the benefit of their particular services. However great the need in the direction of any particular calling, the interference of the government is not tolerated, because though it might be supplying a public want, it is considered as invading the domain that belongs exclusively to provide inclination and enterprise." See also Cooley, *Taxation* (1st ed., Chicago, 1897) 90.

4. App. A #4 at 210.

5. (a) App. A #50, #58; 33 AG 21 (1944); 34 AG 127 (1945); 36 AG 206 (1947). / (b) App. A #50. / (c) App. A #51; 31 AG 37 (1942); 35 AG 394 (1946); 36 AG 116, 528 (1947); 39 AG 391 (1950); 42 AG 18, 133 (1953). / (d) App. A # 48, #56, #76. / (e) App. A #48. / (f) App. A #48, #52. / (g) App. A #52. / (h) App. A #48, #55. / (i) 38 AG 546 (1949); 39 AG 391 (1950). / (j) 38 AG 265 (1949). / (k) 34 AG 127 (1945). / (l) 32 AG 109 (1943). / The case has also been cited for the proposition that informational and educational work fulfills a public purpose. 37 AG 526 (1948).

6. Department of Veterans' Affairs: 35 AG 394 (1946). Veterans' Housing Authority: 36 AG 528 (1947); App. A #51.

7. An elaboration of this paragraph is in Note, "The 'Public Purpose' of Municipal Financing for Industrial Development," 70 *Yale Law Journal* 789; n. 29, p. 794 (1961). For recent cases upholding industrial promotion provisions, some of them embodied in the state constitution, see *ibid.,* n. 15, p. 791. For constitutional provisions specifically announcing a public purpose doctrine, see *Index Digest of State Constitutions,* Legislative Drafting Research Fund of Columbia University, especially under "State Finances" pp. 977–78 (New York, 2nd ed., 1959).

8. *Criticism:* "As might be expected in a private enterprise society, public industrial financing has met strong opposition. The Investment Bankers Association has recommended that its members 'exercise extreme caution in underwriting or marketing [industrial financing] bonds.' Others have joined in the opposition [citing, among other things, resolutions of the American Bar Asso-

ciation's Section on Municipal Law and of the Municipal Finance Officers' Association]. The federal income tax exemption of income from municipal obligations, particularly revenue bonds, has been under persistent attack. Commentators allege that public financing has been emphasized at the expense of other factors far more crucial to industrial site location. There is also a genuine concern that the use of of public credit to finance private industrial expansion will hamper the ability of state and local governments to improve other community services. Furthermore, to the extent that public industrial financing becomes a weapon in the interstate struggle to attract new industry, the public participants may find that their losses from tax exemptions and hampered borrowing power exceed their gains." David E. Pinsky, "State Constitutional Limitations in Public Industrial Financing: An Historical and Economic Approach," 111 *University of Pennsylvania Law Review* 265, 274 (1963). / National Municipal League, *Salient Issues of Constitutional Revision* (1961) 140.

9. Nor are we concerned with the non-economic promotion represented by educational efforts with respect to obscenity in books (an effort for which the *WDA* case was cited as authority in 37 AG 526 [1948], or the ideological promotion involved in the duties of the Governor's Commission on Human Rights (*Stats.*, 1961, Sec. 15.85).

10. The *amicus curiae* brief of business and taxpayer interests supporting the Supreme Court's first decision has a tabular indication of aid to those agricultural societies receiving aid in 1937. Aid to a few other agricultural groups is shown in the Appendix of the *amicus curiae* brief of the Wisconsin Agricultural Authority. As of 1962, the basic statutory provisions for aids to agricultural societies were *Stats.* 1961, Secs. 20.140 (25)–(30), 20.365 (3), 27.30 (5) (state aid) and Sec. 60.80 (3) (town aid). On farm cooperatives see Chapter I. Concerning other miscellaneous agricultural aids, see for example, (1) some of the provisions governing loans by the state annuity board, *Laws* 1921, c. 459, sec. 3, par. 42.32; *Laws* 1925, c. 368; *Laws* 1933, c. 126; (2) the appropriation to the Wisconsin Home and Farm Credit Administration for drought-relief farm loans through county boards, *Laws* 1937, cc. 25, 38; (3) the tax advantages available for certain types of land, *Laws* 1921, c. 374; *Laws* 1923, c. 101; *Laws* 1927, c. 164; *Laws* 1933, c. 423. See generally on twentieth-century aid to farmers, Lewis R. Mills, "The Public Purpose Doctrine—Part I," 1957 *Wisconsin Law Review* 52–57. An early and extensive program for the loan of state funds arising from the sale of the federally donated school and university lands was launched under *Laws* 1849, c. 212, Sec. 62 *et seq.*

11. Perhaps the earliest executive promotion was Governor Doty's suggestion to the Territorial Legislature in 1841 for tax exemption of sheep and their fleeces for a term of years in order to encourage wool production. HJ 18–19 (1841). Governor Randall in 1858 suggested aid to lead and mineral interests. SJ 30 (1858). And in 1861 he proposed a tax exemption for five or ten years for newly established or expanded industries which develop the state's raw materials. AJ 27 (1861). The latter proposal was made again the following year by Governor Harvey. SJ 28 (1862). In 1864 Governor Lewis asked for a program of publicizing the state's economic opportunities to Eastern capitalists and enacting laws that would "remove impediments and hold out . . . inducements." AJ 19 (1864). In 1870 Governor Fairchild suggested the possibility of legislation to aid manufacturing, though stressing that a patronize-home-products policy is better than tariff manipulation. AJ Appendix 19 (1870). Two years later Gov-

ernor Washburn briefly suggested the encouragement of manufacture through state legislation and appropriate tariff policy. SJ Appendix 26 (1872). Governor Kohler in 1929 stressed the need for an expansion of industry and said that the state must remove any apprehension of unfriendliness on the part of the state to industry, though without granting "special favors." SJ 301 (1929). Governor La Follette in 1937 went further by asking for a state department "devoted to assisting in the prosperous development of Wisconsin industry, business and commerce, protecting their legitimate interests and welfare, and aiding in the solution of their problems. Such a department could do much in advancing the industrial progress of the state," SJ, SS, 68–69 (1937). Similar urgings in behalf of state promotion of industrial development were made by Gov. Walter Kohler, Jr. SJ 29 (1955); Gov. Vernon Thomson SJ 22–24 (1957); and Gov. Gaylord Nelson SJ 68–71 (1959).

12. See Robert S. Hunt, *Law and Locomotives* (Madison, 1958), 83–84, 144; 85–87; 147–48 on favorable state tax treatment, enactments authorizing local aid, and the cited developments in the seventies and eighties. See also Lewis R. Mills, *supra* note 10 at 49–51.

13. Fairs and expositions: RS 1878, Sec. 1465; *Laws* 1879, c. 242; *Laws* 1885, JR 15; *Laws* 1889, c. 234. Steam Wagon: *Laws* 1875, c. 134; *Laws* 1876, c. 182; *Laws* 1879, c. 193. Promotional corporations: *Laws* 1893, c. 403. / Tariff memorials: *Laws* 1899, Memorial No. 5 asked repeal of the duty on hides, the raw material for the Wisconsin tannery industry. *Laws* 1878, Memorial No. 14 objected to reduction to the tariff on wool or lumber. (But *Laws* 1909, JR 50 requested *removal* of the lumber tariff because "keeping out of lumber products of other countries stimulates and compels the destruction of our own forests and nullifies" the conservation efforts of the state forest department.) / The point in the last sentence of the text is illustrated in Lewis R. Mills, "Government Fiscal Aid to Private Enterprise in Wisconsin: A Quantitative Approach," 1956 *Wisconsin Law Review* 110, especially pp. 114–115, 122–24; "The Public Purpose Doctrine in Wisconsin—Part I" 1957 *Wisconsin Law Review* 52–57; Erling D. Solberg, *New Laws For New Forests,* Chaps. VI–XI (Madison, 1961). / That tax exemptions are generally regarded as not violating the public purpose limitation or the equal protection clause, though they are sometimes held to violate state constitutional provisions on uniformity and equality in taxation is shown in Note, "Legal Limitations on Public Inducements to Industrial Location," 59 *Columbia Law Review* 618, 625–29 (1959). This article also considers problems connected with such alternative methods of economic promotion as general obligation bonds and revenue bonds (629–38), private development organizations with bond-issuing powers (634–35), development credit agencies (638–40), acquisition of industrial sites by eminent domain (640–42), advertising and public relations (643–44). Further comprehensive discussion is in David E. Pinsky, "State Constitutional Limitations on Public Industrial Financing: An Historical and Economic Approach," 111 *University of Pennsylvania Law Review* 265 (1963). See also Note, "State Constitutional Limitations On A Municipality's Power to Appropriate Funds or Extend Credit to Individuals and Associations," 108 *University of Pennsylvania Law Review* 95 (1959); Note, "Financing Industrial Development in the South," 14 *Vanderbilt Law Review* 621 (1961).

14. Dairy products: *Laws* 1935, c. 518; Potatoes: *Laws* 1935, c. 289; Conservation Commission activity: *Laws* 1935, cc. 365, 526; Department of Commerce:

Laws 1937, SS, c. 8 (for description see WBB 565 (1937), repealed by *Laws* 1939, c. 12. / The interim committee was created by *Laws* 1953, c. 395. The committee was given $10,000 for the study and was composed of two senators and assemblymen appointed as are standing committees, and (to be appointed by the governor) one representative each from the executive branch, industry, agriculture, small business, labor, banking and finance, and the University of Wisconsin.

15. Coordinating committee on advertising: *Laws* 1951, c. 345, amended by *Laws* 1953, c. 251, secs. 1, 12 (*Stats.* 1953, Sec. 1478). / The staff report was entitled "Preliminary Research Report to the Committee on Industrial Development, Sec. III, Oct. 20, 1953." (1) It referred to the "farm products promotion" program of the Department of Agriculture, on which about $100,000 would be spent that year, and which included out-of-state programs in twelve to fifteen areas, special product campaigns (butter, potatoes, etc.), radio broadcasts, the "Alice in Dairyland" program, food preparation advice by nutritionists, seasonal campaigns (e.g., June dairy month), outdoor advertising at entrances to the state, souvenir cheese distribution at conventions throughout the U. S., state fair and state convention promotional work. (2) The Conservation Commission was expected to spend about $203,000 that year in advertising Wisconsin recreation, scenery, etc., in thirty-four newspapers, twenty-three national magazines, Chicago TV and billboards in the Chicago area, and exhibits at out-of-state outdoor sports and travel shows. (3) The Bureau of Community Development, University of Wisconsin, was described as having been, since 1946, the state bureau most closely connected with industrial development in Wisconsin, on a budget of some $30,000 a year. In the School of Commerce of the University of Wisconsin was the Bureau of Business Research and Service, organized in 1945 and spending about $20,000 annually. Its research was of a broader type, with less field work than the bureau last mentioned. (4) Other state agencies mentioned were the State Planning Division, Bureau of Engineering, which had broad developmental functions under *Stats.*, 1953, Sec. 15.85 (4), (5), but had generally forwarded "industrial development" matters to the above-mentioned Bureau of Community Development; and the Industrial Commission which furnished statistical data on labor-supply, etc., to business. (5) Municipal aids had been given under *Stats.*, Sec. 66.04 (3). (6) Some private programs had functioned through the state Chamber of Commerce, local Chambers of Commerce, individual industries, and "development corporations." / Division of Industrial Development: *Laws* 1955, c. 271; *Stats.*, 1955 and 1957, Sec. 15.535, 15.536, 20.360. The division, aided by an advisory committee of legislators and interested private groups, was "through research and promotion" to foster the most desirable growth and diversification of agriculture and industry in the state"— e.g., aiding plant location, researching into taxes, markets, and other factors affecting industrial development, aiding local communities in organizing for and obtaining new business. For the July 1957–59 biennium, the division's budget had risen to some $130,000, plus an additional $100,000 for "advertising and promoting industrial development." / The new Department: *Laws* 1959, c. 442; *Stats.* 1959 and 1961, Sec. 109 *et seq.* For budgetary information, see *Stats.* 1961 Sec. 20.705 A report covering the first two years of operation, under the dynamic leadership of Director David Carley, was published in 1962. / Formed under *Laws* 1955, c. 656, the Wisconsin Development Credit Corporation was given, from the general fund, $4,000 on July 1, 1959, and another $4,000 on

July 1, 1960. *Stats.* 1959 Sec. 20.885. For the national picture on this type of corporation see *Development Corporations and Authorities,* Committee Print, U.S. Senate Committee on Banking and Currency, 86 Congress, 1st Sess. (1959).

16. Examples of enterprises thus aided are: a water company (Milwaukee), *Laws (P. and L.)* 1853, c. 116; *Laws (P. and L.)* 1855, c. 335; a gas company (Oshkosh), 1857, c. 47; a hotel (Hudson), 1867, c. 75; a bridge company (various towns), 1867, c. 62; 1883, c. 231; a river improvement company (various municipalities), 1866, c. 295; 1870, c. 268; a dry dock company (Sheboygan), 1871, c. 410. Sometimes the authorization was for levying a tax rather than issuing bonds, 1867, c. 537 (hotel in Prescott). Sometimes the local subscription to stock in the enterprise was required rather than merely authorized (Marathon County subscription to stock in improvement and steam navigation company), 1853, c. 301.

17. Portage: *Laws* 1889, c. 158 / *Caveat:* The Prairie du Chien Common Council was authorized to "aid and to offer ... such inducements and ... privileges as are not repugnant to the constitution of the state ... for the erection and maintenance of ... manufacturing industries and all other institutions and industries as in the opinion of the Common Council, may be of great public benefit...." *Laws* 1889, c. 491, Sec. 38, par. 41. / *Laws* 1915, c. 276; *Laws* 1921, c. 396 (becoming Sec. 66.04 of the Statutes), repealed by *Laws* 1953, c. 245. / Concerning the league's position, the previously cited staff report of the 1953 interim committee, said: (p. 23) "The legislature repealed this section [i.e. the general 1915 authorization to municipalities] as a result of the opinion of the League of Wisconsin Municipalities that if this type of expenditure was legal, it was legal under the general powers of municipalities rather than under Sec. 66.04 (3). The ... legality of this type of expenditure is determined by the purpose of the expenditure rather than the agency expending it. It is the opinion of the attorney for the League of Wisconsin Municipalities that a city may spend money for industrial development with no limit to amount, as long as the purpose is general development and not directed to a particular business or industry. No data as to number of cities appropriating money for such purposes was available." / Industrial sites: *Laws* 1957, c. 98; *Laws* 1961, c. 75.

18. *Laws* 1937, c. 291 (became Sec. 66.04 (3a) of *Stats.,* by *Laws* 1939, c. 107); *Laws* 1953, c. 245 (also re-numbered the section, so that it became Sec. 60.80 (2) of *Stats.*)

19. See Mills, 1956, note 13 above, esp. 117–18, 122, 126–27.

20. See App. A #40, #45, #49, #60. / The attorney general had previously condemned municipal subsidies to particular firms on the basis of earlier cases on the public purpose doctrine. 9 AG 170 (1920). See also 18 AG 599 (1929); 23 AG 14 (1934). Counsel for the League of Wisconsin Municipalities has also not sanctioned such subsidies (see Knight study, cited in note next below, pp. 6–7; and quotation from Staff Report in note 17 above).

21. W. Donald Knight, *Subsidization of Industry In Forty Selected Cities In Wisconsin* 174–75 (Wisconsin Commerce Studies, vol. 1, no. 2, Madison, 1947). This was published as a Bulletin of the University of Wisconsin by the Bureau of Business Research and Science, of the School of Commerce. The Bulletin observed (p. 1): "The inducements offered consist of the gift, outright or conditional, of buildings, sites or cash bonuses, the payment of moving expenses or repair and installation costs, the provision of buildings for low or

nominal rents, tax concessions, the sale of plants or sites at low prices, the provision of services and facilities, and the financing of new enterprises through land contracts or the sale of securities. The element of subsidy or outright gift involved varies in amount from $100,000 or more in the earlier cases of gift or low rental of buildings to a negligible amount or to nothing, in recent cases of the sale of sites at cost, or the financing of buildings on a profit basis." The author, who feels that, on the whole, the subsidization has been economically justifiable, is aware of the legal problem. "If the use of municipal funds in subsidization programs is to be continued, both a redefinition of the legal principle based upon the concept of a public purpose and closer adherence of municipal practice to that principle seem desirable." (p.v.)

22. For an elaboration of the above-mentioned factors to be considered, see Note, "The 'Public Purpose' of Municipal Financing for Industrial Development," 70 *Yale Law Journal* 789 (1961). Mississippi and Tennessee legislation does require prior administrative agency approval of a project. *Ibid.,* 797. For further general recommendations on the proper approach to promotion and public purpose see Note, "Legal Limitations on Public Inducements to Industrial Location," 59 *Columbia Law Review* 618, 644–47 (1959).

23. See Appendix B for text of article VIII, section 10, of Wisconsin constitution, including its twentieth-century amendments. / Mississippi's ban in 1832 was the first; Wisconsin's in 1848 was the second; some five more states adopted it in the fifties, some six more in the sixties, and some five more in the late nineteenth and early twentieth centuries. See tabulation in Waldron, *supra* note 2, p. 449. / For smaller number of current prohibitions, see esp. pp. 573–74 of *Index Digest of State Constitutions, supra* note 7.

24. A letter of E. G. Ryan of Racine, a Democratic leader and later Chief Justice of the Wisconsin Supreme Court, observed of the opposition to the 1846 constitution, "The opposition may talk about married women and exemption, but here along the Lake Shore, at all events, the real opposition is to the restrictions against banks, internal improvement, and state debt." Milo M. Quaife, *The Movement For Statehood* 46 (Madison, 1918). The Madison *Wisconsin Argus,* March 30, 1847, gave as a reason for supporting ratification of the 1846 constitution with its internal improvements ban the fact that it would devote to education, the proceeds of the 500,000 acres of state land granted by Congress for internal improvements (Congress having changed the grant accordingly); and if the present constitution were rejected, a later constitutional convention might devote the proceeds of this acreage to internal improvements, and lift the ban on state participation therein, for the "Whig party hold most tenaciously that government shall undertake and carry on works of this kind." Milo M. Quaife, *The Struggle Over Ratication* 343 (Madison, 1920). At the 1846 constitutional convention, the Committee on Internal Improvements recommended: "Internal Improvements shall forever be encouraged by the government of this state. But the legislature shall in no case create or incur a state debt for that object, without at the same time providing means for the payment of the interest thereof, and the final liquidation of the same." Milo M. Quaife, *The Convention of 1846,* 81 (Madison 1919). But the convention tightened the restriction by striking out all after the word "object," and also rejected a proposal that the legislature should never encourage internal improvements in any shape whatever. *Ibid.,* 323–24. As later modified and adopted by

the convention, the provision declared that the state "shall encourage internal improvements by individuals, associations, and corporations, but shall not carry on, or be a party in carrying on, any work of internal improvement except" that "when grants of land or other property shall have been made to the state, specially dedicated by the grant to particular works of internal improvement, the state may carry on such particular works, and shall devote thereto the avails of such grants so dedicated therto; but shall in no case pledge the faith or credit of the state or incur any debt or liability for such works of internal improvement." *Ibid.*, 404, 745.

25. At the 1847–48 convention, the committee submission of the 1846 internal improvements ban was accompanied by a minority report, whose sentiments were represented by the Sanders proposal to permit improvements of navigable waters leading into Lake Michigan and the Mississippi, subject to popular approval at a referendum, and subject to a $300,000 debt limit; and the Fox proposal permitting the state to undertake some single project with two points of termination, provided there is a tax sufficient to enable completion within ten years, and provided that there is popular approval at a referendum. The Sanders proposal was defeated 54 to 9; a provision similar to the Fox proposal carried by vote of 30 to 29, but was then defeated 36 to 28. Adopted was a Morgan Martin amendment which loosened the provision on state internal improvements through the avails of land grants, by saying that the state could also pledge the revenues from the work to those who would complete it. See Quaife, *The Attainment of Statehood* (Madison, 1928), 301–302, 415–20; 426, 443, 581–88. In addition, as finally adopted, the provision that the state should "encourage" internal improvements was omitted, and the provision against being a party to carrying on such works was expanded by a prohibition against contracting debts for internal improvements. Moreover, article VIII, secs. 4, 6 also prohibited the state from incurring a debt (except for extraordinary expenditures, up to $100,000). For the text of the internal improvements provision as finally adopted in article VIII, section 10, see Appendix B.

26. The sentiment on financial ruin, etc., as reflected in contemporary newspapers, is reported in Quaife, *Movement For Statehood,* 252, 283, 426; *Struggle Over Ratification,* 20, 211, 321, 508, 598–600, 665; *Attainment of Statehood,* 37–39. For judicial recognition of this sentiment see App. A #2, #33, #68. As Democrats dominated both conventions (see Quaife, *Convention of 1846,* 800; *Attainment of Statehood,* 931), it is significant that a resolution at a meeting of Democratic members of the legislature opposed "the power to contract any debt for the purposes of internal improvement, holding that it is the object of a state government not to transport freight or passengers, but to make and administer equal and just laws." Madison *Wisconsin Argus,* Feb. 16, 1847, in Quaife, *Struggle Over Ratification,* 321.

27. Fairchild and Seibold, "Constitutional Revision in Wisconsin" in 1950 *Wisconsin Law Review* 201, 226–29; Comment, "Wisconsin's Internal Improvement Prohibition: Obsolete in Modern Times?" 1961 *Wisconsin Law Review* 294. The related issue of state indebtedness is analyzed in the light of recent developments, in A. James Heins, *Constitutional Restrictions Against State Debt* (Madison, 1963); Morris, "Evading Debt Limitations With Public Building Authorities: The Costly Subversion of State Constitutions," 68 *Yale Law Journal* 234 (1958); Note, "Obligations of a State-Created Authority: Do They Constitute A Debt of the State?" 53 *Michigan Law Review,* 439 (1955). The pro-

posal that the Wisconsin restriction on state debt be eased by constitutional amendment was strongly urged by Governor Nelson, elected in 1958 and 1960.

28. The state has gone on strengthening the Portage levee in spite of the decision. This is discussed in the history of the Portage levee detailed in the present writer's unpublished study of the Fox-Wisconsin Rivers Improvement. The definition is set out in the digest of the *Froelich* case, App. A #30.

29. On authorization: see *Clark* and *Bushnell* cases, App. A #63, #64. For prior legislative opinion favoring such authorization, see *Report of a Majority of Judiciary Committee on Power of Legislature to Authorize Towns, etc., To Aid in Construction of Works of Internal Improvement,* SJ Appendix 3–12 (1854). For the contrary view see *Report of Committee on Expiration and Re-enactment of Laws, In Relation to Ass. Bill. No. 364 to Authorize Certain Towns to Aid in Construction of A Railroad,* AJ Appendix 1–8 (1854). / On compulsion: see *Jensen* case, App. A #66. / The 1959 *Canepa* case (App. A #79) involving the Redevelopment Authority of the City of Madison, which was authorized by state law, and created and largely controlled by the city (and apparently involving no *state* financial aid) cited the *Clark, Bushnell,* and *Jensen* cases to the effect that the internal improvements ban was inapplicable to governmental units created by the state and functioning within particular areas of the state.

30. Importance of the encouragement-of-others rationale has been recognized in attorney general opinions, e.g., 35 AG 394 (1946); 36 AG 528 (1947); 37 AG 360, 363 (1948). The rationale was not stated in the veterans' housing case (App. A #51) though the court quoted approvingly from 35 AG 394 (1946) which in its unquoted portion had invoked the rationale, giving it the narrower construction. In the 1954 state office building case (App. A #76) and the 1955 case on University and other state buildings (App. A #77) the court ignored the encouragement-of-others rationale, preferring to rest on the ground that the buildings involved were not internal improvements. The 1953 turnpike corporation case (App. A #75) furnished little occasion for use of the rationale, since the state was not even "encouraging" the turnpike corporation's activities (other than through the statutory authorization for its formation and operation and for its tax exemption) and was devoting no funds thereto (the appropriation being for the commission's *study* of a turnpike project). All that the court felt it necessary to say was that the internal improvements ban "applies only to such works as may be engaged in by the state" (265 Wis. 185, 206). It may be, of course, that the encouragement-of-others principle will in the future be given narrower scope than that which the *WDA* case thought was justified by the precedents, and not be construed to cover encouragement by way of financing the cost of improvements by others. WDA's own encouragement activity was not of that kind, and the court's rationale did not have to go that far. Nor, as again argued in Chapter VI, did the precedents require it. However, the 1960 shopping center case, to be discussed shortly, does seem to point in the direction of a broad encouragement-of-others principle.

31. The arguments appear, for example, in the *Report of President's Commission on Intergovernmental Relations* 37–38 (Washington, D.C., 1955); Walter E. Sandelius and Ray L. Nichols, *Constitutional Revision in Kansas: The Issues* (Governmental Research Center, University of Kansas, 1960). For the further argument that the constitutional restrictions on fiscal powers are anti-democratic, see, for example, Carleton F. Chute, in W. Brooke Graves, ed.,

State Constitutional Revision 277 (1960); Frank M. Landers, "Constitutional Provisions on Taxation and Finance," 33 *State Government* 39 (1960).

32. *Report of the Governor's Commission on Constitutional Revision* 9, 10 (1960). See also Comment, "Wisconsin's Internal Improvements Prohibition: Obsolete in Modern Times?" 1961 *Wisconsin Law Review* 294, for the view that the prohibition should be repealed by constitutional amendment.

33. See the tabular analysis, in the *amicus* brief of seventeen corporations receiving state aid, showing starting dates of legislation making grants of funds to agricultural and other societies.

34. Dissenting Justice Eschweiler had further contended that the internal improvements clause was violated, but he did not take note of the *Froehlich* case rationale (App. A #68) according to which undertakings for the primary purpose of facilitating governmental functions would not be internal improvements, nor did he note the observation at p. 36 therein. On this point, see with respect to government office buildings the 1954 decision in the *Giessel* case (App. A #76), and with respect to university buildings the observation at p. 373 of the veterans' housing case (App. A #51), and the 1960 shopping center case (App. A #80).

35. See, e.g., *Laws* 1947, c. 28; *Laws* 1949, c. 604; *Laws* 1953, cc. 253, 403, 508; *Laws* 1955, c. 144.

36. Carter v. Carter Coal Co., 298 U. S. 238, 311 (1936); Schechter Poultry Corp. v. United States, 295 U. S. 495, 537 (1935). These stressed delegation of "legislative" power, the WDA opinion, "executive" power.

37. In the turnpike case the *WDA* decision was relied on in these ways: (1) At. p. 191 the court quoted the first *WDA* opinion's sanction for a state's having a highway constructed privately if essential matters as to location, etc., are determined by the state; (2) at p. 192, the court quoted the *WDA* opinion's language adopted from a Delaware court: "We are unable to see that the state is parting with a part of its sovereignty by providing that a private corporation may construct and give it to the state, when it is done by authority of the state, without expense to the state; (3) at p. 199, the court invoked the *WDA* decision for the proposition that article VIII, section 3 of the constitution against giving or loaning the state's credit applies only where the state has a legally enforceable obligation to pay to one party an obligation owed him by another party; (4) at p. 196, the court, after pointing to the *WDA* court's stress on the fact that the corporation had not been given any powers it didn't already possess under its articles, observed: "Here the same principle applies in that the turnpike corporation when formed derives its powers from the general provisions of the act, Secs. 182.30 to 182.48, and the mere fact that the end result will be the construction of certain highways to which the state will eventually have title does not result in making the private corporation a state agency or instrumentality." This last reference to the *WDA* case seems not appropos except as an *a fortiori* argument. For the principle referred to arouse out of the granting of state funds to a private corporation for the fulfillment of functions which the corporation could legitimately exercise under its articles, whereas the turnpike corporation case is easier; no funds were being granted to the corporation; there was merely a statute authorizing its formation and operation.

38. See the digest of the *American Legion* case, App. A #48. / Some unfavorable delegation cases decided before the advent of WDA were: Gibson Auto

Co. v. Finnegan, 217 Wis. 401 (1935), invalidating the statute providing for formulation by the private industry involved (though subject to the governor's approval) of a code of fair competition having the force of law; Wagner v. Milwaukee, 177 Wis. 410 (1922), invalidating an ordinance providing that wages of city employees and of contractors doing work for the city were to be determined by the labor union wage scale (a proviso specifying, as a condition, the city council's approval of the union scale, was apparently construed as ineffective in view of other provisions unqualifiedly adopting the union scale); State ex rel. Carey v. Ballard, 158 Wis. 251 (1914), invalidating a statute requiring a town board to levy a highway tax whenever a group of citizens requested state highway improvement within the town and at least half of the town's share of estimated cost had been paid. But some cases were more favorable. Just prior to the *WDA* case there had been upheld as not an invalid delegation, a provision of the Fair Trade Act permitting a manufacturer of competitive trademarked products to establish by contract with retailers a minimum price below which any contracting or non-contracting retailer could not sell. Weco Products Co. v. Reed Drug Co., 225 Wis. 474 (1937). More recently upheld was a provision adopting as the definition of "drugs" for purposes of a statute prohibiting the sale of drugs except under supervision of a registered pharmacist, the definition as it appeared in existing and future issues of the *U. S. Pharmacopoeia,* a compendium issued by a private institution. State v. Wakeen, 263 Wis. 401 (1953). Before that, the court had upheld a law requiring that a majority of the state board of dental examiners be members of the state dental society and providing that any appointee "may be selected by the governor from among such persons as may be recommended" by the state dental society. State ex rel. Milwaukee Medical College v. Chittenden, 127 Wis. 468 (1906). Perhaps as extensive as any delegation to private parties was the particularly broad form of eminent domain power conferred by the mill-dam legislation upheld in Newcomb v. Smith, 2 Pin. 131 (1849); Pratt et al v. Brown, 3 Wis. 603 (1854), though the determination of validity was only reluctantly adhered to (see Fisher v. Horicon Iron and Manufacturing Co., 10 Wis. 351 (1860); Newell v. Smith et al, 15 Wis. 101 (1862)).

Valuable discussions of the general problem of delegation to private parties will be found in Louis Jaffe, "Law Making By Private Groups" in 51 *Harvard Law Review,* 201 (1937); Notes, 37 *Columbia Law Review* 447 (1937); 67 *Harvard Law Review* 1398 (1954); 1954 *Wisconsin Law Review* 500. The Jaffe article was cited by the *WDA* court on rehearing as showing "the pressure which the complexities of modern life have put upon all governmental agencies, particularly those of an administrative character, and the demand that relief be sought by delegating to private groups some of the functions of the government." (228 Wis. at 166). The article, which is favorable to such delegations, had been referred to in the *amicus* brief of the law professors on rehearing.

Chapter VI

1. Another facet of the predictability issue is the *definition* of law in terms of predictions of what the courts will do—a definition most prominently associated with Holmes. Oliver Wendell Holmes, Jr., *Collected Legal Papers* (New York, 1920) 173. One of the criticisms of this definition has been that while it may accurately describe the mental process on the basis of which a legal coun-

sellor advises his clients, it errs in ascribing a predictive process to the functioning of the advocate or the judge. Yet the advocate selects his arguments in the light of his predictions as to what they will lead the court to do. And the judge in considering the relative virtues of alternative decisions has to make forecasts of the impact of the decision on the behavior of himself and future judges faced with new situations to which the decision might be deemed relevant. Another aspect of the predictability controversy is the suggestion of Herman Oliphant that more reliable predictions can be made by studying not the "vague and shifting rationalizations" embodied in judicial doctrines but rather "what courts have done in response to the stimuli of the facts in concrete cases before them." Herman Oliphant, "A Return to State Decisis," in 14 *American Bar Association Journal* 71; 159 (1928). For a critique, see Patterson 310–315. There has been discussion also of the predictive duty of the legislature and executive in considering whether a bill presented for approval could successfully survive a judicial test of constitutionality. See Sidney P. Simpson and Julius Stone, *Law And Society* (3 vols., St. Paul, Minnesota, 1948–1949) 2:1461–62. Jerome Frank's major emphasis on legal unpredictability has been with respect to trial court rather than appellate court decisions. See Frank 1930 and 1949, *passim*.

2. MS April 9, 1937.

3. The Frank observation on Cardozo is in 13 *Law and Contemporary Problems* 369, 374 (1948). / Cardozo 1924, 60; Cardozo 1921, 35. / Llewellyn 1960, 25n, 45, and 14 *University of Cincinnati Law Review* 208, 219 (1940). / Patterson 590. / Clark, Book Review, 57 *Yale Law Journal* 658, 661 (1948).

4. On the continental system see Rudolf B. Schlesinger, *Comparative Law Cases and Materials* (Brooklyn, 2d ed., 1959) 287–322; Arthur Von Mehren, "The Judicial Process—A Comparative Analysis," 5 *American Journal of Comparative Law* 197 (1956). / Cardozo 1921, especially. / The spearheading "realist" articles were by Llewellyn: "A Realistic Jurisprudence—the Next Step" in 30 *Columbia Law Review* 431 (1930) and "Some Realism About Realism" in 44 *Harvard Law Review* 1222 (1931). A related approach was in Frank, 1930.

5. The point was classically made in Oliphant's presidential address to the Association of American Law Schools in 1927. He suggested the symbol of an inverted pyramid to represent the ever-broadening propositions that can logically be erected out of a particular decision. Oliphant *supra* note 1 72–73. Later elaborations of the point are in Julius Stone, *Province and Function of Law* 186–191 (1946) and Llewellyn 1951, 66–69.

6. On *sub silentio* rulings, see authorities cited in Note, 29 *New York University Law Review* 1122 (1954), and in note 5d of Judge Frank's separate opinion in Gardella v. Chandler 172 F. 2d 402, 411 (2nd Cir. 1949). / App. A #46, 193. / Reference to the *New Richmond* case briefs shows that the issue was treated in a minor way by the attorney general and argued at somewhat greater length by the city of New Richmond.

7. The rule of law must cover "a group of fact-situations, including as a minimum, the fact situation of the instant case and at least one other." Oliphant, *supra* note 1, 72.

8. App. A #46, 163.

9. See App. A #1, 178, 179, 180, 192; App. A #19, 45, 50; App. A #4, 182, 183, 184, 185, 186–87, 203, 207, 210; App. A #9, 695, 697; App. A #11, 371;

App. A #13, 466–67, 468; App. A #26, 644, 648–49; App. A #27, 157, 160–61; App. A #29, 573, 574, 575; App. A #30, 139, 142; App. A #33, 125, 126, 127; App. A #36, 232, 238.

For detailed treatment of the influence of the treatise writers on the public purpose decisions, particularly the works of Cooley and Dillon on constitutional law, municipal corporations, and taxation, see Clyde E. Jacobs, *Law Writers and the Courts* (Berkeley, 1954), Chaps. 4–6; Ellis Waldron, *The Public Purpose Doctrine of Taxation* (Ph.D. Thesis, University of Wisconsin, 1952), 424–439. Cooley had also written the opinion in the leading Michigan case of People v. Salem Township, 20 Mich. 452 (1870), which applied the public purpose doctrine against an issue of township bonds as a loan to a railroad; and Dillon wrote similar opinions against local donations to a railroad (Hanson v. Vernon, 27 Iowa 28) and to an iron manufacturing company (here as the federal circuit judge who was affirmed by the U.S. Supreme Court in Loan Association v. Topeka, 87 U.S. 655 [1874]).

10. App. A #4, 216. / App. A #9.

11. App. A #4, 191 (majority), 215 (dissent). The same difference of approach is revealed in the majority and minority opinions in the leading Michigan case decided in the same year as *Whiting,* with the influential Judge Cooley writing the majority opinion. He observed (People v. Salem, 20 Mich. 452, 477): "An object may be public in one sense and for one purpose, when in a general sense and for other purposes, it would be idle and misleading to apply the same term." The *WDA* opinion specifically noted this aspect of the *Whiting* majority opinion. 228 Wis. 147, 179 (1928).

12. See *Bound* and *Herreid* cases, App. A #12 and #17.

13. App. A #6, 357; App. A #15, 119.

14. Sentiments similar to those of Justice Fowler were voiced in the *Donald* case, App. A #33, 127, 136, and in public purpose cases outside of Wisconsin, e.g., Loan Assoc. v. Topeka 20 Wall. (U.S. 1874) 655; Opinion of the Justices 58 Me. 590 (1871). / Derivation of the state purpose doctrine was thus described in the *WDA* case (App. A #46, 183); "Sec. 5, VIII . . . requires the legislature to provide an annual tax sufficient to defray the estimated expenses of the state for each year, and it has been held in [here citing App. A #29, 30, 33] that an appropriation by the legislature must not merely be public in purpose but a proper expenditure by the state."

15. App. A #71, 278. The quotation from the attorney general is from 30 AG 343, 346 (1941).

16. On legal fictions see Morris R. Cohen, "Fictions," in VI *Encyclopedia of the Social Sciences* 228 (1931); Lon Fuller, "Legal Fictions," in 25 *Illinois Law Review* 363, 513, 877 (1931). It has been said that the purpose of a legal fiction is to reconcile a desired result with some accepted premise or postulate— i.e., to avoid the appearance of departure from the latter. Thus, the premise that people should not suffer legal liabilities for conduct occurring when they were unaware of the applicable law is reconciled with the actual visitation of such liability by the obvious fiction that everyone knows the law; it is said that everyone is "deemed" or "presumed" to know the law. Thus if the court in the *New Richmond* case (App. A #29) had phrased its determination (that the calamity befalling New Richmond was "state-wide") in the form of a statement that when a local event is of sufficiently calamitous nature it is a state-wide event, this would have been a clearly false generalization, characteristic

of the legal fiction. In *Loomis* v. *Callahan* (App. A #41) the court might be said to have treated the debt incurred by the Building Corporation to the Annuity Board on the basis of the fiction that state officials acting in a corporate form are not state officials. In neither case did there seem to be a clear and open use of fictions. A court will prefer to create an exception to a rule or otherwise expressly modify a prior rule, or (by one of the many devices we have previously analyzed) modify it *sub silentio, without* making a concededly or palpably false generalization of fact.

17. Cardozo 1921, 167–68. / Compare, however, with the *New Richmond* decision the fact that contemporary courts of other states refused to find even a *public* purpose in the use of public funds as loans to aid those affected by a disaster overcoming a substantial area. Lowell v. Boston, 111 Mass. 454 (1873); Feldman and Co. v. City Council of Charleston 23 S.C. 57 (1884) (both cases involving fire in large areas of a city); State ex rel Griffith v. Osawkee Township, 14 Kan. 418 (1875) (drought in large area of Kansas). If the explanation is that the *New Richmond* case reflected a later temper of the times, being decided in 1902, it is to be noted that a roughly contemporary Minnesota case looked the other way. (Deering Co. v. Peterson, 75 Minn. 118 [1898]).

18. The court found it unnecessary even to mention the *LaFebre* case where state payment of a sub-contractor's unpaid claim of $878 against a contractor who had abandoned work on a school building had been upheld. For equities in that case not present in the *Consolidated* case see App. A #25.

19. For some of Llewellyn's remarks on "situation-sense" and "situation-types," see Llewellyn 1960, 59–61, 200–201, 220–21, 260–61, 268. Abstract criteria in such terms as "conscience," "judgment," and "life essence" are suggested at 426–29.

20. Pound, "The Economic Interpretation and the Law of Torts," 53 *Harvard Law Review* 365, 367 (1940); "The Theory of Judicial Decision," 36 *ibid.* 641, 644–51 (1923); I *Jurisprudence* 323 (1959); Llewellyn, 1960, 22–23, 185, 214–22.

21. For elaboration of the ideas in this paragraph, see Walter Murphy, "Marshalling the Court: Leadership, Bargaining, and the Judicial Process," 29 *University of Chicago Law Review* 640 (1962).

22. Llewellyn 1960, 35–45, 62–64; "Remarks On the Theory of Appellate Decision and the Rules or Canons About How Statutes Are To Be Construed," 3 *Vanderbilt Law Review* 395, 396 (1950).

23. Wiener, *Effective Appellate Advocacy* (New York, 1950), 20–42.

24. Warner, "The Responsibilities of the Lawyer," 19 *American Bar Association Reports* (1896) 319, 326.

25. In the rehearing opinion, virtually an entire paragraph comes from the WDA brief: at 228 Wis. 147, 148, the general proposition which opens the first full paragraph, and the long string of case citations which follows are verbatim duplicates of material in the WDA brief (pp. 97–98); and so is the subsequent lengthy quotation from the *Carmichael* case (228 Wis. 147, 178–79) a duplicate of subsequent material in the WDA brief (pp. 100–101).

26. See, for a sampling of pros and cons in this field, Glendon A. Schubert, *Quantitative Analysis of Judicial Behavior* (1959); Lee Loevinger, "The Element of Predictability in Judicial Decision-Making," in Edgar Jones, *Law and Electronics* (New York, 1962), 249–302; Frederick B. Wiener, "Decision

Prediction by Computers: Nonsense Cubed—And Worse," 48 *American Bar Association Journal* 1023 (1962).

27. Wigmore said this: "The promoters of a corporation circulate a prospectus in which erroneous statements are recklessly made; an investor loses money by trusting to the prospectus. One legal question is whether the accepted doctrine of the law of deceit, as hitherto laid down *logically holds* the promoters liable; i.e., whether twenty-five prior decisions on various groups of circumstances *logically are consistent* with such a result. This is nomocritics. But if we ask further whether by accepted standards of ethics or economics the rule of law *ought* to hold the promoter liable, *regardless of the logic* of prior decisions, we are traveling into Nomo-thetics or Nomo-politics." (Emphasis added.) Wigmore, in Symposium volume, *My Philosophy of Law* (1941) 317–318.

In Williston's celebrated treatise on contracts (as Fuller observes) the fundamental attitude—which Fuller describes as characteristic of contemporary legal thinking—is that recognition for the demands of policy is deviational: "if we ask at what point in Prof. Williston's method 'policy' becomes relevant, it will be found, I think, that in general he admits 'policy' only where 'logic' has failed, that is where a syllogistic marshalling of traditional concepts fails to yield a certain answer, or occasionally ... where the answer yielded seems too unjust to be acceptable." Fuller, "Williston on Contracts" in 18 *North Carolina Law Review,* 9–10 (1939).

28. His statement of the four methods is in Cardozo (1921), 30–31. It seems clear that the very process of determining whether an "analogy" exists—i.e., whether the two situations should be governed by the same policy—involves use of the "method of sociology." He was not unaware of this. In his subsequent discussion of the methods, he observed: "Logic and history and custom have their place. We will shape the law to conform to them when we may; but only within bounds. The end which the law serves will dominate them all .... I mean that when [judges] are called upon to say how far existing rules are to be extended or restricted, they must let the welfare of society fix the path, its direction and its distance." And although in some fields of law, courts are more concerned with consistency and adherence to the past than with the social value approach embodied in the method of sociology, "in a sense it is true that we are applying the method of sociology when we pursue logic and coherence and consistency as the greater social values." Cardozo (1921) 133, 75.

29. Julius Stone in *The Province and Function of Law* (1946), 190 puts it this way: "Ultimately it is not by achievement of logical certainty that the system of precedent is to be justified; but by the insistence on regarding particular situations in the contexts for which experience in administering justice already exists in the form of precedents. The contexts rarely provide a ready-made answer in a novel case; indeed, they often provide conflicting answers. The contexts do usually ensure that what official experience there is relevant to such situations is examined; but they do not themselves logically compel any particular answer in a new case."

30. This analysis is quite consistent, of course, with Wasserstrom's painstaking attempt to demonstrate that judicial decision is ideally a "two-step" procedure involving (1) rules, which are (2) always subject to critical evaluation. See Wasserstrom, *The Judicial Decision* (1961).

31. Compare Edward H. Levi, *An Introduction to Legal Reasoning* (Chicago 1949) 2–3: "The problem for the law is: When will it be just to treat different cases as though they were the same? A working legal system must therefore be willing to pick out key similarities and to reason from them to the justice of applying a common classification .... The kind of reasoning involved ... is one in which the classification changes as the classification is made. The rules change as the rules are applied."

32. Llwellyn 1960, 108–117.

33. The relevant language in the *WDA* opinion was (228 U.S. 147, 193): "And that such encouragement is not prohibited by that Section was held in Jensen v. Board of Supervisors of Polk County 47 Wis. 298 ... ; State ex rel New Richmond v. Davidson, *supra;* and Appeal of Van Dyke 217 Wis. 528, 545 ... , by sustaining legislative enactments by which the state promoted or encouraged the making of such improvements, even though such encouragement in the two cases last cited was by appropriations of state funds. See also State ex rel Hopkins v. Raub 106 Kan. 196 ... in which it was held that the promotion and encouragement by the state of the construction of highways by political subdivisions thereof by an appropriation of state funds to pay for activities which consisted of educational, advisory, regulatory, and co-ordination activities relating to such construction, were not prohibited by the provision in the constitution of Kansas which is similar to Sec. 10, Art. VIII Wis. Const."

The *Jensen* case (App. A #24) had upheld a state law compelling taxation *by,* and consequent expenditure by, *counties and towns* for construction of roads. The *Van Dyke* case (App. A #72) upheld state reimbursement of counties and cities for part of public works' labor cost, on the theory that the state's "primary purpose" was to assist in unemployment relief rather than be party to works of internal improvement. The *New Richmond* cyclone case (App. A #29) upholding use of state funds to help a city relieve distress from a cyclone, had not discussed the "internal improvements" issue at all. Thus the broad doctrine announced by the court was not necessitated by these prior cases.

34. Holmes, "The Path of the Law," 10 *Harvard Law Review* 457, 467 (1897). / A few examples of other areas where courts talk more openly on policy issues than in the usual common-law case are: 1) cases dealing with statutes, where a court discusses the policy behind the statute,—whether in connection with the presumption of constitutionality supporting its policy, or as part of the process of construing and applying statutes, independently of constitutional issues; 2) cases where some kind of behavior, notably the formation of a particular kind of contract, is objected to on the specific ground of its being against common-law traditions of "public policy," e.g., a gambling contract, and the court therefore was forced to talk specifically in terms of policy; 3) cases where, as Leon Green has put it (in *The Study and Teaching of Tort Law, 34 Texas Law Review* 15, 16 (1956)), the court is trying "to justify ... not taking some bold step .... "

35. See the dissenting opinion of Justice Brandeis in Burnet v. Coronado Oil and Gas Co. 285 U.S. 405, 406–10 (1932).

36. The practice is discussed in Auerbach, Garrison, Hurst and Mermin, *The Legal Process* (San Francisco, 1961) 172–81.

37. Llewellyn, 1960, 119. We should note here, too, that in making a rough separation of the preliminary and later thought processes we are not assum-

ing that the former is so different in kind from the latter as to be completely "non-legal" in character. It surely is not entirely free from the influence of legal concepts and rules that are part of the judges' mental equipment. See, e.g., Stone, *The Province and Function of Law* (1946) 206, note 320; Llewellyn 1960, 104–05, 116–17, 118–19, 201–03.

38. Max Radin, "The Method of Law," 1950 *Washington University Law Quarterly* 471, 489. One of the earliest analyses along these lines is in John Dewey, "Logical Method and Law," 10 *Cornell Law Quarterly* 17 (1924). *Cf.* a psychologist's observation: "When men rationalize their actions they are nearly always striving to do more than hide their real motives. They are expressing their ideals of what the motives of such actions ought to be. Most rationalizations need to be viewed therefore as themselves actual or potential motives. If they are not motives when they first arise, their mere repetition is likely to establish them as such." Edward S. Robinson, *Law and the Lawyers* (1937) 147.

39. Arnold's views are in "Professor Hart's Theology," 73 *Harvard Law Review* 1298 (1959). Justice Stewart's view contrary to Arnold's is reported in Griswold, "Foreword: Of Time and Attitudes—Professor Hart and Judge Arnold," 74 *ibid.* 81, 84 (1960). On the effect of circulating majority and minority drafts, see remarks of Chief Justice Vinson, 20 *Oklahoma Bar Association Journal* 1269 (1949) and Chief Justice Stone, 26 *Journal of American Judicature Society* 78 (1942), and the examples cited in our earlier discussion of the "kind of court" variable. Arnold had been skeptical of the efficacy of the Supreme Court's devoting more time to its cases—more individual study as well as more group deliberation. Apropos of the former, see the examples cited in Murphy, *supra* note 21 at 646–47, of Supreme Court justices who, having been assigned to write the Court's opinion, reported back that additional study had changed their minds the other way, sometimes carrying the majority along to the changed decision.

40. Cardozo 1924, 95. Justice Stone thought in 1936 that "whether the constitutional standard of reasonableness of official action is subjective, that of the judge who must decide, or objective in terms of a considered judgment of what the community may regard as within the limits of the reasonable, are questions which the cases have not specifically decided." However, the judge must "ever be alert to discover whether [the two standards] differ and, differing, whether his own or the objective standard will represent the *sober second thought of the community,* which is the firm base on which all law must ultimately rest." Stone, "The Common Law In the United States," 50 *Harvard Law Review* 4, 25 (1936). [Emphasis added.] See also Frankfurter, "Some Observations on the Nature of the Judicial Process of Supreme Court Litigation," 98 *Proceedings of American Philosophical Society* 233 (1954).

41. Concerning rules for construction of constitutions, see *American Digest System* (as supplemented to 1962), Constitutional Law keynote numbers 11–49; Cooley, *Constitutional Limitations* (8th ed. 1927), Chap. IV. On statutes, see Sutherland, *Statutory Construction* (3rd ed. Horack 1943); "Symposium on Statutory Construction," 3 *Vanderbilt Law Review* 365–584 (1950).

42. For discussion of some restraining constitutional traditions in the Supreme Court other than the basic one mentioned, see Alexander Bickel, "Foreword—The Passive Virtues," 75 *Harvard Law Review* 40 (1961). The controversy over "activism" may be sampled from Kurland, "The Supreme

Court and Its Judicial Critics," 6 *Utah Law Review* 457 (1959); Kadish, "A Note On Judicial Activism," *ibid,* 467; Lewis, "The Supreme Court and Its Critics," 45 *Minnesota Law Review* 305 (1961); Rodell, "For Every Justice, Judicial Deference Is A Sometime Thing," 50 *Georgetown Law Journal* 700 (1962).

43. The classic statement of the misconception discussed in this paragraph is Arthur Goodhart's "Determining the Ratio Decidendi of A Case," 40 *Yale Law Journal* 161 (1930). For criticism see Julius Stone, "The Ratio of the Ratio Decidendi," 22 *Modern Law Review* 597 (1959); Auerbach, Garrison, Hurst and Mermin, *The Legal Process* (1961) 64–65.

44. Erwin N. Griswold, "Foreword: Of Time and Attitudes—Professor Hart and Judge Arnold," 74 *Harvard Law Review* 81, 92 (1960).

45. Herbert Wechsler, "Toward Neutral Principles In Constitutional Law," 73 *Harvard Law Review* 1 (1959).

46. See Paul Freund, "The Supreme Court Crisis," 31 *N.Y. State Bar Association Bulletin* 66, 78 (1959); Llewellyn 1960, 388–89.

47. Llewellyn, 1960, approvingly quotes the German lawyer and legal historian Goldschmidt at 122. But Llewellyn does occasionally recognize that the "immanent law" will not be perfectly clear to all judges; and that there may be reasonable disagreements as to which immanent law is pointed to by "situation-sense" (pp. 127–28, 139, 224). In addition to embracing the concept of "immanent law," Llewellyn makes other seeming departures into the metaphysical (see his reference to the "Platonic" nature of legal concepts, pp. 180–81) and into the metaphorical (note his view of the judges' response to the "urge or flavor or force-field of a rule or concept," pp. 189, 191, 222, and to the "life-essence" of a situation, p. 426.)

48. The controversy between Fuller and Nagel is part of a larger one appearing in 3 *Natural Law Forum* 68–104 (1958) and 4 *Natural Law Forum* 26–43 (1959).

49. While the writer has made detailed studies of the two nineteenth-century projects, they are as yet unpublished, and references to them here will be undocumented.

50. George R. Taylor, *The Transportation Revolution, 1815–1860* (New York, 1951) 381–83, 48–52, 90–94; Louis Hartz, *Economic Policy and Democratic Thought: Pennsylvania 1776–1860* (Cambridge, 1948) 104, 289–90, 307–08; James N. Primm, *Economic Policy In The Development of a Western State: Missouri, 1820–1860* (Cambridge, 1934) 124–27; Milton S. Heath, *Constructive Liberalism: The Role of the State in Economic Development in Georgia to 1860* (Cambridge, 1954) 9, 231, 388–89. A not altogether clear but perhaps similar picture appears in Handlin and Handlin, *Commonwealth, A Study of the Role of Government in the American Economy: Massachusetts, 1774–1861* (New York, 1947) 53–56, 116–17, 184, 226–27, 258–59. The cited Heath study of Georgia reveals that prominence of the state's economic role appeared in cycles. A study of the New Jersey corporation (not so specifically focussed on the present issue as the other volumes) suggests there was no general state financial assistance or stock subscriptions to internal improvement corporations, though there were some instances of the latter, as well as some assistance through liberal tax treatment and authorization of public lotteries. John W. Cadman, Jr., *The Corporation In New Jersey: Business and Politics, 1791–1875* (Cambridge, 1949) 47–49, 51–61. See

also James W. Hurst, *Law and the Conditions of Freedom In the Nineteenth-Century United States* (Madison, 1956) 7–8, 53–55; Robert A. Lively, "The American System," 29 *The Business History Review,* 81–96 (1955).

The techniques used, insofar as the above studies reveal them, were somewhat different from those developed in our two Wisconsin nineteenth-century projects. The Georgia study shows that the devices of state and local aid to railroads and other improvements included stock ownership, money loans, loans of state bonds, endorsement of company bonds, payments for original survey, sometimes accompanied by public representation on the board. (Heath, *supra,* pp. 281, 287–89, 328–35). There was considerable state and local stockholding in Pennsylvania projects, sometimes with public representation among the company's governing officials. (Hartz, *supra,* pp. 82–85, 96–103). The Massachusetts study shows instances of gifts of land for bridges, and state scrip as security for railroad loans (Handlin and Handlin, *supra,* pp. 115, 227–28). There were in Missouri examples of state grants of money and of state bonds under certain conditions, and stock subscriptions by localities (Primm, *supra,* pp. 96–97, 104–13).

51. See Chap. V, note 28.

INDEX

history of rural electrification, 201, 207n*16*; on spite lines and other utility tactics against co-ops, 10, 207n*23*

Clancy, Senator Joseph: offered defeated amendments to Senate bill, 25, 212n22; non-participation in initial voting on WDA bill, 213n25

Clark, Judge Charles E.: view of, on predictability of decisional outcome, 84

Clemens, Eli W.: on 1907 utility law, 3, 201; on beginnings of rural electrification organization, 8, 207n*19*; on utility tactics in resisting co-ops, 10, 207n*23*

Coakley, Senator Maurice: offered defeated amendment to kill WDA bill, 25, 212n22; parliamentary moves by, against WDA bill, 26, 27, 213n*26*; leader of Senate "walk-outs" to avoid effective vote, 26; quoted in press, on Socialist character of WDA bill, 29–30; non-participation in initial voting on WDA bill, 213n25; press comment on his appealing chair's ruling, 213n*26*

Compensation of public officer increase during term, constitutional prohibition against: ruling as to WDA's non-violation of, by Judge Reis and second WDA decision, 36, 52, 220; text of prohibition, 193–94

Cooley, Judge Thomas M.: influence of, on public purpose doctrine, 65, 224n*3*, 235n9, n*11*

Cooperative League of Wisconsin, 20

Cooperatives, agricultural: organization of pre-REA electric co-ops by, 9–10; Wisconsin promotion of, and requirement for teaching essentials of, 10; mentioned in WDA litigation, 34–35, 38, 54, 55

Cooperatives, consumer: Wisconsin requirement for teaching essentials of, 10

Cooperatives, electric: preference to, in federal REA loans, 7–8; 1935–37 promotion of by REC and opposition thereto, 8; extent of REA loans to, by 1938, 9; limited pre-REA existence of, 9; co-ops sponsored by TVA as models for, 9–10; tactics of utilities in opposing growth of, 10; relations of with utilities under Commission rules, 10–11; WDA's contribution to, 57–58, 60. *See also*: Rural electrification

Corporations. *See* Development corporations; Federal public corporation; Private corporation; Special laws granting corporate privileges; State Utilities Corporation

Court decision, process of. *See* Judicial process, appellate

Court litigation on WDA. *See* Wisconsin Development Authority

Court techniques. *See* Judicial process, appellate

Credit of state, constitutional prohibition against loaning or giving: ruling as to WDA's non-violation of, by Judge Reis and second WDA decision, 35, 52, 220n*45*; text of prohibition, 194

Crow, William L.: on municipal ownership under 1907 utility law, 4

Daugs, Assemblyman Palmer: resolution of, for attorney general opinion on WDA bill, 22–23; offered defeated amendment to Assembly bill, 23, 211n*18*

Davidson, Governor James O., 3

Davlin, Thomas F.: 1941 report to WDA meeting, 60–61; WDA incorporator, 208n*31*; WDA secretary, 222n7

Debt of state. *See* State debt

Delegation of judicial power to Secretary of State: ruling on, by Judge Reis and in second WDA decision, 36, 52, 220

Delegation of sovereign power: injection of issue into WDA litigation by *amicus* briefs, 38; treatment of, by counsel and Supreme Court opinions, 38, 39–48, 54; summary and evaluation of case-law, 77–79, 232–33n37, n*38*. *See also*: Private corporation, use of for government function

Dempsey, Senator Chester E.: 213n25

Department of Agriculture and Markets. *See* Wisconsin Rural Electrification Coordination Division

Department of Resource Development, 69, 227n*15*

Development corporations, 227–28n*15*

Dietrich, William H., Jr., 216n*24*

Division of Industrial Development, 69, 227n*15*

Doty, Gov. James D., 225n*11*

Duel, Senator Morvin: anti-WDA statement 30; vote against WDA bill, 213n25

Duncan, Thomas: testimony of, at hearing on WDA bill, 17; comment on "propaganda" of, by Assemblyman Thomson, 24; press characterization of, 29

Electric cooperatives. *See* Cooperatives, electric

Estabrook, Experience: influence of opinion as attorney general, upon Fox-Wisconsin project, 124

Evjue, William T.: attacked by Kannenberg, 28; municipal competition bills, 205–6n*11*

Faber, Louis, 210n*12*

Fairchild, Justice Edward T.: dissenting